Acknowledgements

This volume gathers the results of a research project titled "Transnational Poetics: Racialized Women Writers of the 1990s" funded by the International Academic Relations Division of the Department of Foreign Affairs and International Trade (DFAIT) within the International Council for Canadian Studies' "Canadian Studies in Europe: Institutional Research Program" in 2004. We are thankful to this Canadian institution as well as to the Spanish Ministry of Science and Innovation and to our respective universities, University of Huelva and Univerity of Vigo, for providing the funds that allowed us to carry on our research in Canadian and European universities. Our gratitude is also due to Erín Moure and Diana Brydon for their letters of support for our project, for their continous encouragement and friendship. Other Canadian writers and academics have also helped us in different ways during the years that this manuscript has taken to see the light, sharing their wisdom with us in illuminating conversations and intellectual discussions. Heartfelt thanks to Larissa Lai, Hiromi Goto, and Fred Wah.

Some sections of the chapter on Indo-Canadian women writers appear in extended form in the essays by Belén Martín-Lucas "'Grammars of Exchange': The 'Oriental Woman' in the Global Market" (in *Cultural Grammars of Nation, Diaspora and Indigeneity in Canada,* ed. Melina Baum Singer, Christine Kim, and Sophie McCall. Waterloo: Wilfred Laurier UP, forthcoming 2011); "'Mum Is the Word': Gender Violence, Displacement and the Refugee Camp in Yasmin Ladha's Documentary-Fiction" (in *Feminism, Literature and Rape Narratives: Violence and Violation,* ed. Zoe Brigley and Sorcha Gunne. London: Routledge, 2010) and "Territories in Dispute: Cultural Contamination and Sexual Purity in Feminist Indo-Canadian Fiction" (in the proceedings of the "India in Canada, Canada in India: Managing Diversity" International Conference, Córdoba 2009, forthcoming). Previous drafts of sections of the chapter on Japanese Canadian women writers first appeared in Pilar Cuder-Domínguez's essays "The Politics of Gender and Genre in Asian Canadian Women's Speculative Fiction: Hiromi Goto and Larissa Lai" (*Asian Canadian Literature Beyond Autoethnography,* ed. Eleanor Ty and Christl Verduyn. Waterloo: Wilfrid Laurier UP, 2008), and "Nation, Narration, and the Abject Self in Japanese Canadian Women Writers" (*Her Na-rra-tion: Women's Narratives of the Canadian Nation,* ed. Françoise Lejeune and Charlotte Sturgess. Nantes: CEC-CRINI et Université de Nantes, 2009).

TRANSNATIONAL POETICS

Asian Canadian Women's Fiction
of the 1990s

Pilar Cuder-Domínguez

Belén Martín-Lucas

Sonia Villegas-López

We acknowledge the support of the Canada Council for the Arts for our publishing program. We also acknowledge support from the Government of Ontario through the Ontario Arts Council.

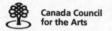 

Cover Image: René Mansi/iStockphoto
Cover Design: Peggy Stockdale

Library and Archives Canada Cataloguing in Publication

Cuder Domínguez, Pilar
    Transnational poetics : Asian Canadian women's fiction of the 1990s / by Pilar Cuder-Domínguez, Belén Martín-Lucas, Sonia Villegas-López.

ISBN 978-1-894770-68-2

    1. Canadian fiction (English)--Asian Canadian authors--History and criticism. 2. Canadian fiction (English)--Women authors--History and criticism. 3. Canadian fiction (English)--20th century--History and criticism. 4. Identity (Psychology) in literature. 5. Minority women in literature. 6. Ethnicity in literature. I. Martín Lucas, María Belén II. Villegas López, Sonia III. Title.

PS8191.I3C83 2010   C813'.5409928708995   C2010-904830-X

Printed and bound in Canada by Coach House Printing

TSAR Publications
P. O. Box 6996, Station A
Toronto, Ontario M5W 1X7
Canada

www.tsarbooks.com

Contents

INTRODUCTION:
GENDER AND RACIALIZATION IN CANADA   *vii*

I. INDO-CANADIAN WOMEN'S FICTION IN ENGLISH:
FEMINIST ANTI-RACIST POLITICS AND POETICS THAT
RESIST INDO-CHIC
Indo-Canadian Fiction in English and the Larger World   *3*
Transnational Feminist Fictions: Diasporic Trails   *12*
The Many Violences of Racism   *31*
Conclusion   *41*

II. RACIALIZED BODIES:
CHINESE CANADIAN WOMEN'S FICTION
Introduction   *47*
Femininity and Its Discontents   *55*
Sex and the Body   *66*
Addressing Race, Reading Ethnicity:
   New Assessments of Exoticism and Hybridity   *71*
Exploring Genre and Aesthetics: Autobiography, History, Fantasy   *82*
Conclusion   *91*

III. BEYOND REDRESS:
JAPANESE CANADIAN WOMEN'S FICTION
Introduction   *95*
In the Shadow of Obasan: The Trauma of Internment   *97*
An Absent Community: Dispersal, Isolation, and Assimilation   *100*
A Conspiracy of Silence   *109*
Alternative Communities: (Female) Body Politics
   and the Challenge to Heteronormativity   *113*

Enemy Aliens: Japanese Canadian Masculinities   *122*
Japan, or the Attempt to Fix Identity   *132*
Politics and Poetics: Innovations in Genre and Aesthetics   *136*
Conclusion   *143*

NOTES   *145*

WORKS CITED   *158*

INTRODUCTION
GENDER AND RACIALIZATION IN CANADA

Racial identity has been the subject of much scrutiny in Canada in the second half of the twentieth century, particularly in connection with the definition of a national identity. During the 1960s and 1970s Canada severed its last colonial ties with Britain while it engaged in the construction of a coherent national image (flag, anthem, and related symbols) that was distinctive from both their old imperial centre (the United Kingdom) and their powerful neighbour (the United States). There emerged then the notion of the "Canadian mosaic," a symbol of inter-ethnic and inter-racial cooperation that gave the lie to the "American melting-pot" by reconciling differences instead of fostering assimilation into a normative white European identity. However, at the same time, Canadian political institutions such as the Royal Commission on Bilingualism and Biculturalism subscribed to the bilingual, bi-national identity of the country, thus raising paradoxical questions, as Marnina Gonick has observed:

> Language has played an integral role in the imagining of the nationalist project in Canada. Canada's present understanding of itself as a society composed of two languages and many cultures is both a souvenir and an erasure. It is a reminder of the historic struggle between the English and the French that was perceived by themselves as the struggle between two races (Ng 1993), and as members of the nations competing for hegemonic control over the geographic territory that was to become the country Canada. At the same time it obliterates the presence of the several hundred languages spoken by the aboriginal groups that peopled the same geographic space prior to the arrival of either the English or the French ... [Moreover] this move left undesignated and therefore outside the boundaries of the nation those citizens—that is, immigrants and their children—whose first language is neither English nor French. (100–01)

Even though the notion of the "two founding nations" has proved extremely resilient and quite impossible to debunk, this framework opened up to other races and ethnic groups during the 1980s. In that decade, the writing of "visible minorities" in Canada attracted major media and academic attention for the first time. They became central to the project of displaying the pluralist makeup of Canadian society and culture as articulated in the Multiculturalism Act of 1988 and promoted from the institutions. Anthologies such as *Other Solitudes* (ed. Linda Hutcheon and Marion Richmond, 1990) as well as collections of interviews (e.g. Makeda Silvera's *The Other Woman*, 1995) have since contributed to construct an ethnic counter-canon around such figures as Michael Ondaatje or Joy Kogawa. Furthermore, critical studies and publishing practices have participated in the creation, transmission, and legitimization of the cultural mosaic by means of the circulation of token writers who have stood for their respective ethnic and racial backgrounds.

But the later 1980s were the time when, as Smaro Kamboureli states, "ethnic literature in English Canada was slowly beginning to establish its own ground; it was also the time when multiculturalism, already in its second decade as an official policy, entered a 'new' stage as Canadians began vigorously to express their opinions on the merits and perils of officially sanctioning ethnicity" (vii). Marnina Gonick too expresses what she considers the failure of multiculturalism: "As the makers of ethnic ascription, those claiming anglo identity have projected ethnicity onto others and thereby naturalized their own as generically Canadian . . . Despite multiculturalism's declarations of its relevance to all Canadians, it has done little to disrupt the normative notion of Canadian identity" (96). According to Paul Kelley, true multiculturalism cannot result from such imposition of a norm, but through the mutual interaction of all ethnic and racial groups:

> To live in a 'multicultural' society means that no one can be exempt from thinking about race and culture, about their histories and relations, for one cannot, in such a society, fail to think about, and respond to, the other. (187)

Critics and writers both expressed reservations pertaining to an official policy of multiculturalism that unproblematically celebrated "difference" without undertaking to analyze the unequal access to power of these social groups. As Stasiulis warned in 1993:

> Several intellectuals from Aboriginal and minority groups are voicing some scepticism about what Edward Said (1989: 213) regards as an ominous trend involving the "fetishization and relentless celebration of 'difference' and 'otherness.'" Writers of colour, and particularly Native writers, are at risk of being treated as "otherness machines, with the manufacture of alterity as [their] principal role" (Appiah 1991: 357). The growing demands that the literature of women writers of colour be produced

and recognized increase the risk of their being read from the vantage point of "politically correct" feminist dogmas such as the now ubiquitous mantra "race, class and
gender." (54)[1]

As a result, such ethnic/racial groups and their representatives have become frozen
in the position of Others to white Canadian culture, and their work ghettoized and
commercialized under the label of being "ethnic." In the case of women writers,
the interface of gender with race, sexuality, and culture has further repercussions,
insofar as white feminist discourses have tended to exclude or stigmatize minority
women. Although women writers like Marlene Nourbese Philip or Dionne Brand
have obtained wide recognition, both in sales and awards, they continue to offer a
critique of the representation of racialized subjects in Canada, not only through
their creative writing but also in their essays on current issues and in their
activism. Another important step in that direction was the 1994 conference "Writing Thru' Race" held in Vancouver, whose exclusionary politics—it was meant only
for First Nations and Writers of Colour—caused some media uproar. However,
these writers demanded their own space to think through those issues they were
involved in:

> By inscribing this space exclusively under the conjoined sign of "First Nations and
> Writers of Colour," by specifying and particularizing it this way, by repeating and
> multiplying a nationalism and a pluralism in a nationalism and pluralism, other
> possibilities for speech, governed by other kinds of logics, are to be made free.
> (Mookerjea 122)

Out of these debates there arises throughout the 1990s a new conceptualization
of racial identity that starts by re-examining the very terms used for it, steering
clear of those that have absorbed undesirable associations. Didi Khayatt explains:
"The assumptions implicit in the categories of 'immigrant woman,' 'woman of
colour,' and 'visible minority' conceal real differences in experience and do not
account for nor distinguish between the various levels of oppression. They
assume a homogeneity of background amongst all people who fall into those various groupings" (8). The term that has acquired more currency in the final years
of the twentieth century, "racialized," was introduced by the Japanese Canadian
author and critic Roy Miki in his 1994 essay "Sliding the Scale of Ellision: 'Race'
Constructs/Cultural Praxis," written shortly after and reflecting on his chairing
the above-mentioned Vancouver conference "Writing Thru' Race," and later collected together with other essays in his book *Broken Entries*. Here is how he
defines the term:

> "Racialization" . . . applies to the imposition of race constructs and hierarchies on
> marked and demarked "groups" whose members come to signify divergence from the

normative body inscribed by whiteness. The subject racialized is identified by systemic categorizes that winnow the body, according privilege to those glossed with dominance and privation to those digressed to subordination. (127)

Such racialization has affected Asian Canadians since their arrival in Canada over a hundred years ago. As Glenn Deer says in his editorial to a special issue of the journal *Canadian Literature* devoted to Asian Canadian writing, "Asians in North America . . . continue to be interpellated as stereotypical and simplified Others by an historical narrative that includes acts of exclusion, internment, disenfranchisement, and discriminatory taxation" (5).

As an academic field of study, Asian Canadian Literature has a relatively short history. The writings of the pioneers at the turn of the twentieth century, the Eurasian Eaton sisters Edith (using the pen-name Sui Sin Far) and Winnifred (known under the pen-name Onoto Watanna), have been understudied until very recently, with interest in them sparking after the publication of Joy Kogawa's *Obasan* in 1981. Guy Beauregard has examined the history of the discipline, that according to him has developed on the basis of the theory of Asian Canadian constituencies "coming to voice" after a long period of silencing and marginalization. However, Beauregard finds such a theory wanting in many respects. He contends that the reliance

on a "coming to voice" narrative pre-empts the necessary task of investigating the terms on which and through which certain texts are admitted into the circuits of Canadian publishing, reviewing, teaching, and so on. In short, a "coming to voice" narrative, despite (or perhaps even because of) its celebratory tone, may not be able to address the potential containment of cultural difference in a Canadian "multicultural" context. ("The Emergence" 56)

Beauregard's argument is, following Bhabha, that such writing should be seen as disturbing narratives of the nation rather than simply adding excluding histories. More recently, Lily Cho has expressed her own reservations. She observes that "we cannot ignore the trenchant critiques of Canadianness embedded within [minority] literatures . . . These explicit markings of difference call attention to a desire to be considered *both* within and without the nation . . . Moreover, minority literatures in Canada insist on an engagement with histories of dislocation that are differentially related" ("Diasporic Citizenship" 93, 97). The tensions between such diasporic histories and the very concept of the nation have been productively explored in contemporary Asian Canadian women's fiction, as Beauregard perceptively points out:

[M]uch of the most engaging Asian Canadian cultural work . . . addresses narratives of nation and their fissures: Hiromi Goto's novel *Chorus of Mushrooms* (1994), for example, narrates the story of Naoe, an energetic elderly Japanese Canadian woman who sets out to inscribe her name on the icy roads of Canada; and Jin-me Yoon's postcard series *Souvenirs of the Self* (1991) uses postcards to engage with the highly ambivalent "place" a body racialized as "Asian" and gendered as "female" occupies in the landscape of Banff, a landscape that stands in metonymically for the nation. Goto and Yoon both actively renegotiate their location in racialized and gendered representations of Canadian national culture, and refuse to accept the Canadian nation as "finished product" from which they are inevitably excluded. ("The Emergence" 57)

Such is precisely the field of enquiry we have set out to examine in this book. The general aim of our research is to determine to what extent the new generation of Asian Canadian women writers who started publishing in the 1990s feels at ease or at odds with a cultural climate that markets their writing as being exotic, and in what ways they relate to the poetics and politics of their predecessors. The choice of this decade has not been arbitrary. Rather, we concur with Eleanor Ty that towards the 1990s one can establish a shift in the literary articulation of Asian North American identities:

[C]reative works shifted from those that were mainly auto-ethnographic to those that are no longer tied to ethnic and national identities. There is a growing body of works with more experimental forms, structures, and contents: narratives with protagonists who are either less identifiably Asian or whose plots are not necessarily concerned with the struggle between the traditions of the Old and New worlds. (*Un/Fastened* xviii)

Within this general framework, we have attempted to pay special attention to several issues. First, we aim to disclose these women writers' perception of themselves within the context of Canadian literature, and to study their contributions to the new theoretical corpus on race and writing in Canada that we have been discussing in this Introduction.

Second, we focus on the attitude of the new generation toward the role models of the older generation of women writers who have obtained local and international acclaim. Among the writers publishing their first works in the 1990s there is an important group of young women who look up to the writers of the 1980s as role models for their involvement as activists in their own communities. Yet, there is also among new writers an anxiety about old strategies that might be not as useful in the contemporary context of globalization as they were in previous times. The appropriation of the discourses on race and gender by the dominant classes— the cooption of the "politically correct" ideologies—is seen by many feminist racialized writers as a threatening move that requires new strategies. These are the reasons that have led us to study the proposals offered by the new writers in their essays and in their creative works.

Third, we address the patterns of inter-generational and intra-generational relations among women (of similar or different racial backgrounds) in their writing. Earlier generations of feminist writing have focalized inter-generational relationships among women. The purpose was to bring to the spotlight the heritage of women, often by means of plots that followed the lives of several generations of women within a family, i.e., from grandmother to mother and then to daughter. This pattern is also apparent in the writing of racialized Canadian women, once more in an attempt to unveil what is specific to their ancestry and life experiences, like diaspora, forced transportation, slavery, etc. However, our working thesis is that the younger women writers have been steadily moving away from this kind of literary mode, perhaps because it has been "over-ethnicized," and instead they are focusing more and more on the relations among women belonging to the same generation.

Fourth, the sexual identities of Asian Canadian women come into focus. Among the new writers of the 1990s there is an increasing number of lesbian writers who have achieved recognition. In their theories and textual practices, these lesbian writers problematize dominant conceptions of identity, not only in terms of race and gender, but also of sexual identity. In their creative works, authors like Shani Mootoo, Larissa Lai, and Hiromi Goto play with metamorphosed women in order to call attention to the performative body as a site of identity. We will therefore engage in an analysis of lesbian politics and poetics in the texts of racialized women in the 1990s.

Fifth, our study brings together the politics and poetics of this Asian Canadian women's fiction, undertaking an analysis of their innovations in genre and aesthetics. While in previous decades what was labelled as "ethnic" writing had as a priority issue in its agenda the inscription into the literary canon of the experiences of the ethnic communities that had been previously excluded, and thus favoured testimonial literature, in later years the new writers are openly defying the aesthetics and genres associated by (often white) critics with "ethnicity." Although in Canadian literature there has always been a general trend towards experimentation with genres that has given rise to forms categorized as typically Canadian—the long poem, the short-story cycle—the subversion of generic conventions becomes an aesthetic feature loaded with political implications in the hands of racialized women. In the 1990s resistance to categorization is imperative.

Finally, whenever possible, we will examine the reception of these works by the critical apparatus and reading public and their marketing. Reading Canadian literature from Spain, we approach these texts as foreigners. As such, we are aware of the filter that the book market posits for any book buyer, but even more so for the international reader. The weight of availability in a global market is not a light one. At a moment when publishing and distribution are in the hands of a few big corporations, the decisions taken on which books will be printed, in which number, and for how long, are crucial for a Canadian book to cross the Atlantic. Most of the Asian Canadian women writers under analysis here have received critical attention within Canada, and many have received important prizes and awards. However, it is difficult to get copies of these texts from Europe since they disappear from the Canadian publishers' catalogues soon after their publication. Only in the second-hand or rare book market on the Internet may we find scarce copies of these texts. Even those that make it into translation disappear soon after. The marketing of these texts as "exotic" for consumption by global readers may favour a rapid ascent to popularity of the writer, but it certainly does not help the text's permanence in the long term, within the canon.

This book is organized into three chapters, each of them focusing on one ethnic constituency within Asian Canada. The first chapter is devoted to the fiction of South Asian Canadian women. Here we will look at the sudden outburst of fiction works written by Indo-Canadian women published during the decade. Compared to other racialized groups, Indian writers in Canada have received more critical attention and wider distribution in recent years; the international success of Rohinton Mistry, Anita Rau Badami, and Shauna Singh Baldwin is ample proof of the interest of Western markets for these authors, a phenomenon that must be considered within the wider context of the new Orientalist fascination of the Western market for Indian fiction in English, and more specifically within the preference of the West for diasporic Indian authors. We will look at the reification of Indian women in the strategies employed for the marketing of these texts and the authors' resistance to their commodification as "exotic others."

Looking at the increasing number of Indo-Canadian women authors published by large and small companies in Canada since 1991, we will establish the common traits that their texts share as diasporic narratives. Moving across borders, both within and outside India, these works of fiction problematize national identity in the singular, in the Asian subcontinent, in the Caribbean, in Africa, in Europe, or in North America. The borders they cross are not only physical, they also move between languages, cultures, and gender codes even if they never move from their home. Intergenerational rupture, displacement, racism, gender violence, and sexual identity are recurrent common issues developed in these narratives, focusing especially on their specific effects on women's lives.

The novels and short stories here studied articulate the conflict between generations that the changes brought about by migration and globalization are intensifying. The female body often becomes the site of dispute between tradition and modernization, which in the Indian context is expressed as the confrontation between cultural purity and contamination by exposure to allegedly Western ideologies. Allying feminism with foreign intromission, the rebellion against gender restrictions is understood often as "westernization" and rejection of Indian culture. Contrary to this reductionist cultural fundamentalism, most of these narratives express the dilemma of contemporary diasporic subject pressed by different national traditions to fit in. The analysis of the feminist politics in the texts will occupy a substantial part of the chapter. Two forms of gender violence recurrent in some of these works are studied in relation to patriarchal nationalism: war rape and incest.

Another recurrent problem examined in diasporic fictions is the position of the migrant in the host society. Many of these stories contest the benevolent image of Canadian multiculturalism through the racism faced by immigrants. However, these authors do not offer simplistic victim narratives. Canada, the USA, and Great Britain also represent new opportunities of personal fulfilment and most of their characters are successful in their new countries. The personal and communal struggle between generations, languages, and cultures is, though painful, a positive one. The chapter will offer an in-depth examination of these issues drawing examples from the fiction of the nineties by Shauna Singh Baldwin, Anita Rau Badami, Shani Mootoo, Rachna Mara, Yasmin Ladha, and Shree Ghatage.

Chapter Two involves the analysis of Chinese Canadian women's fiction during the following years. The works of the three authors analyzed in this chapter— Evelyn Lau's *Fresh Girls and Other Stories* (1993) and *Other Girls* (1995), Larissa Lai's *When Fox Is a Thousand* (1994) and *Salt Fish Girl* (2002), and Lydia Kwa's *This Place Called Absence* (2000) and *The Walking Boy* (2005)—cannot be considered in isolation from the writing community from which they have undoubtedly benefited and got inspiration. The beginning of the chapter is therefore devoted to the study of the efforts made by the whole collective of writers, professionals, activists, and intellectuals in the early nineties to consolidate a Chinese Canadian tradition in writing and to establish this newly created tradition into a source of academic interest, acknowledging the paramount influence of key texts and authors such as Sky Lee's *Disappearing Moon Cafe* (1990) and Wayson Choy's *The Jade Peony* (1995).

Though following their example and recognizing their legacy, the members of this new wave of Chinese Canadian writers that we propose for this study open new ways, experimenting with the concept of genre—autobiography and history writing—and reassessing the question of race. References to skin colour and visibility are ever present, more obliquely in the case of Lau's work, and openly in Lai's and Kwa's novels. After years of colour-blind politics promoted by multiculturalism, Lai's characters in particular are not ready to admit their difference without a fight. Lau is more subtle, but nonetheless makes a point about the configuration of the prostitute as an exotic object of consumption. Similarly, Kwa works ex-centric figures like the prostitute and the hermaphrodite.

In all cases, the sense of community and the need to find ties of affection—whether at the heart of heterosexual or homosexual relationships—become commonplace. Lau's writing problematizes the lack of those connections, whereas Lai and Kwa foster alternative and companionate notions of collectivity that include the dialogue between women belonging to past and present generations. The three women explore different realizations of identity, which escape fixed definitions and work instead "towards a collectivity with permeable boundaries" (Wong, "Jumping on Hyphens" 119). Gender is therefore another category that is foregrounded in their productions. In the case of the writers proposed they reject traditional constructions of femininity: Lau provides the most exceptional departure from this construction, her character the unruly Canadian-born daughter of Chinese parents who leaves home and works eventually as a prostitute. Not only that, she exposes herself by writing about her experience. Lai speaks as a woman and about women, and also as a lesbian, thus setting up the queer perspective as another discursive site to take into account. Kwa follows the same track and includes "out-of-the-norm" characters who evade straightforward definitions. As rigid categorizations of identity are expressly rejected, these writers seem to enjoy, or at least to accept, their in-betweenness, "the hyphen between Asian and Canadian" (138).

In Chapter Three, the analysis of Japanese Canadian women's fiction must start with the dispossession, internment, and dispersal of their community under the auspices of the War Measures Act in World War II. This was the starting point for a long period of silence and invisibility that would be masterfully broken by Joy Kogawa's *Obasan* in 1981 and by the success of the Redress Movement in 1988. Since then, as this chapter argues, some Japanese Canadian women writers like Kerri Sakamoto have followed Kogawa's lead in addressing the trauma that has become their cultural heritage. Sakamoto's fiction thematizes the fragmentation and silence of the Japanese Canadian community in the pre-Redress period in her first novel, *The Electrical Field* (1998), while in the second, *One Hundred Million Hearts* (2003), she has her characters in the 1990s search for answers to the mysteries of the 1930s and 1940s both in Japan and in Canada. Moving across decades and oceans, Sakamoto manages to trace the communal fissures and gaps through the twentieth century and beyond. Other Japanese Canadian writers, though by no means eluding these issues, prefer to look into other problems. Those who came to Canada after World War II are less likely to develop an interest in these events and often turn to the experiences of the new immigrant. Such is the case of Hiromi Goto, particularly in her first novel, *Chorus of Mushrooms* (1994). They may also examine the idea of an alternative community, usually by addressing same-sex love. Nevertheless, both groups of writers share common interests. Like other racialized authors, they emphasize issues of visibility and invisibility, and of the need to come to terms with an ancestral land that is neither native nor home. In Japanese Canadian writing this is often embodied in an older generation—often the Nisei—that either keeps silent or else actively puts obstacles in the path of the younger generation's attempts to get to know and understand the past. The characters of Sakamoto, Goto, and Kobayashi often feel frustrated in their efforts. Visiting Japan appears as a productive alternative, and as such it features in Sakamoto and in Sally Ito, but the visit fails to give an easy or definitive answer to the problem of racial identity and national belonging. Instead, it opens up new questions and lines of enquiry, a new journey into the dynamics of sameness and difference between the Japanese and the Japanese Canadians. Last of all, this chapter highlights the aesthetic choices of these women writers, in particular their innovative use of hypertextual elements and the complex layering of languages and their written representation.

Our efforts throughout the book have followed the path described by Beauregard in the conclusion to his article on the current state of the field of Asian Canadian Literary Criticism: "To the extent that we can train ourselves to read the collective acts of resistance ... against the exclusions and structural contradictions of the Canadian nation-state, Asian Canadian literature can become an important site in which to rethink connections between history, representation, and social change" ("The Emergence" 68). We subscribe to this critical practice, and we are certain that Asian Canadian women writers of this younger generation have an important contribution to make, if only we listen to their words intently.

I.
INDO-CANADIAN WOMEN'S FICTION IN ENGLISH: FEMINIST ANTI-RACIST POLITICS AND POETICS THAT RESIST INDO-CHIC

1. Indo-Canadian Fiction in English and the Larger World

In 1991, Rohinton Mistry's first novel, *Such a Long Journey*, won the Governor General's Award. This recognition constituted an important step towards the incorporation of Indo-Canadian writing—most notably, of fiction—into the literary canon. However, the decision was not happily celebrated by some authors and critics who saw this irruption of "ethnic" writing as a menace to the normative and essentialist nationalism of "Canadian" fiction.[2] Thus, some responses to Mistry's award were charged with hostility against the "foreignness" of his novel, a story set in Bombay and about Parsi Indian characters. Curiously enough, the previous year's winner of the same award had been Nino Ricci's *Lives of the Saints*, a novel about an Italian family set in a small Italian village that ends with the protagonist's migration to Canada. Although Ricci's award had already stirred some negative criticism, comparing the reactions to the awards, both given to books by "ethnic" writers and set abroad, one cannot avoid suspicions of racism. The Canadian literary world became highly charged, with cross accusations of appropriation and racism versus censorship in the pages of newspapers and at conferences.

It is important to clarify at this point that the labels "South Asian" and "Indian" used here are as uneasy and open to interrogation and to border slippage as the political frontiers of the Indian subcontinent have proven to be. The term "South Asian" is used in the broad sense in which McGifford uses it in the anthology *The Geography of Voice*, to refer to those authors publishing in Canada

who trace their origins from one of the countries of the Indian subcontinent: writers who have come directly to Canada from one of these countries or indirectly by way of Britain or a former British colony, usually East or South Africa, or the Caribbean, or the Pacific Islands ... The term South Asian then refers only to origins—not, for example, to a single geographical location, a particular national group, or a specific religion. It's worth noting that many of the writers here have never seen the South Asian countries of their ancestors and in some cases several generations of a family may have experienced transcontinental shifts, say from India, to England, to Canada. (ix)

All the authors studied in this chapter are related by Indian "origins"[3] and carry with them the "psychic spaces"[4] of India and its diasporas in one way or another, and in all cases they produce transcultural narratives.[5] It is fair to the writers to record here their resistance to be ascribed an Indian identity based in some cases exclusively on skin colour, as Shani Mootoo has repeatedly expressed:[6]

> From day to day, her skin colour being her primary identifier, she is constantly reminded by certain others of her Indian past. Not by Indians born and bred in India, who insist that she is in fact not truly Indian (adding to her rootless and confused floating), but by certain others. Brown equals Indian equals India, they had carelessly assumed. So how come, these certain others want to know, she is so ignorant of things Indian? And she becomes angered by the answers. "Indians stem from India, even if they weren't born there, or their parents either. That is where their roots lie." This logic has become inscribed on her fast-obliterating self-image. She wants to know why it is that all that she has of her Indian heritage are her name, Sushila, and her skin colour, both of which are lies about her identity. She yearns for an understanding that digs deeper than the well-known facts of British Will and Empire. (*Out on Main Street* 61)

In fact, movement across borders, be they national, ethnic, racial, sexual, or religious, is the predominant common trait in these narratives and problematizes any attempt at establishing a stable identity of any kind. Besides, the historical reality of the division of the Indian subcontinent points to the risky use of "Indian" as a national category for literature. My use of the term "Indo-Canadian" does not pretend to sweep over the traumatic divisions in the subcontinent. While in the work of some authors "India" is a specific state that corresponds to its contemporary political demarcation (for example in Shree Ghatage's stories or in Badami's *The Hero's Walk*), in others it refers to the territories of the Indian subcontinent before the Partition wars of 1947.

Mistry's international success opened the doors of mainstream publishers to other writers of South Asian origin in Canada. For instance, Shani Mootoo's *Cereus Blooms at Night*, first published in 1996 by the feminist Press Gang Publishers, was reprinted in 1998 by McClelland & Stewart; Shauna Singh Baldwin's *English Lessons*, published first in 1996 by Goose Lane in Canada, was published again three years later by HarperCollins India; Ven Begamudré's memoir *Extended Families* appeared in Viking/Penguin in 1997. From 1991 to the present we have witnessed a remarkable proliferation of narratives by women of South Asian origin. Among them, Anita Rau Badami and Shauna Singh Baldwin have been published in mainstream publishing houses; they have received multiple awards and distinctions; and they have also achieved international recognition.

This recent attention from publishers, critics, and readers on Indo-Canadian fiction requires a wider contextualization in relation to the "Indian boom" in the international cultural markets. The Rushdie affair and Arundhati Roy's Booker Prize were two main catalysts for the contemporary success of Indian fiction in English. Their frequent appearances in the media served to promote Indian fiction in English all over the world, and most especially in the West, a success confirmed by VS Naipaul's Nobel Prize in 2001 and the more recent Man Booker Prize awarded to Kiran Desai in 2006, together with the important number of Indian novels translated into other languages in recent years.

Translation constitutes an important marker of status in the economic and cultural global system as it determines the range of the circulation of texts and therefore their span of reception. In our own country, Spain, there are scarcely any Canadian titles available in translation from racialized writers. However, as a significant proof of international interest on Indian women's writing, we do have Baldwin's *What the Body Remembers* and Badami's *The Hero's Walk* available not only in Spanish, but also in Catalan. Mootoo's *Cereus Blooms at Night* was translated into Spanish in 1999; unfortunately, it is now out of print, which demonstrates that literary success and commercial interests do not always maintain a long-lasting relationship. It is the destiny of most works of fiction, prizes and awards notwithstanding, to disappear from bookstores in a brief while, which complicates the teaching and therefore the canonization process of contemporary writing. The same has happened to Rachna Mara's *Of Customs and Excise*, translated into Galician in 1998 thanks to the personal insistence of its translator, María Reimóndez (a reputed Galician writer and translator[7]), though not into Spanish, and which is also out of print.

In this world of globalized consumerism, the taste for Indian products is not limited to the literary sphere, and many denounce it as renewed orientalism in the globalist age.[8] We dress "Indian" from head to toe, with henna, nose rings, colourful silks, and chappals,[9] and Indian novels reach the top ranking among our literary best sellers, in particular, diasporic fiction in English.[10] After the initial recognition of diasporic Indian male writers, like Salman Rushdie, VS Naipaul, and Vikram Seth, the turn came for Indian women to enjoy the pleasures of international distribution. Among them, Gita Mehta, Chitra Banerjee Divakaruni, Anjana Appachana, Jhumpa Lahiri, Abha Dawesar, Kiran Desai, Meera Syal, and Sunetra Gupta.[11] The controversy and subsequent promotion following Arundhati Roy's Booker Prize confirmed and increased even more the interest of the West in Indian fiction in English. This same phenomenon can be found in film, with the international successes of directors like Deepa Mehta, Mira Nair, and Gurinder Chadha, and in popular music, a field where the fusion of traditional Indian rhythms with Western ones has reached all styles.

It is within this general context that Indo-Canadian women writers have started to receive the critical attention that was denied to their predecessors in the seventies and eighties,[12] when Indo-Canadian women fiction writers were rare phenomena in the literary market, most of them published in small alternative presses. The only author of fiction to reach the mass market was Bharati Mukherjee, in part due to her polemics of racism, becoming then "the first South Asian woman in Canada to gain economic and cultural capital, publishing . . . with large publishers like Penguin and Random House" (Rahman 99, 86).

In the nineties, the fruits of the eighties activism on the part of the then-labelled "ethnic" writers started to be reaped, and new voices appeared on the literary front that questioned the politics of official multiculturalism, replaced the milder theoretical discourse of ethnicity for the more radical one of race, and experimented with new genres. In the area of Indo-Canadian fiction, Rachna Mara inaugurated the decade with her short-story cycle *Of Customs and Excise* (1991), her first and so far only work of fiction for adults. Mara is a pseudonym of Rachna Gilmore, who had previously published fiction for children and young readers.[13] Her choice of the short-story cycle constituted a significant irruption in a well-established Canadian tradition. It was, together with Makeda Silvera's *Remembering G and Other Stories* of the same year, the first short-story cycle published by a racialized woman in Canada. Silvera and Mara reclaimed then for the immigrant woman writer a form that had served until then as a more than suitable mode for the reconstruction of the white Anglo-Canadian *Lives of Girls and Women*.[14] In 1997 Shree Ghatage published her first collection of linked stories, *Awake When All the World Is Asleep*, winner of the Thomas Raddall Atlantic Fiction Award in 1998. Ghatage's collection may seem at first sight less "unified." Its eleven stories may show less recurrent characters and looser links; however, they all deal with a group of characters connected by the space of residence, the Maya Apartments. Ghatage's book can thus be included in what I've analyzed elsewhere as "place cycles," dealing with a group of people inhabiting a common space, in the line of Katherine Govier's *Brunswick Avenue* or Sandra Birdsell's *Agassiz Stories*. Ghatage's collection opens and closes with a recurrent character whose visit to India from Canada frames the space of the cycle as a diasporic text. In the current decade the genre stays alive, as is proven by the publication in 2002 of Nalini Warrior's cycle *Blues from the Malabar Coast*—which won the Quebec Writers Federation McAuslan First Book Award—and more recently of Nila Gupta's *The Sherpa and Other Fictions* (2008), which includes recurrent characters and other looser links between different stories.

There is no question, looking at the number of collections, that the preferred genre by Indo-Canadian women authors is the short story. Besides the aforementioned cycles, the following short-story collections were published in the last decade: Farida Karodia's *Coming Home and Other Stories* (1988) and *Against an*

African Sky (1997), Shani Mootoo's *Out on Main Street* (1993), Shauna Singh Baldwin's *English Lessons and Other Stories* (1996) and *We Are Not in Pakistan* (2007), and Uma Parameswaran's *What Was Always Hers* (New Muse Award 1999 and Canadian Authors Association Jubilee Award 2000, containing one novella and short stories) and *Riding High With Krishna and a Baseball Bat and Other Stories* (2006). Playing with different narrative forms, including short fiction, autobiography, criticism, and poetry, Yasmin Ladha's collections *Lion's Granddaughter and Other Stories* (1992) and *Women Dancing on Rooftops Bring Your Belly Close* (1997) resist genre categorization and can be considered the most innovative texts of the decade. The first volume resembles a loose short-story cycle, connected by the narrator's repeated address to her *Readerji* and recurrent characters in some of the Tanzanian stories, while the second is even more experimental in the mixture of genres.

Uma Parameswaran has seemed to specialize in the novella form, with the publication of *The Sweet Smell of Mother's Milk-wet Bodice* (2001, reissued in 2007), and the more recent *Fighter Pilots Never Die* (2007) and *The Forever Banyan Tree* (2007). However, she also continues to write short stories as noted above.

Finally, the less frequent but most publicized of fictional texts are, undoubtedly, the novels, and they have brought international fame to their authors. In 1986, Farida Karodia published her first novel, *Daughters of the Twilight*, in London (Women's Press), followed by *A Shattering of Silence* (1993) also in the United Kingdom (Heinemann). Shani Mootoo's *Cereus Blooms at Night* and Anita Rau Badami's *Tamarind Mem*, both published in 1996, received excellent reviews and were soon published internationally.[15] Shauna Singh Baldwin's *What the Body Remembers* won the Commonwealth Writers Prize for the Canada-Caribbean Region in 2000, and the following year Badami's second novel, *The Hero's Walk*, won the same prize, confirming the inclusion of Indo-Canadian women into the international Indian boom.[16] Soon after, in 2002, Uma Parameswaran's first novel *Mangoes on the Maple Tree* was published by the Canadian independent publisher Broken Jaw Press. New authors have started to be published in the present decade, for example, Ramabai Espinet, with *The Swinging Bridge* (2003); Sikeena Karmali, with *A House by the Sea* (2004); Nalini Warriar, with *The Enemy Within* (2005); Farzana Doctor, with *Steeling Nasreen* (2007); and Padma Viswanathan, with *The Toss of a Lemon* (2008). Besides, Farida Karodia has continued writing novels while splitting her time between South Africa and Canada, publishing *Other Secrets* (2000) and *Boundaries* (2003).

Badami's and Baldwin's careers have been unusual and spectacular. Badami was the first of these authors to have been published initially by an international company, Viking Penguin, and she is the first non-white writer to receive the Marian Engel Award (2000), and the youngest, a superb achievement for someone with only two novels published. Her latest novel, *Can You Hear the Nightbird Call?* came out simultaneously in five countries (Canada, India, France, Holland, and Italy) in 2006. Shauna Singh Baldwin has received numerous awards and distinctions, including The Writers' Union of Canada award for short prose in 1995 and the CBC Literary Award in 1997; her latest novel, *The Tiger Claw* (2004), was shortlisted for the Giller Prize. Shree Ghatage has also published her first novel, *Brahma's Dream* (2005) internationally with Random House, while Shani Mootoo published her second, *He Drown She in the Sea* (2005), with Grove Press and McClelland & Stewart.

Despite these successes, one has to be aware of the ways these books are being marketed and generally reviewed. Larissa Lai has cautioned that

> It is becoming increasingly evident that the Canadian publishing industry has a taste for particular kinds of narratives. There is a preference for texts that, if they speak of Canadian history, speak of histories rooted in past injustice, or else treat brutal histories of "over there." This is not to disparage the merit or political value of any of these books; however the cumulative result of their being foregrounded over others has the effect of producing new tropes of the marginalized subject as, on the one hand, equivalent with violence or, on the other, as the old stand-by staple of exotic faraway adventure. (2001, 42)

The exotism of the narratives is further reinforced by their colourful book covers that often include women in sari, the paramount reification of Indian women. In this trendy Indo chic, silk and cotton saris wrap beautiful bodies of South Asian women who become the main appealing bait for the Western consumer (see Rahman 99, 88). The "woman in sari" has become a sort of trademark, where we can easily identify the old nationalist trope of woman as the embodiment of the motherland. Henna-painted hands and feet and beautiful saris appear in almost every single book from Indian authors,[17] and Indian women authors are, perhaps, the most photographed of all. In this commercial strategy the body of the author herself becomes an object of exhibition.[18] These paratextual elements employed in the wrapping of the books (the design of the covers, titles, and other promotional devices) reveal the exploitation of the South Asian woman as a sign of sexual exoticism that commodifies these women's narratives in English for massive consumption in the West. It is important to take into consideration here that the writer's control over the marketing of her book is, except in very rare occasions, nil. Publishing houses have professional teams that decide the strategies to follow regarding book-cover design and title, negotiating with the writer's agent. Publishers sometimes use different titles (and often different cover designs) for the same literary text sold in different countries. An example is Anita Rau Badami's first novel, published in Canada as *Tamarind Mem* (1996), which became

Tamarind Woman in its American·and British editions (2000), keeping the exotic taste of the tamarind while targeting it more clearly to a feminine audience. In France it was published as *Memsahib*. The book covers of the different editions "might lead a prospective book buyer to believe that in the book a South Asian woman presents an exotic tale set in an exotic land, India" (Rahman 99, 89). The literary value of these novels is thus paradoxically put into question by the very system that promotes them, depoliticizing the voices of the marginalized and silenced experiences that the fictions present. By foregrounding the victim/object (the exotic woman in sari), the reader's attention is directed away from the political issues raised by these narratives, such as anticolonialism, antiracism, and feminism, and, of course, the Indian woman as subject. A clear example of this attempt to political neutralization is pointed out by Shazia Rahman in reference to Badami's first novel:

> This marketing strategy functions by capitalizing on the author's status as an ethnic woman writer to sell the book by promising a stable ethnic subjectivity that will narrate an exotic story about a misty, faraway land. However, this marketing strategy is in direct conflict with the book's actual argument, which posits mobile, diasporic, and feminist subjectivities. (90)

Chandra Mohanty's incisive criticism of the stereotype of "the Third World Woman" in her "Under Western Eyes" lists the expectations conjured up by this cliché in Western readers:

> The "third world difference" includes a paternalistic attitude toward women in the third world ... third world women as a group or category are automatically and necessarily defined as religious (read "not progressive"), family-oriented (read "traditional"), legal minors (read "they-are-not-still-conscious-of-their-rights"), illiterate (read "ignorant"), domestic (read "backward"), and sometimes revolutionary (read "their-country-is-in-a-state-of-war; they-must-fight!"). This is how the "third world difference" is produced. (72)

In a similar vein, Yasmin Jiwani has analysed these strategies in the realm of film, exposing the exploitation of the symbolic values of South Asian women's bodies in Western mainstream culture and which, from our point of view, constitute the ideological basis for the use of these visual representations in the marketing of Indian fiction:

> The woman is appropriated as a sign, and a sign infused with meanings that have their roots in the historical relationship of inequality and otherness. The symbolic value of the South Asian woman as a "sign" in the system of visual signs that form the language of the cinema lies in its ability to evoke this chain of association [that] has

become entrenched over time and now forms the taken-for-granted stock of knowledge of contemporary Western societies. [T]he South Asian woman is both "exotic"
and "dangerous," both attractive and repulsive. She is woman like her white female
counterparts, and yet not a woman because of her race. Her difference is what makes
her exploitable as a spectacle. (Jiwani 45)

These stereotypes are still predominant in the dominant culture of the West
and severely affect cultural expectations on racialized women. Those narratives
that tell a woman's story of courage and defiance in an old-fashioned context of
barbaric oppressive traditions soon make it to the best seller list. That many of
these texts are conveniently used to perpetuate the racist stereotypes of nonwhite
cultures as primitive and barbaric is not often part of their critical acclaim; on the
contrary, they are often praised for their positive examples of individual heroism.
The cumulative effect of this marketing device, with its promotion of tragic and
violent stories set in a remote place and/or time, reifies these women's resistance
to specific patriarchal practices in their cultures and to imperialism as a product
for quick consumption that obliterates very real and both historical and contemporary injustices.

Indo-Canadian fiction in English may fit into these categories, with violent stories of war, prosecution, and violence against women exerted in remote countries
filling their abundant pages. The Partition wars, the religious prosecutions and
massacres, and gendered violence of all kinds, including rape, war, incest, and
homicide for "crimes of honour" do figure in some of these narratives. However,
the fact that they are understood "natural" or "normal" in "those cultures" and, in
contrast, monstrous exceptions in the "civilized" West only confirms the racism
and sexism that permeate the dominant ideology of the publishing industry and
its targeted audience.[19] It is worth mentioning as an example, that Shauna Singh
Baldwin's second novel, *The Tiger Claw*, deals with the war in Europe that was taking place at the same time as the events in her previous novel, *What the Body
Remembers* (1937–1947). On the back cover of that first novel (Vintage Canada,
2000), the violence of the Partition is foregrounded along with polygamy and
described in the following dramatic terms: "separatist tensions between Hindus
and Muslims trap the Sikhs in a horrifying middle ground." This line in the promotional summary of the novel emphasizes the horrors of ethnic and religious
violence, while in the book the actual events only occupy the final section. In contrast, on the back cover of *The Tiger Claw* (Vintage Canada, 2005), the summary
does not include any adjective in reference to "the Nazi occupation after the German invasion of France in 1940," while describing the story as romantic: "[an]
extraordinary story of love and espionage," "an *astonishing* search through the
chaos of Europe's displaced persons camps," "an *unforgettable* denouement" (my
emphases). The contrast is a telling one. The case is made even worse by a blurb

from *The Gazette:* "*The Tiger Claw* muses on the dangers of tribal intolerances." While some forms of gendered violence are specific to certain cultures, all patriarchal societies exert violence on women in different ways. Every feminist writer will denounce the many forms of violence women experience in her specific culture. That the patriarchal ideology dominant in the culture industries attempts to neutralize feminist revelations of violence against women by numbing audiences with the victim cliché should not deter us us from acknowledging, studying, and neutralizing this violence.

The paratextual elements we have commented on here are just a few obvious examples of the Orientalist fault in the dominant Eurocentric view of racialized people which, in my opinion, resides at the heart of liberal multiculturalism's hypocritical celebration of cultural "diversity," and that must be taken into consideration when analyzing Indo-Canadian women's fiction. In the field of theory and criticism, the invaluable work of Himani Bannerji, Arun Mukherjee, Uma Parameswaran, and Aruna Srivastava have set the standards for the study of South Asian literature by women in Canada. Their involvement with scholars, writers, and artists and their activism has produced an indispensable critical corpus that intends to rescue Indo-Canadian women's writing from cultural commodification.

2. Transnational Feminist Fictions: Diasporic Trails

Whether set in North America, East Africa, the Caribbean, or the Indian subcontinent, all these texts share the traits of diasporic cultural identities. Moving constantly between Canada and India and beyond, whether imaginatively or physically, the characters in these narratives show the impossibility of single national cultural ascriptions in the contemporary world. Although diasporas are no new phenomena, recent conditions have exceptionally reinforced migration flows across the world.[20]

The case of the Indian diaspora is complex in its historical development and the diverse backgrounds of the authors discussed here prove the variety of this phenomenon. The great multiculturality of the Indian subcontinent does not allow any reductive approach to "Indian" identity, much less to an Indian diasporic one. Whether they are descendants of indenture labourers in the Caribbean or refugees in the subcontinent, whether they come as exiles from Africa or cheap labour in the United Kingdom and North America, or qualified professionals, students, and intellectuals, the experiences of Indian diasporic characters in the "host" countries are diverse. There has been much criticism directed against the privileged group who write in English, with accusations of elitism and removal from Indian "reality."[21] The group of Indo-Canadian women studied here are university-educated, and their narratives often deal with upper-class women of Indian origin or nationality, but they also portray the women around them: ayahs, servants, and migrated daughters who study and develop professional careers in Canada, in India, and in other countries. The social spectrum portrayed in these narratives includes members of different classes, castes, and religions, and each text is at least bilingual, sometimes multilingual; although predominantly urban, there are also a good number of stories about characters in rural settings. They are woman-centred narratives that share the common themes of diasporic writing enumerated by Roger Bromley: "generational conflict, the loss of family languages

12

and traditional practices, and the tensions caused by acculturation, inter-racial relationships and social and geographical mobility" (39), focusing on their specific effects on women's lives from a feminist perspective.[22]

Displacement

People like her were neither here nor there. Roots diluted, language lost.
Religion held onto only by the thin straps of festivals.
—Shani Mootto, *Out on Main Street,* 63

Movement is, naturally, a recurrent motif in diasporic fiction, and all of these texts present multiple displacements and travels: from village to the city, from one city to another, across national borders or across oceans. Some characters follow their husbands, like Saroja in Badami's *Tamarind Mem;* in many cases they go as sponsored wives, like Parvati in Mara's *Of Customs and Excise,* Kanwaljit in "English Lessons," and the Sikh wife in "Montreal 1962," two of the stories in Baldwin's collection, and Vijai in Mootoo's "A Garden of Her Own." Some migrate as girls with their families, for example, Mala in *Of Customs and Excise* and the girl narrator of "Be a Doctor" in *Lion's Granddaughter;* others have escaped from war and persecutions, as is the case of Asha and Sundri in *Of Customs and Excise,* and Roop in Baldwin's *What the Body Remembers,* and the Kashmiri refugees in the stories by Yasmin Ladha and Nila Gupta. We also find a number of girls who are sent away from their homes, like Bridget in *Customs and Excise,* born in India and sent "back home" to England because she is going "too native"; Veena in Ghatage's "Shantabai" is expelled from Bombay to Poona to separate her from her lover; in Gupta's "The Tin Bus," a twelve-year-old girl is sent to Delhi from Kashmir to save her from "land mines, ambushes, stray bullets, random executions" (161). Others choose to study and work abroad: Kamini in *Tamarind Mem;* Shaila in the opening and closing stories of *Awake When All the World is Asleep;* Simra, Jaya, Piya, and Prem's unnamed wife in "The Cat Who Cried" in Baldwin's *English Lessons.*

In all cases, their movement causes change and disruption, which is tragic and the most traumatic in the case of war refugees, and culturally acute in the cases of migration to the West. However, even those who do not move are affected by other people's displacements. Thus, the return of the migrant forces a family to change customs or views, and there is of course the change in Indian life as it gets modernized. A good example of such a sense of displacement of those who do not travel but experience changes occurs in Badami's *The Hero's Walk,* analyzed by Heike Härting as a representative example of "the formation of diasporic identities as an empowering process shaped by multiple changes on the local level rather than by transnational mobility" (43); or the widows and ayahs abandoned and/or exploited in their old age by their children in Baldwin's *English Lessons*. In her first story, "Rawalpindi 1919," the old mother illustrates the changes brought to her home by her son's university education in Vilayat when she says, "You will need to buy chairs for this house when he returns . . . And we will need plates" (3).[23] Her words express the preoccupation with inadequacy that those "left behind" might experience.

Cultural Contamination and Sexual Purity

> Can there be anyone or anything that can remain pure and survive?
> —Shauna Singh Baldwin, *What the Body Remembers*, 280

One of the most recurrent themes these authors explore is the traumatic disruption of the mother-child relationship (mostly daughters, though not exclusively)[24] caused by the adoption of "foreign" values and customs, whether by the "modernization" of India (often seen in terms of Westernization) or by their experiences in Western countries.

The "tradition vs modernity" dichotomy is best articulated on the site of the female body. The discussion of arranged marriages and women's (sexual/emotional) freedom is a recurrent topic in these narratives and constitutes a clear marker of intergenerational and intercultural clash. The subject of arranged marriage symbolizes the separation between mothers and daughters that reflects most explicitly the change in Indian women's social roles. In a number of cases, an arranged marriage is seen by parents as the necessary corrective to their daughter's excessive modernity, a way of recovering the estranged daughter; some women see in the arranged marriage an imposition and claim their right to independence, while others express their love, loyalty, and sexual desire towards the husbands chosen for them; some stories present the growth of love and desire in arranged marriages, while others show unlawful sexual relations. The expression of sexual desire in their writings constitutes in itself an important rupture with social and religious mores that deny women sexual agency. Some of the stories break old taboos and transgress racial, sexual, class, and even family limits, unveiling the hidden sexual lives of Indian women. Consider, for example, the abundant examples of forbidden mixed-race relationships, such as that between Parvati and her Goanese Christian lover in Mara's "Parvati's Dance." Parvati will get pregnant with Mala, who in turn will choose to have an equally forbidden sexual relation with a white friend. Similarly, we find an affair between Aisha's Indian mother and her black father in two stories in Ladha's *Lion's Granddaughter*. Saroja, the wife and mother in Badami's *Tamarind Mem*, has a white lover, and Shaila is in love with the white Canadian Simon in the two stories that open and close Ghatage's cycle.

In the latter collection we find frequent transgressions of the rules of "licit" sex, as is the case of the twin sister who has an affair with her sister's husband in "Awake When All the World Is Asleep" and "Shantabai," or the young wife who desires her father-in-law in "I am the Bougainvillea." Lesbian relationships appear frequently in Mootoo's narratives, for instance in the stories "Lemon Scent," "Out on Main Street," and "The Upside-Downness of the World," and in the novel *Cereus Blooms at Night*. Nila Gupta has her characters transgress both racial boundaries and heterosexual normativity in "The Mouser," where three teenagers—two girls and one boy—of diverse racial origins form a sexual trio.

All the narratives focus on family relationships, and most of them deal with the tensions created by the dilemma of individual freedom versus family duty. The interference of Western individualist ideologies in the traditional schemes of honour and duty provoke most of the conflicts in the stories. Honour and duty are demanded of the younger generations, especially the women, the traditional carriers of symbolic purity.[25] Thus, the young women become often the territory of dispute, pressed by parents and young husbands to accept their traditional roles. Mothers teach their daughters to remain silent and hide their intelligence and desires; even when they provide their daughters with university education in Western countries, they wish their girls to marry nice Indian boys of the same caste, class, and religion and return to India. The fear of cultural "contamination" is expressed in many stories through references to the daughter's body and family dishonour, following the logic of patriarchal possession of women's bodies.

A good example can be found in Baldwin's story "Simran," which shows how the families that send their daughters to be educated abroad expect them to return unchanged and accept their parents' decisions. Simran is nineteen and unmarried, and studies in an American university. Two narrative voices, in separate pieces, write about Simran—her mother, Amrit, and Mirza, a man in love with Simran (though she does not love him). We never get Simran's thoughts or feelings; symbolically occupying the traditional place of the silent daughter, she is spoken about, the site of contention, and they all try to manipulate her and make decisions for her. Simran is, like the girl narrator in "Family Ties," a victim of her family and of her friend; no one cares for her own wishes. Amrit, the mother, is afraid her Sikh daughter will lose her traditions and goodness because she will be Americanized, since "[i]n America, children learn that they can blame their parents for everything and then they all, parents and children, spend years in psychotherapy" (37). To avoid this contamination she tells Simran "to stay clear of Americans and make friends with other foreign students" (37). When Simran returns home for holidays, her mother observes her anxiously:

Was it my imagination, or did she laugh a lot more and louder since she came home?

Even her limbs imitated American indiscipline; her gestures were wider, and when she wore a sari I was dismayed that she no longer walked with a graceful glide, but strode as firmly as any shameless blonde woman. For this I sent her to America? (41).

Contrary to the "English lessons" in the book title, these mothers teach the language of silence. Amrit notices that her daughter is becoming too bold with words, arguing with her father all the time:

He'd brought it on himself by wanting her to have this American degree. I never studied in America and I have been content because I have always known instinctively and naturally just how far I can push the men around me, when to be winsome, when to be silent, when to become visibly sick with internal pain rather than unbecomingly obstinate. In four months in "the States," as she called it, Simran had lost all restraint, all decorum. (44)

It is made clear in several stories, as we have seen above, that Indian women should not dare express their views and opinions, and that Western women are considered "loose" not only in sexual terms, as Amrit suggests in the quotation above, but because of their tongues.[26] Mara offers a very similar situation in "Market Analysis" *(Of Customs and Excise):*

Her mother had whispered that morning that she was going to cook his favourite *russ-gulla,* and talk to him about McGill after dinner. But it took so little to set him off. If she was silent, *Answer me, show some respect.* If she said anything, *Don't you talk back to me. I will not have you acting like those white girls, always being disrespectful.* (37)

University education, especially if it implies "leaving home," is, for many parents in these works, at best a secondary asset to a bride's prospects, and at worst a waste of money and a menace to their daughters' reputations and therefore to the patriarchs' honor. In Mara's *Of Customs and Excise,* Mohan, as we have seen above, strongly opposes her university education:

You want her to be like the girls here? All they are talking about is sex, sex, sex! If she is going to Montreal, what will she get up to? *Pagal hai, ladki,* she is young and silly and totally unreliable . . . McGill! God knows what that girl will get up to. Ruin herself. Is that what you want for your daughter? So no decent boy will want her? . . . French will not improve her value as a bride. She should have gone into Domestic Science, like you. (44–45)

In this story, symbolically titled "Market Analysis," Mala criticizes the patriarchal view of woman as the father's property that can be exchanged with another man for money, and is devalued if she loses her virginity. In her reflections Mala gives a similar argument to that in Irigaray's chapter "Women on the Market" in *This*

Sex Which Is Not One (1985). Irigaray's discourse, which combines Marxism and psychoanalysis, applies to the recurrent images of woman as a market product in the short story, as in "Virginity was priced" (41), "French will not improve her value as a bride" (45), or "No spoilt goods, no seconds, nothing damaged" (46), that refer to Mala's value as a bride. For Irigaray, this commercial transaction between men is possible thanks to the incest taboo, which is the basis of all commercial operations. In "Market Analysis" the ghost of incest is also recurrent, as will be discussed below, and the influence of Irigaray's analysis is hardly casual. The logic of the male exchange of women's bodies is thus a fundamental aspect of patriarchal cultures with devastating effects on women's lives that will be further analyzed here in relation to violence against women.

In Baldwin's "The Cat Who Cried," an Indian grandmother, Mataji, distrusts her daughter-in-law because she has studied in America: "That my parents sent their daughter to study in America was an indication of a family tendency towards wasteful spending" (129). Years later, Mataji thinks it is stupid to put a Saraswati statue in her granddaughter's room and moves it to her grandson's, "where she will do some good" (131). As the old woman explains, Sarawasti will inspire him to learn. But the mother of the children, her daughter-in-law, is firm: "I said nothing, but the next day I moved Saraswati back to Sheila's room. I refuse to apologize for wanting my daughter to be educated" (132). Remembering her own times at Boston University, she says: "Being single while I was there and fearful of damaging my reputation at home, I stayed close to the Indian students and didn't mix with many Americans" (131).

Cultural purity, though affecting women more extremely in these fictions, is also contested by young men, especially in Baldwin's stories. In "Dropadi Ma," a young man who has migrated to Montreal refuses to be married "to someone my grandfather had decreed acceptable" (8). The story is set in 1966, and Sukhimama, the narrator's uncle, does not want to marry someone he does not know at all. His father's angry words reveal the generational fracture opened up by migration around individual choice and family duty, best exemplified in the case of marriage:

> What will come of knowing her, may I ask? And if, after this "knowing her," you think you do not want her, what will we do then? By then her reputation will be ruined and I will have to pay her parents to find a lesser match. Did they addle your brain in Canada? You should have stayed in England, sir. The English understand these things. (9)

While for the Indian father marriage is a family business—the bride has a certain price, and the son must be dutifully obedient—for the son marriage is an individual's option. The allusion to the English reveals that despite their occupation of India, the British did not interfere much in the "private" sphere and did not force Indians to change their marriage customs, which the father obviously prefers to the Canadians "brainwashing" his son.[27] When the son escapes to Montreal in the last minute, his parents bemoan their luck, "We are ruined . . . We are ruined," thinking both of their good name and of "how much money we will have to pay the girl's family" (11).

The lessons these parents consider most suitable for their daughters are those of silence and submission, and the mothers themselves are the best models of behaviour. As the narrator of Mootoo's "A Garden of Her Own" says, "Wiping up, scrubbing, making spotless these areas, and others, before he returns, are her evidence that she is diligent, that she is, indeed, her mother's daughter" (*Out on Main Street*, 16). Mala also describes her mother Parvati as an ideal if unreal model: "My mother, the perfect wife" (106) and "I can see the burden of my mother as the perfect wife, impossible, fanatical virtue" (Mara 108).[28] The goddess Parvati, according to Emily Kearns, "stands for 'normal' values and the married state of the householder, in opposition to behaviour that transgresses social norms" (198). However, both her affair with a Goanese Christian—Mala's biological father—and especially the lie she lives with all her life with regard to this paternity are severe transgressions that subvert the myth. When Parvati, in the short-story cycle, decides to accept the marriage her parents have arranged with Mohan, she consciously takes on the role of the perfect wife that the myth represents, as a penance, though not as an ideal:

> I must obey my husband, it is duty. But for me it is more. When I married Mohan, I prayed to Vishnu, Vishnu the Preserver, to save my baby and me. If he spared us, I would never let my husband regret marrying me, be the best Hindu wife, always obey my husband, make him happy. I made that oath, I made it freely. I had learned then only old ways are best. Useless to try to change karma.
> Vishnu spared us both. Always I kept my oath, always I will. Maybe it will make up for some of my sin. (50)

In her iconographic representations, the goddess Parvati appears subordinated to her husband, depicted either as a diminutive, submissive figure at his side, or with half of her body joined to half of his; but despite her submission, she preserves a distinctive identity of her own (Kearns 200). Unlike her husband Shiva, this goddess has a certain human trait: she wants to be a mother. Parvati's son Ganesh is hers only, not her husband's (Kearns 212). In *Of Customs and Excise*, Mala is also a daughter without a father, as Parvati admits: "My daughter, all mine, not Mohan's" (50). Between her child and her husband there is a terrible jealousy that emerges in family disputes, both in the myth and in the cycle. Nevertheless, this strife-torn mythic family is considered the ideal Hindu family, and the union of Shiva and Parvati the ideal marriage. Curiously, the traditional Hindu family in the myth, represented here by Parvati, Mohan, and Mala, is displaced to Canada; the transposition of the myth to an alien culture is paralleled by the strong sense of displacement of this migrant family. The problems between Mohan and Mala arise mainly from Mala's deep desire to be integrated into the new culture and Mohan's resistance to it. They hold antagonistic positions with regard to their new nationality. While Mala, in her adolescence and youth, wishes to be subsumed into "normal" Canadian life, not to stand out as different, Mohan and Parvati try to preserve their Indian roots. The desire for assimilation opens a chasm between mother and daughter:

> It is hard for her. She has Canadian friends, goes to Canadian university. Does not understand our ways, almost like a stranger sometimes. Never speaks our language. When I say something in Hindi, she is looking ashamed, always answering in English. She does not want to learn Indian cooking, never wear saris, never even *salwar khameez*, or *bindi*. For years I have saved my good saris for her marriage, nice temple saris, thick, old silk. When I hear her foreign voice, I wonder if she is really baby [sic] I sang Hindi lullabies to. (54)

The clash between the two cultures and their joint pressure on second-generation Canadians causes confusion, giving rise to anger and hatred for their parents, those "misfit outcasts." Mala's anger at her parents' iron attachment to the "old" Indian ways is not so much a rejection of their foreignness as a response to what she perceives as the weak and demeaning position of women in Indian society. Mala finds in Canada a more propitious atmosphere for personal development—in comparison to her obedient Indian mother—and a chance to achieve independence through education and professional training. Her family, more emphatically Mohan but also Parvati, wishes to arrange a marriage for her in the traditional manner, thereby securing her economic future at the expense of individual freedom and submission to a stranger. Although other women in this cycle transgress patriarchal rules by seeking independence and liberation in different ways—Asha remains single to avoid the burdens of motherhood and male tyranny, and Parvati follows through with her unlawful pregnancy—it is Mala who, "contaminated" by Western feminist discourses, explicitly articulates this oppression and fights it.

> *How could you send me to a strange man's bed to be raped on my wedding night.* I wanted to snap that gold chain off her neck, rip those saris she was saving for my wedding, tell her, get better, take care, stay well, drop dead, I don't care. (62)

The antagonistic mother-daughter relationship is not exclusive to the Indian family in the cycle, but it is extended, in Mara's typical balanced way, to the white English family too. Bridget is sent to a boarding school in England, since "'she's getting too native'" (67) in India, according to the British rules of ladylike behaviour as embodied by her mother. Bridget's parents are always absent, away somewhere in India or in Europe, in the service of the British army. Bridget's ayah Heera becomes a surrogate mother, from whom she is taken away at the age of six. In one of her characteristic binary contrasts, Mara uses opposing characters, Bridget's two mothers (Imogene and Heera) and their attitudes towards Bridget to represent British and Indian cultures, respectively. Imogene's cold, polite manners stand in strong contrast to Heera's warmth and love:

> My mother is kind but remote . . . Everyone admires my mother, even the servants. She treats everyone with the same disinterested, gentle courtesy. Heera loves me best. Mother says she spoils me . . . At the station my father hugs me and says, "Chin up, biddy."
> My mother smiles her cool, beautiful smile, pecks me on the cheek and touches my hair lightly. Normally she is not a demonstrative person. "There's a good girl, no tears now."
> That last night I cling to Heera and we both weep. Heera smooths the hair off my forehead, strokes my cheek, "Never mind, missy Sahib. You will come back one day and I will still be here. You will come back." (68)

Bridget's situation is similar to that of the migrant protagonists in Badami's, Mootoo's, Ladha's, and Baldwin's narratives. The psychic space of these child-characters, displaced as they are in another country which will gradually become their home, is occupied by another land and culture that they claim as home. Thus, although Imogene sends Bridget to England because, "after all, she's going home" (67), Bridget desperately asks to be allowed to return *home*, which for her means India: "During the worst of it, I manage to send off one furtive letter to my mother. I'm not very old, I can't spell many words. Enough to beg her to let me come home" (74).

Although the mother-daughter plot is a recurrent one, it is not the only one employed by these authors to comment on the changes in contemporary women's lives. It is important, from my point of view, not to lose track of the fact that conservative traditionalism is not a matter of age, but of ideology, and neither are all mothers "traditional" nor are all daughters "modern." Badami's *Tamarind Mem* offers a wonderful reversal of the typical situation when Saroja, the mother, avoids surveillance of her daughter by symbolically breaking the umbilical cord that ties them together (in the form of a telephone cord), to be, at last, a free woman with "a room of her own":

> Once I travelled because my husband did. Now it is time for me to wander because *I* wish to, and this little apartment with the gulmohur flowers will be here for me to return to when I am tired of being a gypsy. My daughters are surprised and not a little

annoyed at this decision. So many years I refuse to visit them, and now, all of a sudden, I chart out a pilgrimage around the country, a *jatra.*

"Go where, Ma?" ask Kamini and Roopa together on one of those ridiculous conference calls where everybody yells together . . .

"Anywhere," I say and cut off the call. Then I pull the phone cord out. Hunh! They hop from plane to plane, go here and there, and I am supposed to sit at home and wait for them. What is that phrase the boy in the flat downstairs uses? No way, honeybun! I do not belong to anyone now. I have cut loose and love only from a distance. My daughters can fulfil their own destinies. (265–66)

In Baldwin's *What the Body Remembers,* older Satya dares to confront Sardarji's masculine authority while the younger Roop is submissive and obedient; in her short stories Baldwin often resorts to opposing pairs of characters of the same age group. Thus, for example, in the story "Gayatri," Gayatri's husband supports his younger sister Reena's decisions contrary to tradition because "[s]he's a modern girl" (30). It is his wife Gayatri who resents the risk to the family's reputation. Gayatri and Reena stand for the old and the new values. Gayatri has followed the path laid for her by her family; her parents arranged her marriage through an advertisement and she has fulfilled her duty by giving her husband two male descendants. Reena, on the other hand, has found a good job as stewardess after finishing college, "making two thousand rupees a month and flying all over the world" (31). It is obvious to Reena (and to the reader) that Gayatri is jealous of Reena's life of freedom. But she cannot admit that her own life is being wasted; to Reena's suggestion that she should take a job, she replies,

Of course I'm bored. If I had been interested in working, my parents could have found me a poor man. But since they wanted me to marry a rich man, they protected me so I had a perfect reputation when I married your brother. My mother always said, "A girl can't be too careful with her reputation." (32)

The association of reputation and wealth that Gayatri mentions here is made explicit at the end of the story. When Reena announces that she has married an American man, her brother is happy and dismisses her outcry with a laugh, saying, "Well, times have changed, Gayatri. Your parents didn't have such a lot of money, so reputation was very important. Now in Reena's case, no one will dare to say much" (35). When they find out that Reena has married a black man, Gayatri feels vindicated, foreseeing a great tragedy, but her husband is as supportive of his sister as ever: "She will need all the help we can give her" (35).

Thus, racial prejudice, always an important issue in Baldwin's stories, is counterbalanced by brotherly affection and the old restrictive customs give way to new interracial families, as happens also in the story "Nothing Must Spoil this Visit."[29] In this story, Kamal resents his white sister-in-law's "asking questions as though she had a right to the answers" (100). Kamal is angry and envious that his elder brother has "removed himself so easily from the responsibilities of love and obedience" (100) in Canada while he remains in Delhi and measures achievement "by the extent of Papaji's or Mumji's approval" (109). He has married the woman chosen for his brother in order to avoid a scandal that would damage the family's reputation. The two wives are compared throughout the story. Janet, the white Canadian, has a professional career at the Royal Ontario Museum and was educated by her mother Anyu, a Hungarian refugee, to be a free woman:

> Janet imagined herself telling Anyu that her daughter had poured mustard-seed oil on a wood threshold and touched the feet of her husband's mother. Anyu, who had lived under Communists, would say, "You start bowing your head once, it gets easier and easier." (96)

Janet cannot understand Chaya's submissive attitude. When she finds out Chaya had been Arvind's fiancé, she wonders, "Would the Arvind she knew today have been happy with so passive a woman? Never an opinion, never any talk. Spoken at but mostly ignored. Rewarded with jewellery and sweetness for that silent, respectful obedience. And always that beautiful, ephemeral, meaningless smile" (110). Ironically, her husband Arvind thinks of Janet in similar terms; he believes Janet has grown up in Canada overprotected from any evil and unaware of the risky lives of other people. He finds her naïve and sometimes looks at her paternalistically: "It must have been Anyu who'd made her daughter this seeker of beautiful things, past and present. Anyu, who must have taken a vow on arriving in Canada to fashion her Janet's life into a procession of perfect, agreeable, beautiful experiences. Somehow, Anyu had protected her daughter's illusions through the seventies, and now he had the job" (95). Janet's puzzlement at Chaya's silent compliance contrasts with Kamal's view of Janet's assurance; in the following passage, Kamal compares his own wife to Arvind's, exposing his sexist traditionalist standards:

> [Chaya] was always slow. It really didn't matter—she came from good blood and she had given him a son. What more was there? At least she wasn't like Janet, brash and talkative . . .
> What did Arvind see in Janet? A woman who appeared not to need a man. These foreign women, though, they talk their heads off against male chauvinism, but they really like it, they like surrendering to a real man. Look at their movies—full of gaunt red-lipped women thrusting their come-hither pelvises at every eye. No sweetness, no kindness, no softness. Unbroken fillies. (100)

The derogatory vocabulary of domestication and control that Kamal uses is not as violent, though, as the method employed by the family doctor to "domesticate" poor Chaya into silent obedience. Although Janet sees Indian women as passive by nature, we are given in this story one more instance of the violence women face everyday. Chaya is "an adjustable woman" because she's been forced into submission and silence by violent threats to have her tongue cut, literally and not just symbolically. She is often reminded that she is lucky to be "protected" from worse dangers by her husband's family, and "her old college friends said there were worse mothers-in-law" (98).

A similar lesson in self-protection is given by a mother to her daughter in "The Cat Who Cried." As previously mentioned, here America is considered dangerous territory for unmarried Indian women who acquire wrong ideas about their independence and future possibilities. When the narrator returns to her parents' home because she's angry at her husband's family, her mother admonishes her:

> "Yes, you are going back. And you are going to be silent. No one will ever be able to say that you were raised to be troublesome. Do you want them to say that all your education only made you like some American feminist?" . . .
> "I want them to be fair. And what is so wrong to be a feminist?"
> My mother thought for a while. Then she said, "Be careful when you use that word. Men become afraid. If you want to survive, you must always let a man believe he has you under control. Silence is an excellent instrument, beti. Use it well." (133)

This is the only instance in the collection where feminism is explicitly mentioned and associated with North America, although in many of the examples we have seen it was suggested that women's desire for freedom and choice is a foreign intromission. Tony, in the story that gives title to the book *English Lessons*, warns his wife's teacher about the limits he wants in her learning:

> I will not like it if you teach her more than I know. But just enough for her to get a good-paying job at Dunkin' Donuts or maybe the Holiday Inn. She will learn quickly, but you must not teach her too many American ideas. (126)

Nevertheless, whether explicitly stated or not, the desire for freedom is recurrent among the women in these narrations. As the narrator of "The Cat Who Cried" states, "there are limits to silence" (133). Although the preservers of cultural purity would do anything to avoid change, "as if change were some terrible catastrophe that had so far been deftly averted" (134), change is inevitable and feminists demand it everywhere. The price paid by women in the name of "culture" and "religion" is too high.[30] Yasmin Ladha writes, denouncing crimes against women in the name of Islamic religion,

> When Allah turns chauvinistic, he fits me into male hands, who in turn, banish me to the couch when I talk back . . . Only a mother is pure, and like the Prophet said,

heaven is at a mother's feet. There has been this spill spewed on-and-on about the broad-minded Prophet and the progressive charter of rights he drew up for women in the Mecca-Medina century. The Prophet has passed on and today a Muslim woman's dusty rights might as well be displayed in a museum. Today, the movers of and shakers of Islam (now a *mujahideen,* now a *mullah*) insist on painting a woman's windows black, to barricade loin-drools either from the man or the woman's side. In the name of Allah, a *mujahideen* killed a middle-aged woman who served soup to a soldier, not her brother or husband. Lock her up, a woman is a rose for your eyes only. This is a Muslim woman's mirror in parts of my world. It glitters of spanking tight new crotches all over her body. Naturally, it is the iron-locked chastity belt for her, which only the husband may unlock. Anytime. When he is inside her, he does not face the holy direction of Mecca.

. . . Only mother is pure and heaven is at a mother's feet. Contemporary *mujahideens* throw acid on purdah-naked woman. Nowadays, frustrated middle-class Egyptian men relish the practice. With tight housing, soaring prices, and no sex before marriage, dare a woman reject or break the engagement, the frustrated man throws acid on her face. If he cannot have her, no one else can. Such tyranny against women. They drown in a cesspool of sorrow created and monitored by men. (*Women Dancing on Rooftops* 107–08)

War Rape

In war, a woman renunciates without aid or glory. She ropes her pain with her own intestines. Mum is the word.

—Yasmin Ladha, *Women Dancing on Rooftops,* 99

In patriarchal nationalist discourses, the female body is primarily conceived of as an instrument regulated by the state to preserve national purity, as Mary N Layoun has pointed out: "No subsidiary category or secondary concern of nationalism, particular and specific boundaries of gender and sexuality are, rather, its sine qua non. They are fundamental to its very emergence and formulation" (14). Layoun considers that "the question of woman—and of women, and of men—is the foundation of nationalism. The very basic rhetorical and organizational principles of the nation are tropes for and expressions of gendered power" (14). The violence exerted on women at times of war, when the raped woman stands for the invaded nation, is a clear consequence of such a conceptualization of the nation and of the metaphor of the motherland that represents it.[31] Baldwin employs this metaphor in Roop's criticism of British responsibility during the Partition:[32]

She does not wish to read *The Stateman's* words about Indians. She knows what they will say—that they are doomed, that no European would have behaved as they have in the past few months, that the years of British rule and British authority kept the lid

on the inborn savagery of Indians. That India will never last.
Nowhere in their editorials will they acknowledge their own rape and plunder of India. (*What the Body Remembers* 480; italics in the original)

Rape has been a war crime extensively perpetrated in the Indian subcontinent, as in many other international and interethnic confrontations. According to Beerendra Pandey, "at least one hundred thousand women are said to have been abducted and raped by all the three parties involved—Muslims, Hindus and Sikhs. The representation of gendered violence, which remains effaced in the history textbooks of both India and Pakistan, receives a central treatment in Partition fiction by women writers, especially the survivors" (105). War rape figures prominently in Baldwin's texts and in Rachna Mara's *Of Customs and Excise,* where Asha's childhood memories are of "voices wailing, crying, whimpering, shouting. The long stream of carts, people walking, heading from the border area. Both ways, Hindus, Muslims. The terrible things they've seen, heard, the talk. Women weeping, dead bodies by the roadside, naked women, blood between their legs" (32).

In Baldwin's "Family Ties," the codes of duty and honour are presented in these most tragic terms. With the context of the two Partition wars as the background for the story, a girl narrates the process of developing her awareness of her Sikh identity and what it means to be a woman in the context of war. She is told stories of persecution and martyrdom where the Muslims are the enemy and stories about her father's family being killed in the Partition war of 1947. Now, in 1971, the menace is directly over her, due to the new war against the Muslims for Bangladesh. Although her father "doesn't wear a saffron turban or carry a big kirpan" (13), he does follow the rules of his family's code of honour. He has kept his sister hidden because she was abducted by Muslims during the war and gave birth to a child. Desperate at having been rejected by her brother, this woman murders her baby in the hope that her brother will then take her back, to no avail. Now, when his own daughter is only ten, she must face this terrible decree: "[Handing him a gun] he tells my brother, 'If the Muslims come and your sister is in danger, you must shoot her rather than let her fall into their hands'" (17). [33] Shocked to realize that her brother unquestioningly accepts his "duty," the girl acknowledges then that patriarchy places women at risk also within the family: "A plane roars over the house and, for the first time, I feel no rush of fear; far more is the danger from those within" (17). Now that they have been taught a cruel lesson about gender division, sister and brother cannot look at each other as happy siblings any longer: "We are rice saplings separated for transplanting" (18). The little girl wonders: "Is it worse to be caught, converted, killed or raped by Muslims than to be killed by a brother? A brother—my brother—who said 'I will' in the voice of his warrior ancestors without once asking his usual everyday everlasting 'Why?'"

(18). This chasm between the two will become larger and larger as they are also physically separated; her brother is sent to a boarding school "because Dad says he needs to be taught some more what it means to be a man" while "I stay in Delhi because I have begun to know what pain it means to be a woman" (18). The girl cannot understand why her brother who loved her so much is turning to despise her. He's been given absolute power over her, and he grasps this superiority as a victory at a time when everything else around him makes him feel weak and angry:

> He was told I belong to him, that he has the power to will me to live or to die.
> I say, "Don't talk that way, Inder. I am your sister, and I love you."
> ... "No one loves anyone else in this family. It's all a show."
> "I do. I love you."
> "What does your love matter? You're just a girl."
> I let the tears come as I ponder his words under the eucalyptus tree. He's right. I'll be twelve soon, and my love or hate, bravery or fear doesn't matter. All that he and I have in common now is blood and honour. (23–24)

However, despite this terrible situation, the girl is offered glimpses of other possibilities for young women through the character of her teacher, Miss Shafi. Although her mother is always anxious about getting her married and the many drawbacks she faces to attract a good nice boy (she is fat, she needs glasses, her brother takes drugs), she wants to be like Reza Shafi, who is in love with her boyfriend and doesn't care about her reputation. When her mother complains, "We will never be able to get you married," she replies "I never want to be married" (35), thus refusing to accept the submissive role they all expect of her and therefore breaking away from that strangling chain of "duty and honor" that is at the heart of such violence. As Bharati Ray writes,

> Women's bodies are considered by Indian men, Hindu, Muslim or Sikh, as the repository of men's honour. 'Power rape,' the raping of women to demonstrate and defeat rival men in patriarchal societies, is quite common in many parts of India, as indeed in many other areas of the world. The rape of a woman is akin to the rape of the community to which she belongs. (Pandey 105)

Yasmin Ladha explicitly links war rape and nationalism in her narrative "Luggage of a Bride, of a Mujahedeen" (in *Women Dancing on Rooftops*) by inserting a quote from Susan Brownmiller[34] that explains the mechanisms at work that operate in the symbolic sphere of a nation through women's real bodies:

> "In one act of aggression, the collective spirit of women and of the nation is broken, leaving a reminder long after the troops depart. And if she survives the assault, what

does the victim of wartime rape become to her people?"

Fehmida *Didi* phones me up at seven in the morning. I'm almost ready. I'll just suck back a couple of Khaliq's cold slices of mangoes and leave. But Fehmida *Didi* says that the nineteen-year-old Kashmiri Muslim girl who has been raped by Indian soldiers doesn't want to talk to me, but relays her message, "Tell her, I am nothing now but an open coffin."

Much later I dare. Dare to ask the question. Fehmida *Didi* shakes her head, "No, no one will marry her."

"But in Islam, our divorcees and widows are allowed to marry, I mean it is one modern thing about our religion, *Didi*, so why . . ."

"They say, one who is raped has been well chewed on, like a bone." (98–99)

That the woman's body is the "coded text" of male power can also be seen in a brief but forceful exclamation by the narrator's father expressed in Ladha's *Lion's Granddaughter*, when President Nyerere of Tanzania nationalized Asian businesses and properties: "Nyerere, I will kill you . . . I will rape your mother . . . you dog fucker" (23).

A more physically explicit expression of the motherland metaphor is found in Baldwin's *What the Body Remembers*, when Kusum's body, sliced into six pieces, is found by her husband and he wonders whether she was raped and what the meaning of the dismembering is:

"Her hand was like this—unclenched. Her feet were like this—not poised to run. Her legs cut neatly at the thigh, why they must surely have used a sword or more than one! Why were her legs not bloody? To cut a woman apart without first raping—a waste, surely. Rape is one man's message to another: 'I took your pawn. Your move.'"

Even in death he can see Kusum only from the corners of his eyes. For how can he know, how does he know, if she was raped or not, when he has heard the same stories I have heard? But the cutting up, Jeevan continued, what message could this be?

. . . He received the message. Kusum's womb, the same from which his three sons came, had been delivered. Ripped out.

And the message, "We will stamp your kind, your very species from existence. This is no longer merely about izzat or land. This is a war against your quom, for all time. Leave. We take the womb so there can be no Sikhs from it, we take the womb, leave you its shell." (490–91)

Based on this scene, the novel's title, *What the Body Remembers*, projects a symbolic feminist statement on the re-membering of women's fractured bodies and experiences.

Incestous Rape

The violent exertion of masculine power on the site of women's bodies through rape is not limited, unfortunately, to the exceptional context of war. In the story "A Garden of Her Own," Mootoo inserts a reference to the many cases of raped and murdered women in the news, crimes that do not take place in India, Africa, or the Caribbean, but in North America:

> So often we huddled up in Mama's big bed and read the newspapers about things that happened to women up here—we read about women who suddenly disappeared and months later their corpses would be found, having been raped and dumped. And we also read about serial murders. The victims were almost always women who had been abducted from the street by strangers in some big North American city. (18)

Rape does take place also in the most private of spheres, the home, and even in the most forbidden of cases, across the incest taboo. Sexual abuse of a daughter by a father occurs in three of these books and it is a subject prone to misunderstanding or misinterpreted from a race perspective.[35] Although the publication in Canada of groundbreaking texts such as Elly Danica's *Don't. A Woman's Word* (1990), Trysh Ashby-Rolls's *Triumph: A Journey of Healing from Incest* (1991), Liza Potvin's *White Lies (for My Mother)* (1992), Betsy Warland's *The Bat Had Blue Eyes* (1993), or Janice Williamson's *Cry Baby* (1998) should deter any consideration that incest is not part of white Anglo-Canada,[36] it is part of the dominant ideology to think that these are crimes of more "uncivilized" men, as the following excerpt from Rachna Mara's "Market Analysis" shows:

> "Why wouldn't he let you go [to McGill]?" Mrs Nealy's forehead creased slightly.
> "Because he's determined to keep me under him." The words blurted out.
> There was a long silence, then, "Shirley, be a dear and get my slippers from upstairs."
> As soon as Shirley left the kitchen, Mrs Nealy said, "Mala, what's happening at home?"
> Mala looked down and pushed back a cuticle.
> Mrs. Nealy spoke slowly, carefully, "Mala, is he doing anything? Is there anything . . ." Her voice trailed away.
> It took a few seconds to register. Mala looked up, shocked. "Oh, no, it's nothing like that. I mean he's a bastard, but he'd never do anything like that."
> Mrs Nealy patted her hand. "I'm sorry. I didn't mean to imply . . . But if you ever need to talk, I'm here."
> Mala stared at Mrs Nealy, at the flakes of skin peeling around her reddened nostrils. She'd known Mrs Nealy for years, but that didn't give her the right to pry, to insinuate.

... She tucked the books under her arm, walking swiftly, shaken by the ugliness of Mrs. Nealy's suspicion. Was it possible that Mrs. Nealy thought *those* people did ugly, horrible things? For an instant, Mala's childhood affection for her father rushed to his defense. He may be paranoid and tyrannical but he'd never ... do that. (40–41)

The negative racist steretype upon which Mrs Nealy's question is founded has a traumatic effect in Mala's mind as she interiorizes this image of her father and it comes out in her nightmarish vision of herself with an unknown husband on their wedding night: "An image flashed in her mind, of her lying flat on a marriage bed, on top of her a faceless husband. And on top of her husband, shoving him hard, hard, harder into her, her father, his face distorted with rage. And lust" (46). The risk of rape within the family context is a recurrent topic in the short-story cycle, as Parvati (Mala's mother) is spied on while bathing by her father-in-law and Asha is menaced by her brother-in-law, the alcoholic Tilak.

Shree Ghatage offers a more explicit and "real" incestuous rape in the story "Shantabai," where fifteen-year-old Shanta is raped one night by her father. Shanta's life is depicted as a hunger-struck and solitary one, and the rape scene explains the disappearance of her only companion, her brother and protector, who has failed to save her from their father's assault and runs away into the jungle. Sexual violence in this story is related to extreme poverty and alcoholism, very much as in the case of Asha in Rachna Mara's stories.

Shani Mootoo's *Cereus Blooms at Night* presents a more complex incest narrative that spans for many years and has long-lasting traumatic effects. Rather than the simplified tyrant/victim dyad, we find here a violent and hating man with a history of psychological abuse, dislocation, and humiliation that has excluded him from Paradise (the town's symbolic name). Removed as a child from his family, religion, and culture by Reverend Ernest Thoroughly in an exemplary process of colonization that will be further commented on in relation to racist violence, Chandin Ramchandin falls deeply in love with Lavinia, the Reverend's daughter. Chandin's desire for Lavinia constitutes a first hint at incest in that she is, according to the racist Reverend—who does not want Chandin to marry into his family—his sister, although Chandin knows for sure that she is not. The incest taboo that separates him from his beloved will be transgressed years later as a kind of mad revenge at Lavinia's elopement with Chandin's wife, Sarah. The love relationship of his wife (his subaltern) and his unattainable object of desire (his white colonizer) doubly humiliates Chandin, who then turns to abuse his daughter Mala, his easiest target and innocent victim. In this complex novel of unstable and shifting identities, Mala is also a complex character who plays the roles of both daughter and wife to Chandin and mother to her sister Asha. Mala's strategy for survival is to split her identity into Mala, the protective adult, and Pohpoh, the abused child, which will lead her to the asylum as a mad woman suffering from schizophrenia. Although the "secret" incestuous abuse is not that secret, nobody in Paradise intervenes until transexual Otoh (Ambrosia in early childhood) finds Chandin's rotting corpse. The community, representing mainstream patriarchal heterosexist ideology, does not intervene to protect Mala from sexual abuse. Rather, they merely justify the violence exerted on her as a "misunderstanding": "[Her] father had obviously mistaken her for his wife, and [her] mother had obviously mistaken another woman for her husband"(109), and "they further reasoned, what man would not suffer a rage akin to insanity if his own wife, with a devilish mind of her own, left her husband and children." Incestuous rape is thus justified by a mother's transgression of hetero-normativity, and the daughter is punished for her mother's "sin."

3. The Many Violences of Racism

Colonial Legacies

> The Brits invaded India . . . Stole its heart and soul. Juggled and shuffled our con-
> quered people all over their empire, disregarding traditions, cultures and souls . . .
> Brown skin, the purest legacy left to Indians generations away from India.
> —Shani Mootoo, *Out on Main Street*, 63

One recurrent subject of diasporic fiction is the status of the immigrant. Many of the narratives express feelings of alienation and the racism faced by immigrants in their daily lives; at school, in the office, or in the streets, these characters are attacked more or less explicitly in racist terms. Racism, however, is not simple hatred, it is an expression of power, and the authors under consideration here show how it establishes hierarchies and how it is exerted on the powerless in diverse contexts.

The colonial heritage of many societies and the neocolonial power imbalance in one globalized world can be traced as the source of much of the violence experienced by the characters in the works of fiction considered here. British colonialism in India is pointed out as a crucial trigger of the Partition violence in several of the works. For instance, in Rachna Mara's *Of Customs and Excise*, "The Angrezi-log are leaving the country at last, but they're determined to make Muslims and Hindus fight each other; they have broken the country in two" (31); and Baldwin in *What the Body Remembers* says,

> In the chaos the British have created and are leaving behind, a man will no longer be
> measured by his achievement or contribution, but by his father's blood . . . Cunning-
> ham says, 'Hold on, old boy, the British didn't divide Hindus and Muslims—one
> believes in many Gods and the other believes in just one' . . . *Divide et impera*, he
> reminds Cunningham. *That was the policy, divide and rule. Separate electorates for*

Hindus, Muslims and Sikhs, remember? The Hindu and Muslim faiths were tools, the instruments by which you British divided us, than stood back complaining how we Indians fight, never giving you any peace. (410)

The ongoing effects of the Partition can also be found in the current independence war in Kashmir. Yasmin Ladha in *Women Dancing on Rooftops* exposes Western compliance by omission in the "rape, torture, interrogations, misconduct and generally stripping the self-dignity of Kashmiri Muslim citizens by the Indian military" (80), stating that the plebiscite under United Nations supervision promised by India in 1947 has not taken place and further that "international magazines write of Kashmir in terms of India. They don't carry quotes by ordinary Kashmir folks . . . The CNN lens is brutally shut. Who actually talks to Kashmiris?" (86). Nila Gupta's stories in *The Sherpa and Other Fictions* report the effects of that conflict from several perspectives: the refugees', in "The Flight of the Parrot" and "The Tin Bus"; the civil volunteers', in "The Flight of the Parrot" and "In the House of Broken Things"; the soldiers', in "High Regards"; and those who went away to Canada and feel guilty for their lack of committment, in "In the House of Broken Things." Gupta uses the example of implicated volunteers like Miss Kamla Vati or Anil to provoke reflection on those who have chosen detachment, making characters like Mona and Mohammed overcome their dilemmas and act responsibly towards others.

Colonialism and its violent racist hierarchical dynamics also carry a good share of responsibility in the expulsion of Asians from Africa after "independence," as Yasmin Ladha shows through an offensive comic-show scene in "Be a Doctor" (in *Lion's Granddaughter*[37]):

So this servant one day says to this East Indian Queen Elizabeth of us Blacks, "Mama, my legs are thin, think like spider legs, I can't carry all these utensils on one tray." So the fat darkie Royal Queen advises, "First carry the train in, and then fall all you want!" My brothers and nephews, this is the East Indian mentality. It is nobody's fault, we Africans have slave brains. First the British, Big Bwana and his gun and pipe. And then the East Indian money frog. (22)

Even individual abuse, "domestic violence," such as the incestuous rape of Mala Ranchandin in Mootoo's *Cereus Blooms at Night*, is clearly linked to the history of colonialism, as Coral Ann Howells maintains:

This novel translates the historical traumas of colonial inheritance into domestic terms of dysfunctional families and damaged individual lives . . . The origins of Mala's terrible story lie far back in her father's story in his double betrayal by the English Christian missionary, the allegorically named Reverend Ernest Thoroughly and his daughter Lavinia. Ramchandin is one of colonialism's casualties (while Mala's lover

Ambrose is another), a tragic figure who turns into a monster through grief and rage and self-loathing. (149–53)

Colonialism is funded by an economic exploitation enforced with violence that is justified through mechanisms of inferiorization such as racial discrimination. The racist structuring of society and, more pervasively, the ideology of difference, remain even when the colonizer leaves. In Africa, pigmentocracy "favoured" Asians, who are considered closer to the whites than the Black Africans in the racial scale. At the time of independence, this racial hierarchy targeted Asians in Tanzania and Uganda as "enemies" of the Blacks and accomplices of the white colonizer. Ladha's stories of Aisha in *Lion's Granddaughter* deal with the nationalization of Asian properties in Tanzania and depict it in terms of racial and anticolonial revenge:

> "These East Indians, I tell you, are strange. Who is their God? I ask you my brothers, my nephews, who is their God? A cow! They worship a cow! So what do you expect? This black servant, spindly like spider legs works for one woman. You know her? Oh my brothers, my nephews, you must know her!"
> The audience laughs.
> "Ah, I see you have met her! Who is she? One fat Indian mama. She does nothing; nothing but fans herself. Her black servant cooks, he cleans, he washes, he dries, he shops, he digs—I mean he digs her garden, not in her of course! She is too good for him then!" (22)

In the Indian subcontinent, ethnic hatred was also fomented by British colonialism, and it exploded violently, leading to the Partitions of 1947 and 1971. Muslims and Hindus racialize the Other in order to inferiorize and justify violent extermination of that Other. In Baldwin's fiction, concerned with the historical archiving of the many wrongs done to Sikhs, the visible signs of Sikh masculinity are mentioned frequently as the visual marks of difference that, like "visible" racial colour, target the Sikh body as prey to cultural/ethnic/racial/religious hatred, depending on the specific context. For example, in "Family Ties," the father hides his Sikh background during the war with Pakistan over Bangladesh because "I lost enough in '47" (13), and his son is teased by his Hindu mates at the boarding school for wearing a turban. When the boy is given the female role for a school representation, "forced to dress as a woman and paraded before an audience without the turban that would protect his waist-length hair" (18), the Sikh symbols of masculinity are read by his audience as typically feminine. Since the story deals with the process of acquisition of a gender identity within the Sikh culture, this passage of gender confusion is relevant to understanding the boy's progressive deterioration and his rejection of Sikhism. Similarly Arvind, in "Nothing Must

Spoil this Visit," hides that he is a Sikh at the Punjab border. He no longer wears a turban—for which he is harshly criticized by his conservative brother Kamal—so he passes for a Hindu. When Janet, his white Canadian wife, asks him about it, he reflects on the ignorance of Canadians—safe and sound in their pleasant North America—on the affairs of that other side of the globe, oblivious to the histories of violence in the subcontinent:

> How could he expect her to understand why he hadn't shown the policeman his pass-port with the visa permitting him to enter his home state, the visa so stamped and official? There she was, aglow in that inviolable cocoon of Canadian niceness. Whereas he and the policeman were like twigs of those baskets in the stall—woven together, yet tense with a contained rebellion ... He couldn't talk about possible danger and unpleasantness if it were obvious he was a Sikh, couldn't remind her about the articles she'd clipped from the paper for him—articles on the massacre of Sikhs at the Golden Temple just two years ago, articles that referred to all Sikhs as terrorists. Honesty may be the best policy when you're faced with a Mountie, but here ... (94)

The kind of "danger and unpleasantness" Arvind insinuates here is described in more detail in the story "The Insult," where the narrator explains why her husband does not wear a turban:

> My parents found "a good Sikh fellow" for me to marry in Delhi a few months later, but he had no turban. He'd been driving a jeep home from college on that day in 1984 when every Hindu was licensed to kill a Sikh, and it was lucky for him that they no more than pull him from that wobbly raft and, with his six yards of saffron billowing on the black potholed road, pull down his knot of sleek, long, curly black hair and take a scissor to it. My father says he must have fought like a tiger as the mob plucked out his beard; I have never asked my husband to tell me why he has no need to shave.
>   It is easier to live in Chicago without a turban, though. (138)

However, although for the younger couple not wearing a turban makes life easier in the States, for her parents this reduces the value of the man: "Did you not tell her she did not do her duty to find you a husband on that trip to India? And that it is her fault you are married to a man without a turban?" (140) When looking for a Sikh husband for her daughter, the narrator's mother had discarded American Sikhs because "so many have cut their hair and don't wear a turban" (138).

The menace of "cultural contamination" reaches racist extents on some occasions in Baldwin's stories, as in "Rawalpindi 1919," where an old woman is preparing a goodbye meal for her youngest son, leaving for Vilayat/England where he will study. Her thoughts reflect prejudice and distrust towards the whites, afraid as she is of the changes this visit will cause in her son:

This idea that her son could go to Vilayat, to the white people's country, to learn from their gurus in their dark and cloudy cities—her youngest—and then return to Rawalpindi, and his people would know no difference. (2)

He will have to learn to adjust to white people's "dirty" manners: "he will learn the shake-hand instead of our non-polluting palms-together" (2), she says, opining that for this reason they use white plates, sharp forks, and long knives "to keep themselves distant from their food" (3).

Rachna Mara doubly reverses the attitude of British contempt for the inferior Indian through the character of Asha, in racial and class terms: "It was a mistake, agreeing to work for this Angrezi doctor. So many strange ways she had. The way she spoke. The clothes she wore, such dull colours. And her skin. Not nice and fair so much as boiled-looking, with ugly, dark blotches. Her eyes were pale and watery, and she had no eyelashes to speak of, just a few scrubby, straight hairs, like a cow" (Mara 19), and "Asha mimicked Doctorsahib's Hindi, described her habits. So dirty she was, she never washed properly when she went to the toilet, used paper not water. And she ate with her left hand. *Chee,* imagine not knowing the left hand was for cleaning the body, the right one for eating. The women wrinkled their noses, giggled" (24–25). Asha's opposition to Bridget, who carries, to her eyes, the burden of colonial guilt, is articulated in racist terms with references to her strange looks and customs.

Visible Minorities

Set apart, little brown tiles in a mosaic.
—Rachna Mara, *Of Customs and Excise,* 104

In the Canadian context, as in Great Britain and the United States, all that interethnic, interreligious, racist bigotry is simplified and reduced to a very basic color code: white versus brown. Whatever their nation of origin, their religion, or their language, all people of South Asian ancestry are labeled "Pakis." Their brown skin is the marker of belonging, not to the Canadian nation, defined, as we have seen in the Introduction, in relation to its English and French founders, but to a "visible" minority. Using the common metaphor of weather contrast recurrent in much of the fiction by writers from tropical countries, McGifford makes reference to the antiracist politics of South Asian Canadian writing:

South Asians in Canada usually find that the cold, forbidding Canadian climate is outmatched by the icy, hostile environment where they feel themselves doubly marginalized: first because they are immigrants and second because they belong to racial, often linguistic, and usually religious minorities. Mainstream Canadians may be openly antagonistic, judging South Asians as simply too different, simply the "wrong" kind of immigrant; or the racism and bigotry may be more subtle. Whatever the face of intolerance, the effects are comparable and nobody should be shocked that the alienation of the immigrant and the bitter stings of racism and religious bigotry, painful daily realities for South Asians Canadian writers, are important factors in shaping their lives, politics and art. (McGifford *viii*)

As stated above, the physical signs of Sikhism are mentioned frequently in Baldwin's stories: turbans, daggers, and long hair are understood by Sikh families to be signs of cultural and religious purity, but they mark the Sikh male body as visibly "different," whether in India or in North America. In "Montreal 1962," a Sikh man enoucnters resistance to these markers of his identity: "They said I could have the job if I take off my turban and cut my hair short." His wife's reply quickly exposes the lie in the fairy tale of Canada opening its arms to immigrants:

This was not how they described emigrating to Canada. I still remember them saying to you, "You're a well qualified man. We need professional people." And they talked about freedom and opportunity for those lucky enough to already speak English. No one said then, "You must be reborn white-skinned—and clean-shaven to show it—to survive." (4)

For this couple, the turban, beard, and long hair, the markers of Sikh masculinity, are essential elements of their identities. The term used by the narrator to refer to her treatment of her husband's turbans is "mothering": she feeds them, she massages them, "working each one in a rhythm bone-deep, as my mother and hers must have done before me, that their men might face the world proud" (5), and she touches them with as much care "as someday I will lift my children" (5). Moreover, the red colour of her favorite turban symbolizes the blood of the Sikh martyrs. Thus the woman's insistence on her husband wearing his turban is an assertion of Sikh identity despite resistance.

And so, my love, I will not let you cut your strong rope of hair and go without a turban into this land of strangers . . . My hands will tie a turban every day upon your head and work so we can keep it there. One day our children will say, "My father came to this country with very little but his turban and my mother learned to work because no one would hire him."
Then we will have taught Canadians what it takes to wear a turban. (7)

In another story, titled "Toronto 1984," things have not changed much for the immigrant family. Although the public discourse is now one of multiculturalism and diversity, and "ethnicity" is valued to a manageable extent ("I can have ethnic individualism in my earrings," says Piya in the opening paragraph, 53), there is a clear limit marked by racist standards. Piya's boss is furious when she refuses to stand and toast the Queen ("I cannot stand for the British Queen." "She is Canada's Queen," 55) and insults her: "'You're a damn Paki'. He looked around at all the white faces at the table. 'I would never have hired you if I had known you were a damn Paki'" (56). Piya's refusal to comply with a nationalism founded on British imperialism is confronted by a quick resort to verbal racism. After this episode, Piya is conscious of the racialization that has taken place and now bears the burden of representation: "For now I am not only myself, but I am all of India, Pakistan and Bangladesh. I am a million and a half people sitting in one small office in Mississauga. I wear a label and will take pride in being a damn Paki" (57).

In Rachna Mara's stories, in the character of Mala we can find one of the most explicit articulations of the so-called second generation's discontent with their nation's treatment of racialized citizens. Mala is aware of the subtle forms of racism she faces everyday in Canada, and gives several examples, as in "There were guys who'd never date her. They weren't the type who hissed 'Paki!' in the street, just always saw her kind as strangers. But they'd fuck a stranger" (46); "the last one was Brad, who said the morning after how he loved dark girls, really he did" (57); "It takes a long time to get our ice cream. I feel my father getting restless, angry, and something else I can't name. When we finally get our cones, I say, 'Daddy, that man forgot to say, *Thank you come again*, like he did to the others.' My father says nothing. In the pit of my stomach I realize he feels shame" (108).

She shares ethnicity with her parents, as she does racist aggression. Mara's family takes shelter in the realm of shared memory with other Indo-Canadians. Vanaja Dhruvarajan studied this immigrant phenomenon in two surveys carried out in 1992 and 1996, reaching the following conclusions:

Data reveal that the desire for acceptance by the mainstream was much greater among those who grew up in Canada, while their parents were more preoccupied with preserving their cherished ethnic culture. Most first-generation immigrants were convinced that they were not welcome in this society, and they interacted mostly with members of their own ethnic group. Their reaction to racism was that, since they chose to come here, they must try to make the best of it. Most of them worried about their children going through similar experiences. They felt racism directed against their children was more unfair because their children were born in Canada and grew up here. The second-generation immigrants, on the other hand, were struggling to gain acceptance from the mainstream. Many of them reported experiencing racism, particularly in junior high school. Once they got into university, they found circles in which they were accepted. Many of them felt they were caught between two cultures, because approval from parents and acceptance by peers were equally important.[38] (171)

Mara offers a compelling example of such an inner conflict in the following passage:

I told [mom] about Barb's birthday, that I wasn't invited.

I didn't tell her Barb had invited me, then giggled, *I hope I'll understand your mother when she drops you off, she talks funny.*

I'd torn up the invitation, flung it in Barb's face, spat at her, *I don't want to go to your dumb party, you're a jerk.* I hated her, hated my mother for being different, loved my mother. I wanted to punch Barb, rush home and rock my mother. Most of all, I hated myself for the times I looked away when people stared at Mom in her sari, the times I cringed when I heard her accent in public. (61)

In his review of Dionne Brand's *What We All Long For,* David Chariandy analyzes in depth the creative responses of that novel's racialized youth to racism. His comments on their alienation are relevant to our discussion here:

Some mainstream debates appear to assume that the second generation uncomplicatedly inherits their parent's ethnic legacies, and for this reason alone fails to integrate "properly" into society . . . In contrast, the alienation of the youths in the novel has little to do with the 'foreign' traditions and manners that they have either rejected or adapted towards their own ends, but with the plain and apparently non-negotiable fact of being instantly read, in their country of birth, as racial minority 'others.' (104–105)

Mala is fully aware of the difficulty of defining her nationality. As a member of a "visible" minority, she is always identified as a foreigner, never as a Canadian: "When we lived in Canada and people asked what my nationality was I'd say, 'Canadian. What's yours?' *Where are you from?* In England it's easy. *From Canada*" (104).

Canada as a nation does not easily integrate immigrants of colour, who neither achieve complete assimiliation nor preserve their culture of origin; they are always in-between worlds, permanently displaced, as Mootoo puts it in her story "Sushila's Bhakti,"

For ten years she had been floating rootlessly in the Canadian landscape, not properly Trinidanian (she could not sing one calypso, or shake down her hips with abandon when one was sung—the diligence of being a goodBrahmingirl), not Indian except in skin colour (now, curries and too many spices gave her frightful cramps, and the runs, and in her family a sari had always been a costume), certainly not White and hardly Canadian either. (60)

While a certain degree of exotic difference is not only tolerated but even encouraged in the celebration of multicultural diversity, the persistent definitions of national identity as white exclude all racialized individuals and collectivities from Canadianness. Sitting by a new bride on a flight from London to Toronto,

Mala reflects,

> She's convinced she'll live happily ever after in Canada, wallowing in wealth. What do I tell her? She probably doesn't even know her husband. How can she understand what it'll be like having children there? Watching them fit in, spat upon, rejected, rejecting their parents to fit in. Set apart, little brown tiles in a mosaic, twirling with the other tiles, exotic costumes, dances, food. *Gee, I love your culture. What country are you from?* (104)[39]

Mala's rejection of her parents' culture does not imply an absolute acceptance, in counterbalance, of mainstream Canadian society, nor a complete break with Hindu culture.[40] She exposes the racism latent in Canadian society, and the cruel irony of the multicultural mosaic it pretends to be, which is limited to superficial and "colourful" folkloric images. Nevertheless, Canada is the only country the second generation knows as their home, even if the dominant group stubbornly marks them as foreigners through processes of racialization. After her father's death, Mala is reconciled with her mother, and decides to return, acknowledging that neither India nor England can fill her memories and feelings like the many years shared with her family in Canada. Mala's final words in "Moon Snails" sum up this process of reconciliation both with her mother and her "stepmother" land, Canada: "When I get back to London, Jake and I will look for jobs back in Canada. This is my home. The most home I know" (109). In a similar tone, Mootoo's character Sushila defines Canada as "a country full of rootless and floating people" (*Out on Main Street*, 60) like herself.

Despite their clear depictions of racism, these authors do not offer simplistic victim narratives; as we have seen when looking at cultural restraints in terms of gender, Canada, the United States, and Great Britain also represent new opportunities for personal fulfillment, through education, careers, and less restrictive gender roles. After all, migration is always intended as an act of betterment. As we have seen while commenting on the persecution of Sikhs, migration to North America is presented in some of Baldwin's stories as a way to save one's life. In the case of the migrants from Tanzania in Ladha's stories, Canada is also a shelter and a promise of freedom:

> I remember the thin, tall Canadian who interviews us. So many times, my mother repeats the story of the tall officer who places immigration papers in her lap. Many are rejected and many receive their forms across the table. Mother repeats how this tall body bends to place freedom in her lap. Over the years, she traces him in a gray suit, sometimes charcoal, even green. She does not give him European eyes. They are almond shaped like an Indian beauty's. Her tall sun (he surpasses son) is a lifter and feeder. It is balmy in the north for mother. (*Lion's Granddaughter*, 87–88)

It is relevant here that the narrator's mother recalls the immigration officer as non-white, as if such a welcoming gesture would not be credible if coming from a "normal"—read white—officer. Ladha expresses at different points in her works that ambivalence towards a country that treats racialized people as second-class citizens, while being aware of the privileges that that citizenship, symbolized in the dark blue passport, concedes them. Thus, in her first collection she writes: "He has paid my bride price; now I have been granted a dark blue passport. Now I travel visa-free to most countries because of *Husbandji's* book/seal/clout. Airport officials greet me, 'From Canada, eh? No problem.' Stamp stamp. 'Have an enjoyable stay.' In the same airports, the line marked 'Third World' is full of shuffling" (*Lion's Granddaughter*, 86). In *Women Dancing on Rooftops*, she says, "The affluence of my Canadian passport. To be let through without red alert (I ain't from some tatter-nation, so do fuck off, inspector). My passport, a magical gear" (161), alluding to the practical, political, and economic privileges of (more or less) belonging to a powerful nation in the global scene.

4. Conclusion

Looking at the fiction narratives published in English by Indo-Canadian women from 1990 onwards, I have tried in this chapter to offer an explanation for their appeal to the Canadian readership and to give a critical reading of their politics and poetics of resistance. I suggest here that the international success of the so-called Indo-chic phenomenon, based mostly on an Orientalist gaze over the exotic South Asian Other, has benefited Indo-Canadian authors, opening to them the doors of the big corporations in the culture industry and favouring their international distribution. However, I argue, while in some notable cases the marketing of the texts—most especially of novels—targets them for easy consumption by a large audience, in all cases, and most notably in the collections of short stories published by small independent presses, the texts present narratives of resistance that are strongly political and can be viewed as part of a communal struggle against gender, sexual, racial, and class discrimination.

I have chosen to focus my analysis of the texts around these issues, starting with a general comment on their status as diasporic fictions. The recurrent themes of displacement and cultural purity or hybridity are used to explore the specific cultural values and practices that the women in these narratives want to preserve or transgress. Distance and exposure to other cultural forms help the characters to evaluate their own status within a given class, family, or religion, often also within a given sexuality or a gendered body. Although my study of these works pays special attention to the violence suffered by women of Indian ancestry, and in this I am well aware of the risks of contributing to the pervasive vilification of brown-skinned men as brutal to women, it is my intention to emphasize these authors' feminist denunciations of violence against women within their cultures, while making clear that violence against women is a common characteristic of all patriarchal cultures, and therefore it is also present in the European and North American societies in which these writers and their characters live.

In the narratives set in the Indian subcontinent, often dealing with the Partitions, gender violence takes the form of rape, while in other contexts incest is a recurrent crime. I analyze both forms of violence as having their roots in the patriarchal desire to possess and control women's bodies and its control over women's reproduction capabilities, which is intimately linked to nationalism and the nation's bio-policies. This conceptualization of the nation as a female body, a motherland, explains not only war rape and incest (a taboo that regulates all economy, according to Irigaray), but also the exclusion of racialized women from the Canadian nation, imagined exclusively as a white motherland, as Himani Bannerji has pointed out:

> It is not hard to see that the Canadian state's overwhelming sense of guardianship over women's bodies amounts to a demand for white women to reproduce more and for non-white women to reproduce less ... The fact that the state seeks to hold the white woman's womb hostage has profound repercussions for non-white women. Caught in the same legal labyrinth as their white counterparts, their motherhood is by implication also regulated. (70)

The female body is, in most of these narratives, a site of dispute, a territory where diverse powers struggle for domination, often resorting to other, more subtle, forms of violence. Indoctrination into silence and submission is a recurrent theme, often presented around the conflicting topics of arranged marriages and education. The mother-daughter dyad is a frequent strategy employed by the authors considered here to refer to the changes undergone by the different generations, often in relation to the movements of the characters to other countries, but also due to the ongoing developments in the home culture itself. However, I have intended to demonstrate here that the "tradition vs modernity" paradigm is not exclusively represented in terms of age, as a generational gap, but that it is an ideological clash that takes place between same-age people too, and most explicitly between conservative and feminist positions.

Finally, in the last sections of the chapter, I have looked at the antiracist politics in the stories and novels. Again, the number of texts is substantial enough to offer a varied portrait of the many articulations of racial discrimination. This section focuses first on the hatred among diverse groups in the Indian subcontinent, in Africa (expulsion of Asians from Tanzania and Uganda), and in Trinidad, exposing the crucial role played by the British colonial regime in fomenting pigmentocracy and ethnic divisions.

Colonialism lies also at the heart of the formulation of the Canadian state, which is defined in terms of two European founding nations. In the second part of the final section, my analysis turns to the narratives set in Canada, where we find many examples of verbal aggression and a good number of less explicit racist attitudes. A predominant feeling shared by many immigrants is exclusion from "Canadianness," an exclusion founded on the racist definition of the nation as white despite its contemporary public discourse of multiculturalism. Many of the stories considered here expose multiculturalism as a hypocritical masquerade rather than as a real acceptance of diversity. Despite their contribution to the common wealth of the state (as migrant workers, caregivers, students), the characters in these narratives do not feel they belong to a community that keeps demanding of them an explanation about their "origins." Visually identified as "foreigners" and submitted hence to racialization, the members of "visible minorities" in these stories problematize dominant definitions of the Canadian multicultural nation that still now, in the twenty-first century, rests heavily on its colonial past.

II.
RACIALIZED BODIES: CHINESE CANADIAN WOMEN'S FICTION

1. Introduction

The study of the so-called Chinese Canadian literatures is a rather recent phenomenon, with a brief history of no more than twenty-five years. The first texts by Chinese Canadians can be traced back as far as the late-nineteenth century with the Eaton sisters, but there was no recognizable success in establishing the discipline until the early 1990s.[41] Some of the most relevant critical studies have begun to appear only in recent years, including Lien Chao's "Anthologizing the Collective: The Epic Struggles to Establish Chinese Canadian Literature in English" and *Beyond Silence: Chinese Canadian Literature in English* (1997), and Fred Wah's *Faking It: Poetics and Hybridity* (2000). Furthermore, the influence of the comprehensive politics of official multiculturalism, also known in Canada as the "cultural mosaic," has been paramount, insofar as it managed to dissolve race into ethnicity, and colour into cultural assimilation and homogenization, as many have contended.[42]

In a crucial way, and apart from the efforts made by the academy, the creative productions of Chinese Canadian writers at present, and of women authors in particular, cannot be understood in isolation but as the result of community work. This work has materialized thanks to small publishing companies (Press Gang, Sister Vision, TSAR), writers' workshops (The Asian Canadian Writers Workshop [ACWW], with Paul Yee and Sky Lee), conferences (Writing thru Race, celebrated in 1994, was organized by the Racial Minority Writers' Committee of the Writers' Union of Canada), periodicals (*Gum San Po*, which disappeared after two issues; *Asianadian*, more successful and lasting; and special issues, such as those of *West Coast Line*), and anthologies (*Inalienable Rice*, 1979; *Many-Mouthed Birds: Contemporary Writing by Chinese Canadians*, 1992).[43] The fact that the Chinese Canadian community has preserved its language has worked in favour of a sense of collectivity and has prevented its assimilation into English or French cultures (Chao, *Beyond Silence* 19). At the same time, however, the adoption of English as the language of culture and literature has become a political tool against mainstream efforts to exclude the Chinese.[44]

The great centre of Chinese Canadian literature is Vancouver, where the writers selected for commentary here were either born or have settled. The 1990s saw the publication of a number of memoirs and historical novels problematizing the experience of the first Chinese settlers in Canada.[45] Perhaps the most emblematic historical narrative dealing with this period is *Disappearing Moon Cafe* by Sky Lee, published in 1990, considered the first novel by a Chinese Canadian. The novel is set in present-day Vancouver and illustrates the story of the Wong family, spanning a century, from Wong Gwei Chang's arrival in the country in 1892 up to the birth of his great-granddaughter Kae's first son in 1986. Soon after this cornerstone a remarkable novel by Wayson Choy was published, in 1995, *The Jade Peony*, this time focused on pre-war Chinatown. Judy Fong Bates imagines the context of post-war Ontario in her short-story collection *China Dog and Other Tales from a Chinese Laundry* (1997) and in her novel *Midnight at the Dragon Cafe* (2004).[46] Like Sky Lee before her, but perhaps even more acutely, Fong Bates focuses on the life of Chinatown communities, depicting Chinese Canadians as isolated from their Caucasian neighbours.[47] All these works share the common goal of reconstituting a sense of community that has been essential to breaking years of silence:

> By celebrating the survival and the development of the community, Chinese Canadian literature displays "the collective self" as the sum of its common values and honours individual men and women who have endured unusual physical and human hardships and whose lives constitute a resistant voice against racial discrimination. (Chao, *Beyond Silence* 18)

The works of Evelyn Lau, Larissa Lai, and Lydia Kwa—some of them included in the so-called "Second Wave" of Chinese Canadian writing (van Leuven 40)— seem to depart from this direction and try to open new ways, experimenting with the concept of genre and going further than historical reconstruction. We will see, for example, how Lai plays with a new approach to history-writing that she calls "artificial history."[48] The challenge and renovation of genre goes hand-in-hand with a vindication of "race," except perhaps for Evelyn Lau. We will show how she rejects being classified as a Chinese Canadian writer and working for one ethnic community, but is nonetheless sensitive to issues of colour in her stories. Race is rescued as a valuable political category to be critically reexamined by writers and theoreticians alike. Coleman and Goellnicht argue, for example, that minority literatures in Canada cannot be understood without a perspective on race:

> We argue that the "return of race" to Canadian cultural discourse at the start of the new millennium is a return with a difference because it has been pivotal in establishing

new and complex institutions that have introduced new means of production—from presses and film studios to anthologies and curricula—that can enhance relationships between communication and community. (23)

The question of race and colour, of visibility, is constantly posed by these three writers, as we will see. Lau deals with it only in a subtle way, but Lai returns to it at every opportunity by means of characters who try to find intermediate positions between assimilation and difference. After years of colour-blind politics, Lai's characters are not ready to admit their otherness without a fight. Rather, heroines like Miranda in *Salt Fish Girl*, initially prone to marginalization, state the differences that strengthen them (Ty 2010, 100). For Kwa, race is connected to her own recent immigration experience; like her protagonist in *This Place Called Absence*, she moved to Canada from Singapore in her youth. She is therefore very much aware of racial difference, articulating a sense of racial purity as voiced by some of her Chinese characters.

As Rita Wong says, there are dangers to writing about any ethnic "category," and particularly about Asian Canadian women writers—the dangers of being too inclusive or too exclusive, of being reductive, of creating an idea of sameness. However, the benefits widely surpass the drawbacks.

To link these writers and their texts may be dangerously to ghettoize ourselves once again, yet i [sic] am pushed by a necessity to sketch out some of the tenuous links between these women's writings in my own search for an identity, no matter how brief and historical, no matter how unfinished; *a moment of building an imagined community*, a base for support, for action, since identity exists within a context, a group of women who say to me, yes, i [sic] know that feeling, yes you're not alone. (Wong, "Jumping on Hyphens" 119; my emphasis)

The women share common ground, especially as they interrogate the importance of community, which on many occasions needs to be "imagined." In her groundbreaking study *Beyond Silence*, Lien Chao also addresses the importance of the community for Chinese Canadian writers: "Chinese Canadian literature is characterized by the historical experience of the community; consistent literary tropes and expressions have been developed to reclaim the collective community history and to redefine a collectively shared Chinese Canadian identity" (xi). As Chao aptly observes, in the last twenty-five years the Chinese Canadian literary community has had to struggle to find a place of its own in Canadian letters against the dominant hegemony of European trends—mostly British and French (*Beyond Silence* xiv).

This short history is one of approaching the mainstream, something that the three authors studied here have in common, Evelyn Lau's movement being probably the most definitive. She searches for this sense of community in an oblique way. In spite of adopting an individualistic perspective, Lau creates characters who are in search for bonds. Lai and Kwa foster this very sense, looking for connections, real or fictive, between past and present generations. The three authors explore different realizations of identity that escape fixed definitions and work instead "towards a collectivity with permeable boundaries" (Wong, "Jumping on Hyphens" 119).

Gender is the other category that is foregrounded by these writers, and becomes another focus of difference that they choose to emphasize. Lau behaves as the unruly Canadian daughter of Chinese parents who rejects their traditional constructions of femininity, precisely by leaving home and working as a prostitute. Lai and Kwa speak not only as women and about women, but as lesbians, thus setting the queer perspective as another discursive site to take into account. Furthermore, Kwa seems to fuse both initiatives in her stories, foregrounding individuality but also exploring homosexual relationships and prostitution, two sides of otherness. As rigid definitions of identity are expressly rejected, these writers seem to enjoy or at least to accept in-betweenness, "the hyphen between asian and canadian" (Wong, "Jumping on Hyphens" 138).

Evelyn Lau's biography explains the drive towards the personal and the focus on individuality that characterizes her work. She was born in Vancouver in 1971 in a family of Chinese immigrants with a strong sense of connection with their country and with great expectations for their Canadian-born daughter. As a schoolgirl, Lau suffered the pressure of her parents' expectations for her.[49] Her anxiety was also due to her difficult relationship with her mother, and made Lau leave home at the early age of fourteen, to undergo the traumatic experiences that she would eventually include in her books. In 1989 she published her bestseller *Runaway: Diary of a Street Kid*, an autobiographical account of her experiences as a prostitute. Later, she published a volume of poetry, *Oedipal Dreams* (1992), for which she became the youngest writer to be listed for the Governor's General Award; two collections of short stories (*Fresh Girls and Other Stories*, 1993; and *Choose Me*, 1997); and a novella, *Other Women* (1995). A volume of autobiographical essays, *Inside Out: Reflections on a Life So Far* (2001), followed, comprising some of the recurrent issues from her fiction.

The ten stories included in *Fresh Girls* foreground individuality and isolation. They are told in the confessional voices of women prostitutes in some cases, and women lovers in others. The themes of illicit sexuality and morally-sanctioned relationships seem to permeate the entire volume and illustrate the divorce of the tormented individual from her community. "Fresh Girls," for instance, is the story of Carol's initiation into prostitution at a massage parlour, a setting that inevitably points to gender and race subordination. "Roses" reproduces Lau's basic models of male-female relationships, and it is one of the most autobiographical tales in the whole collection. In an intimate tone, the confessional voice of a young woman speaks about the unconventionality of her relationship with a psychiatrist, a prototype that is endlessly reproduced in the collection. This paternal relationship becomes a master-slave bond that makes the narrator submit to his tastes. At most, the images of community in the collection are reduced to the love triangle between husband, girl lover, and wife, profusely evoked in the stories of *Fresh Girls* and the central issue in *Other Women*.

The latter is Evelyn Lau's only short novel. It tells the story of a brief affair between two people who have recently broken their relationship: Fiona, a young professional woman who is also the narrator of the story, and Raymond, her mature lover. Between the two stands the unspoken presence of Helen, Raymond's wife and an essential desire object in Fiona's imagination. Fiona's love for Raymond turns out to be unrequited, and she feels displaced, an "other," since Raymond confesses to her that he would never leave his wife. In that sense, marriage is invariably connected to ageing, and is seen as a sign of decay and not as a positive bond or an example of community. Lau presents the worlds of family (or domesticity) and illicit sexuality outside marriage as irremediably separate. The wife appears as the figure (if not the individual) in need of protection from the corruption that inevitably the lover represents. On the whole, *Other Women* is a monument to mourning over lost and spent love.

In her essays, *Inside Out: Reflections on a Life So Far*, Lau analyzes the interaction between self and community as far as family relations are concerned.[50] A number of key elements appear in this work, among which I would single out difficult and stormy relations—especially her bond with father figures—her lovers of an age closer to her father's than to her own. Furthermore, she extends the discussion by reflecting on the writer's profession—what it means to be a writer, why she attempted the genre of autobiography in the first place, and the way in which by writing one becomes an "other." There exists as well a conflict between the public and private spheres, most obviously in "The Observing Ego" and "Anatomy of a Libel Lawsuit." *Inside Out* is also about finding a place of one's own, a central Woolfian issue which can be interpreted in Lau's imaginary as finding a flat to let and call it "home." The reason behind this search is, basically, as she implies in the story "In Residence," to create a sense of domesticity, stability, and family security, though without the ties.

In her first novel, *When Fox Is a Thousand* (1995), shortlisted for the Chapters/ Books in Canada First Novel Award, Larissa Lai spins a complex narrative in three voices. The first is that of Fox, who admirably represents the trickster, as she changes shapes, lives between the world of the dead and the world of the living—when the fox is a thousand she becomes immortal—and plays tricks on different characters. Secondly, we read the words of Yu Hsuan-Chi, a Taoist poet and nun of the Tang period, and finally the third-person account of Artemis Wong, a Chinese Canadian woman in contemporary Canada. Formally speaking, each voice is identified graphically by means of a different pictogram, which helps readers to situate themselves and to bridge the distance between past and present. Fox, who travels through time, bridges that gap and is the nexus between the past in China and the present in 1989 Vancouver. She is a wonderful storyteller and often rewrites myth and fairy tale. She creates bonding and community between women across generations, space, and time.

The story of the ninth-century poet Yu Hsuan-Chi in this novel is intentionally fictional (Hilf 128). It is a fractured narrative that Lai has extracted from various sources in translation. The depiction of the nun emphasizes her conviction that all writing (even historical writing) is incomplete and elusive, a conclusion that becomes especially significant when we take into account the legend about Yu Hsuan-Chi killing her servant and being executed for it.

Finally, Artemis Wong stands for the writer's *alter ego*, representing the second-generation immigrant who has apparently assimilated. In spite of appearances, however, she will need to come to terms with her difference.

The conflict between individual and community is also at the heart of *Salt Fish Girl* (2002), Lai's second novel. As in the previous work, the author manages to link different narrative levels and voices. At one level is the story of the mythic goddess of creation, Nu Wa, who wishes to experience the life of the human beings, whom she created, and finally adopts the human shape when she falls in love with a ninth-century young working woman, the salt fish girl of the title. The future is represented by Miranda Ching, living in Serendipity—present-day Vancouver—in 2044. This futuristic society is one in which corporations have taken hold and direct politics and economy. The Pallas Shoes group is one such corporation.[51] Lai plays with the notion of hybridity. Like Fox and Artemis Wong in *When Fox*, Miranda represents in-betweenness in this novel: she is between Serendipity and the Unregulated Zone, between domesticity and the exterior world, and her "disease" situates her in a privileged space between the past and present. Her emaciated and faulty sense of community will be reconstituted when she enters the family of the Sonias, the beings who represent in-betweenness *par excellence*, half-human, half-machine, relying on self-reproduction for survival. As in *When Fox Is a Thousand*, then, Lai plays in her second novel with the idea of biological and gender hybridity, of which Evie and her sisters are cases in point.

In her first novel, *This Place Called Absence* (2000), Singapore-born Lydia Kwa evokes the problem of the self, in perhaps a more astounding way than Lau or Lai. This polyvocal novel opens with the authoritative voice of Wu Lan, a Singapore immigrant for whom the experiences of immigration and loneliness are still too close; the novel ends in the voice of Mahmee, Wu Lan's mother, in Singapore. The "absence" of the title can be variously interpreted in this novel: the absence of her father, who happens to have committed suicide; the absence of the actual mother and of maternal presences amply represented by the "Singapores" of the mind;[52] of the feminine principle, of friendship and company in the country of adoption, Canada; and finally absence refers to the stance of the psychologist—Wu Lan's and Lydia Kwa's professions—before the unknown clients. Furthermore, the subplot of the novel, the story of two nineteenth-century Chinese prostitutes—one of whom commits suicide—provides a metaphor of absence: from history, from public records, and from public life.

In this novel, Kwa reconciles the self and the communal by means of memories. Memories are the only link with the mother country. Like Lau and Lai, Kwa presents family relations at a fracture in both novels. Mahmee confesses that her relationship with Wu Lan is difficult to maintain; communication between them is hardly possible. The distance between mother and daughter grows even wider when she considers Wu Lan's homosexuality. The writer favours bonds between sisters; if not biological ones, then between women who share a common status, like *ah ku*, unofficial women or prostitutes, such as Lee Ah Choi and Chow Chat Mui. Towards the end of the novel, Wu Lan makes the effort to connect with the past and present. At this point, the final act of narration is one of exorcism and liberation. As a psychologist, Wu Lan is a healer and prepares to let her father's spirit go; Chat Mui visits Ah Choi's burial place for the last time before abandoning her profession and becoming a "respectable" woman by marrying.

In her novel *The Walking Boy* (2005), Kwa also proceeds by way of exorcism and renewal. This is a complex narrative in which the personal and the communal are constantly at odds with one another. Kwa refers back to the past; like Lai, she imagines life in China during the Tang period. As in her previous novel, her tormented characters are led to inhabit in-betweenness. Baoshi, the walking boy, bears on his body the sign of otherness. Born a hermaphrodite, he is a cause of shame for his parents, who get rid of him by trusting him to the care of Harelip, a hermit living in Mount Hua. The action of the novel starts when Baoshi is sent by his master on a pilgrimage to find Ardhanari, Harelip's former lover. His fate is intertwined with that of Wan'er, Imperial Secretary and official historian at Nü Huang's court. Wan'er stands for the other site of difference in the novel, branded on her forehead with the character *hua*, meaning "transformation" but reinforcing her subjection to the Female Emperor. In both cases, therefore, individuality and uniqueness are fully realized on the body. Like the *ah ku* in *This Place Called Absence*, difference is visibly marked. Furthermore, ineffectual family relationships are replaced by bonds of true affection, like that between the hermit and his apprentice, or among those belonging to the same marginal group, as in the case of the *jogappas*, male dancers and crossdressers who welcome and help Baoshi to search for Ardhanari.

In the work of these three novelists, there is a clear effort to reconcile the protagonists with their own selves. Evelyn Lau achieves this by looking for a place of her own, both in her life and in her narrative, though that necessarily means renouncing her ties to the Chinese Canadian community and her Chinese ancestry. Larissa Lai and Lydia Kwa explore other ways of reconciliation. The former uses history, myth, and science fiction to find peaceful coexistence between the Chinese and the Canadian, the past and the present. The latter bridges the gap between the private/personal and the public/collective through the lives of her protagonists.

2. Femininity and Its Discontents

Lau seems at times reluctant to reconcile the identities of "woman" and "writer." She rejects traditional views of femininity, and demystifies the figure of the prostitute, at the same time that she seems to argue that bonds between women are difficult to sustain, especially those connected by kin—mothers are absent or ineffectual—and sex relations—the tension between wife and female lover. The vital experiences of Lau's women are irremediably connected to sex. As mentioned above, she focuses on the hardships of the sex worker, but also offers insight into another type of female experience: the young lover, normally represented as the "other" woman, in the lives of mature, professional, or old men who keep on thwarting their dreams of stability and romantic love.

Larissa Lai depicts woman-to-woman relationships in a more favourable light. Nevertheless, her women are also ex-centric beings, at the margins of community and society, as represented by the fox and Artemis in *When Fox is a Thousand,* and Miranda in *Salt Fish Girl.* All are in the process of defining their identity. Lai problematizes the figure of the lesbian, presented as a hybrid—as in the case of the fox—and, in both novels, promotes the reading that ties of friendship and affection between women transcend time and space. However, their relationships are not trouble-free. Contrary to Lau, Lai analyzes the mother/daughter bond in different ways, and enriches the number and variety of maternal figures in her two novels: the fox, Nu Wa (as the mother goddess), Miranda's mother, etc.

Kwa also deals with mother/daughter relationships, like Lai, and the figure of the prostitute, like Lau. In *This Place Called Absence* there is no definite reconciliation between Wu Lan and her mother; rather, it seems that the protagonist has a greater interest in coming to terms with the father figure. In the novel's subplot women's lives are seen in a critical light: the two prostitutes have lived experiences of oppression, both at home before immigration from China to Singapore, and later in their professional life. In *The Walking Boy,* Kwa explores only-masculine and only-feminine ties through the father/son relationship, represented by the ties between Harelip and Baoshi, and the lesbian liaison between Wan'er and Abbess Ling. Kwa also foregrounds the mother/daughter bond, exemplified by Wan'er and Lady Zhen, and by Wan'er and the Empress, with whom she bears a love-and-hate relationship. In each case, Kwa presents female relationships at a fracture.

In defining her social, ideological, and political commitment, Lau resents potential criticism from other Chinese Canadians and feminists. She admits that she sees herself as a writer first, then as a woman (Condé 110). She is interested in depicting the hard life of female prostitutes because one of her major projects is to change society's opinion about the profession: "I wanted to show that prostitutes do have lives and dreams of their own, and they quite often get out of that life again" (107). On the other hand, she rarely explores the woman-to-woman relationship. In spite of the author's insistence in not "taking a stance," she cannot help but do so in the end. In this way, Lau's narrative offers an alternative picture of being a woman, particularly an Asian woman in contemporary Canada. Furthermore, she abandons the study of female individuality for the study of types, which are often interchangeable. Rita Wong argues that most female characters in Lau's fiction could be exchanged for one another:

> This similarity gives rise to ambivalence: on the one hand, they are often like a parade of lost souls, automatons going through the motions of the roles that society has assigned them; on the other hand, in what can perhaps be read as a gesture of evading surveillance, the narrator actually reveals relatively little about them apart from their oscillating emotional states relating to the various men in their lives. ("Market Forces and Powerful Desires" 125)[53]

Context and family are not overtly important, but seem to determine women's lives in practice. Finally, a clear class concern does not exist, although when taking into account Lau's biographical background we can discern a middle-class drive, as in *Inside Out,* where one of her most vivid desires is to own a two-bedroom apartment and to regain a sense of lost domesticity.[54]

In *Fresh Girls,* Lau offers a complete account of the female types most recurrent in her fiction. In the title story, she draws once more on autobiography and makes Lolita a productive sexual icon for the kind of woman she represents in this story and the following ones: "The back room is getting too small, and even the owner's tiring of the pretty girls with their daddy complexes curled up next to the desk where he balances the books and takes half their money; the girls who pull up their skirts and tuck their naked legs beneath them on the chair and fiddle with their long curly hair, pouting" ("Fresh Girls" 7–8). The father/daughter relationship is endlessly reproduced, embodied in this story by client and prostitute and in others by the mature man and his young lover. "Fresh Girls" ends unremarkably by reminding us of the sordid everyday world of prostitution, not looking at the profession itself, but at the woman's experience. "Fetish Night" insists on the absence of ties of affection and sisterhood between women in the same position. In fact, Lau implies that there is competition and rivalry among them, because men prefer women who have the halo of the new and inexperienced (5–6). In the end, the story suggests that men are responsible for drawing women apart. Throughout the collection, a number of female characters inhabit the "margins"—of society, morality, or family—and strive to inscribe their individual stories in larger and more empowering narratives (Hodgson Blackburn 12).

In "The Session," the character of Mary embodies all levels of liminality: she is a coloured prostitute who practices sado-masochism. Mary represents the dominatrix, a fiction of power to which many of Lau's female characters subscribe. Frequently, a woman's subordination becomes more poignant in spite of the control she apparently exerts. "The Session" ends as it began with the image of a woman waiting for a boyfriend who never arrives and whom she imagines safely at home by his wife. In "Mercy," Lau reproduces the typical relationship in her fiction: the respected white married professional man who engages in a secret sexual relationship with a younger liberal woman. While they perform the slave/dominatrix roles, the woman wonders why he needs it: "Perhaps only in the clutches of pain, when your eyes are closed and your lips forced apart, does the day seem long. Perhaps this is what you see, this element of immortality, the way I do by writing poems" (88). "Mercy," as much as "Fetish Night," reflects on the individual's duality by means of transgressive sexual practices that shatter boundaries and social norms. Again, the dominatrix is granted only a fake authority: she is playing the part she has been asked to play.

"Roses" illustrates another case of female submission in which a young woman yields control to a man who is older than her, a professional (psychiatrist), experienced, and patronizing. Their relationship is based on male control and female submission, represented by his obsession with his penis (all pleasure and humiliation are extracted from it). The limits between the father figure and the lover are difficult to set at times. In a humiliating moment, both figures blur, and the obedience paid to the father becomes one with the submission granted to the lover (35–36). The psychiatrist figure is at first comforting and reassuring; the protagonist seems to confide in this man who belongs to the "helping profession" ("Pleasure" 44). The psychiatrist is not only a man but he is also older, which reinforces the idea of protection and security for a young and needy woman. In this light, the narrative twist that follows is much more unexpected and cruel, since instead of a haven, the relationship with the psychiatrist becomes dependent and demanding.

Marriage is a recurrent topic in Lau's fiction and the central *leitmotiv* in the story of the same title, also included in *Fresh Girls*. It becomes the perfect excuse to develop the woman-to-woman relationship between wife and girl lover in Lau's narratives. In "Marriage," the narrator sleeps with a man who wears a wedding ring, which is a sign of belonging, a brand signalling another woman's possession, "the ring as hard as a weapon" (53). The protagonist Fiona is mesmerized by the ring and attracted to it, whereas the man's wife, Helen, is at the same time a symbol of envy and repulsion to Fiona:

> Because I do think of his wife—of the way she must sink into bed beside him in the dark, putting her face against his chest and breathing him in, his scent carried with her into her dreams. I do think of the pain she would feel if she knew, and I am frightened sometimes by the force of my desire to inflict that pain upon her—this wife who is to be pitied in her faithless marriage, this wife whom I envy. (60)

In the end, the father/daughter complex emerges, and to some extent the wife comes to embody the mother figure who is not only a source of nourishment and protection, but fundamentally a rival.[55] Marriage is safe, while sexuality outside its bounds becomes illicit and society sanctions it.

"Glass" is perhaps the most experimental of all the narrations in the collection. Here, Lau explores female consciousness through a narrative voice that detaches "herself from herself," not only thematically (the plight of a woman who is about to commit suicide and seems to speak about the part of herself she does not like) but also from a narrative viewpoint.[56] About this side of herself, she claims: "I'm the only one who can love her unconditionally, but she persists in looking outwards" (67). On one hand, the story insists in the dissociation between sex and a complete relationship based on confidence and love. On the other, by presenting the type of the hysterical and mentally unbalanced woman, Lau denounces once more the way in which women have learned not to value themselves, at least in male terms, with the result of becoming either too dependent or too domineering.

"The Apartments" represents the places that Jane visits in her sessions with her clients. She needs to believe that the middle-class myth of romance ("they married and lived happily ever after") may come true for her, that love has the power to transform:

> Plain Jane. But the man in this apartment wants her, wants her more than just the way a client wants her. Perhaps tonight will be the night he sinks to his knees and tells her that he loves her, that he can't be a client anymore, he wants them to go out on real dates: movies, dinners, walks around the seawall. (98)

Later, she claims, "He will fix her, make things right" (100). She soon discovers that this man is not Prince Charming and becomes disappointed: "Between the waves of nausea it occurs to her that certain things, things that once seemed so possible, are becoming less and less likely with each passing night" (103). The fiction of romance turns out to be another unrealized fantasy. She is ultimately destroyed by her experiences with men, for whom she has been an object.[57] Though at first sight Lau seems merely to evoke the Cinderella plot, Charlotte Sturgess suggests an enlightening interpretation of her work from a female and ethnic perspective:

> It is indeed true that her fictional representations are predicated in the stereotypical grammars of exoticism and pornography, belonging to a sex-industry which contributes to consolidating the image of the Chinese woman as a glamorous object. Yet the conflicted encounter between both codified and more shifting identifications in her work, the way the limits of stereotypical formulas are foregrounded, and the way subject positions are both established and problematized, reveal the complex workings of subjectivity within Western liberalism where hybrid cultural identity is not comfortably contained. (79–80).

In *Inside Out* (2001), Lau hints at the way she speaks of herself as a woman (she never takes the voice of "every woman," but her own). "The Shadow of Prostitution," for example, reveals the mark that her time as a prostitute left on her life, a wound that never healed, in spite of the fact that she sees another woman when reflecting on her younger years: "This stranger whose life seems in so many ways foreign to mine is still inside me, her experiences before and since" (4). Her task from the first chapter onwards is to "empty" herself of her past, of herself. Lau also debates the role of the prostitute: is she a victim or a powerful woman in control of her life? She claims that she prefers the latter definition, although she is aware of the complexity of the prostitute's "empowerment" through sex:

> Does one speak the language of the victim, who sees prostitution as abuse by men, or of the empowered woman who claims it to be an economic choice without any psychological ramifications? There have been enormous psychological and emotional costs for me, but I am uncomfortable with the former position, even though it could be argued that a teenager selling sex to men could be nothing but a victim. (9)

Whether she means it or not, Lau's women inhabit different levels of marginality, a situation that arises not so much from class or ethnicity as from psychological and emotional impairment. Lau's young heroines lose themselves in their search for protection and companionship, which their male lovers fail to provide. Wong interprets this as a lack of ties with other women: "The shape of what is usually present, a displaced daddy fixation, returns me to what relations are absent or marginalized—a mother, an extended family, sister, an aunt, a cousin, a friend, a comrade—and all the cultural histories that have been silenced and denied so that presence can dominate" ("Market Forces and Powerful Desires" 130).

Larissa Lai explores womanhood and focuses on bonds, usually severed by time and distance, between women in her novels. For example, the fox and the poet Yu Hsuan-Chi in *When Fox is a Thousand* and the goddess Nu Wa in *Salt Fish Girl* are related to contemporary female characters. Lai also offers her view on intimate relations between women. She rejects the term "lesbian" due to its racial and ideological implications and instead speaks about "women identified women" ("Political Animals and the Power of History" 149). Moreover, history allows for the reconstruction of the lives of women who share common ground, in this case Chinese women in the West: "It must be artificial because our history is so disparate, and also because it has been so historically rare for women to have control over the means of recording and dissemination" (149). In her study on the interpretation of the gaze in *When Fox is a Thousand,* Morris claims that"Lai propels Artemis towards a collision course with her past in order to question not only the negation of the female story in history but also the representation of Canadian women of Asian ancestry as silent, passive or framed by a privileged white, Western and heterosexual male gaze" (79). In *When Fox is a Thousand* the character of the fox stands as a figure in-between: apart from representing the typical trickster character, an identity sign in Canadian culture, the fox also stands for the lesbian, since it is an extraordinary character that inhabits marginality by taking the bodies of women who have died too soon and engaging in lesbian relationships. Lai explains the potential that the fox's stories offer:

> I find these stories very rich and visceral. They are also politically compelling for a number of reasons. The first is contemporary feminism's struggle with questions of sexual representation. What does it mean for a feminist to embrace the power of seduction? And am I a feminist, or is that also a colonized space? The second is the question of how to deal with sexual representations of Asians in the West where we have been so much exoticized and/or de-sexualized in a society which insists on pathologizing the sexuality of the other. I was compelled to find out what kind of warrior the fox could be in that battle. The third is the possibility of employing the fox as a new trope of lesbian representation, or, if that term and its history reeks too much of its western origins, then as a trope of Asian women's community and power. ("Political Animals and the Body of History" 151)

The fox becomes a useful image representing new and inspiring forms to symbolize gender and ethnicity. In this light, Lai also employs the fox in her revision of the body as a site of difference: she animates the body of the dead. For example, she "breathes life" into the dormant asiancy of the protagonist.[58]

In her first novel Lai plays with the idea of crossing frontiers—whether time, space, or even life and death. In this way, the fox plays her tricks on the living, as with Artemis Wong in the novel and with many other characters throughout history. She takes women's bodies while evading a clear gender association, becoming an empowering figure. However, this results in her ostracism from the society of foxes:

> The foxes of my hole got used to what they called my unnatural behaviour in due time. They did not mind what I did or where I went, although they would never do such things themselves. "But," they said, "do you have to write about it?"
> When I wrote about the thrill of new life that comes from animating the bodies of the dead, they swept their bushy tails in the dirt in disgust and said they didn't want anything more to do with me.
> And that is how it happens that I live alone. (*When Fox is a Thousand* 6)

The fox also stands for Lai's image, the writer, whose occupation not only appears "unnatural" to others, but also speaks out her condition of "otherness." Moreover, the fox's task of "animating the bodies of the dead" applies wonderfully to the role of the historian.

Artemis's search for identity goes hand in hand with the discovery and acceptance of her homosexuality. The bonds between women replace those between heterosexual couples; at one point in the novel, for example, a wife and a concubine begin a relationship that excludes the husband. Relationships between women are established on a more equal basis, often evading the binary system of domination and submission that characterizes heterosexual liaisons (*When Fox is a Thousand* 91–92). On the other hand, Lai also plays with the topic of disguise, particularly through cross-dressing and drag. In her first novel, Lai presents Artemis dressing like a man to attend Eden's men-only party (106–07).[59]

Lai exploits a different aspect of the trope of genealogy, so productive in Chinese Canadian literature, as Chao contends in *Beyond Silence*. Lai's is a female genealogy transcending time and place, as the endless transformations of the fox prove. The poetess Yu Hsuan-Chi also exemplifies the new understanding of female genealogy and her-story that Lai proposes in this novel. Male historiography describes her character in two different ways: either as a lascivious and immoral woman, or as a murderer who killed the maidservant of a young official (150). Lai vindicates her memory by giving her a voice.

Creation and procreation go hand-in-hand in the story of the river goddess Nu Wa in *Salt Fish Girl*. Lai takes us back to a mythical time in the pre-Shang dynasty, where Nu Wa is an earthly goddess inclined to mingle in human affairs. This novel about (re)generation also presents Miranda's birth as an immaculate conception, since she affirms, "my mother was a good eight years past menopause" (15), and conceived her only after eating from the forbidden durian.[60] As in the previous case, Lai explores in depth relationships between women in the bosom of a repressive society. In order to join the salt fish girl, for example, Nu Wa will have to adopt spinsterhood (54), a state that entails self-renunciation. Their love relationship is mirrored by the one between Miranda and Evie, which suggests that history repeats itself. The episode of creation evokes a lesbian liaison, as Miranda's memories of a mythical past reveal:

> I drew a series of images of Nu Wa under water with her mouth open. I drew a series in which Nu Wa was transparent like a long cell beneath a microscope. The first people grew in her belly and pressed out through her skin. I drew Fu Xi as a woman, emerging from the glossy surface of the lake to embrace Nu Wa while she knelt to examine her reflection in the water. (187)

Using further images of transformation that evoke hybridity, Lai proposes a new vision of reproduction beyond normative representations as found in heterosexual couples: the durian stands for this alternative reproduction, while Evie's sisters, living in exile as marginal beings and outlaws, symbolize a women-only society and grow the forbidden tree in their backyard: "Those trees have been interbreeding and mutating for at least three generations since the original work. The fertility those durians provided was neither natural nor controllable. It was too dangerous" (256). Their choice means the only form of adaptation; they become "children of the earth":

> I thought we are the new children of the earth, of the earth's revenge. Once we stepped out of mud, now we step out of moist earth, out of DNA both new and old, an imprint of what has gone before, but also a variation. By our difference we mark how ancient the alphabet of our bodies. By our strangeness we write our bodies into the future. (259)[61]

Above all, the writer vindicates the figure of the hybrid, which appears as genetically different and is considered the only way to survival. The future is written in the feminine in Lai's fiction, especially in her second novel, which ends with the conflict between cloning (male copies of Rudy Flowers) and miscegenation (the new generation of women out of durians). Miranda, after eating one of them, gets pregnant and gives birth to a girl. Her insight into the future is uncertain, but also full of hope: "Everything will be all right, I thought, until next time" (269).

As Lau and Lai preceding her, Kwa offers different insights into what it means to be a woman, paying particular attention to the mother-daughter bond. Demystifying the essentialism of biological bonds, she explores the imposed distance between mothers and daughters, separated by immigration, as in Wu Lan's case in *This Place Called Absence,* or by state politics, as in Wan'er's case in *The Walking Boy.* There are many sites of difference between Wu Lan and her mother, mainly due to their age difference, Wu Lan's access to higher education, and the fact that she left Singapore for Canada twenty years earlier. Yet, in contrast to Lau and Lai, Kwa grants a voice to the mother. She offers as well the figure of the prostitute, who is also a lesbian. Queerness occupies a place of privilege in Kwa's work, and becomes the focus of attention both in *This Place Called Absence* and *The Walking Boy*. Lesbian relationships in these two novels provide relief and communication between women who have been torn from their families and homes, and amount to a valid form of survival. That is the case of Ah Choi and Chat Mui in Kwa's first novel, and also of Wan'er's relationship with Abbess Ling in *The Walking Boy*. In both examples, their "illicit" liaisons provide comfort and balance to otherwise empty lives.

The testimonies of Lee Ah Choi and Chat Mui are delivered in the first person. Ah Choi's story is one of gender violence and sexual abuse while at home. Her past in her native village changes her view of life; she wants to avoid the traditional fate of a woman's life in nineteenth-century China: "I don't understand why many want to return. Oh no, not to the fields and back-breaking labour! Not to that prison of duty to infant mouths and an ugly husband" (10). In spite of that, and in clear contrast to the oppressive atmosphere of the brothel, her relationship with Chat Mui is one of equality. Chat Mui's experience is similar: she has also suffered the hardships of migration. By means of these two types Kwa shows how women's lives are full of sorrow, difficulties and sexual abuse, dramatizing, for example, how Chat Mui was raped several times when running away from home with her cousin.

There is a barrier, a wall of incomprehension and lack of communication between mother and daughter, which remains unresolved even at the end of the novel:

When my daughter speak, she say so little, as if she stand very far away from me, on a beach on the other side, calling out to me, but her shouting reach me only as softly as the pillows I sleep on every night. You have to shout, Lan-lan, I tell her all the time. (20–21)

The distance between them is widened by her daughter's homosexuality, a topic that lurks in the background but is rarely mentioned.

Contrary to what the reader might expect, Chow Chat Mui speaks about the "power" of prostitutes like herself, reminiscent of Lau's stance about the profession:

An ah ku is powerful in many ways that a wife never could be. I learned the various positions of sex acts, that there are many ways for a woman and a man to lie together. Not the routine ways my father touched me, while I lay still, doing nothing. The more I learned the more hopeful I became. I had acquired the powers that would guarantee my freedom. In a world where men's hungers are never sufficiently satiated by their well-mannered wives. Phee! Those women who cannot stand the smell of their armpits and their wet sex-mouths! (36)

Through Chat Mui's experience, Kwa displays a source of hostility between women: the wife and the prostitute, similar to an extent to the conflict that Lau presented in her fiction between wife and lover. The precarious power of the prostitute is based on sex, whereas the wife's respectability (her status as "official" woman) is challenged by the deftly prostitute. Theirs is a world of men, and they have to adapt to it the best they can. The prostitute's life, however, is in constant danger from venereal disease and the opium she takes to soothe the pain of her life, foregrounding the association between femininity, sex, and disease.[62] The life of *ah ku* is also plagued with suicide, a fact that Wu Lan documents by means of historical records. In a critique to the historical discipline, however, she suggests that the true reasons for these women's deaths remain hidden and silent (47): traditional historiography does not deal with the private but with the public, and the versions of history are insufficient to offer a complete view of reality.[63]

Curiously enough, the life of the prostitute resembles that of the nun in many respects in this novel. Special colours are associated with different stages in their lives. For example, red represents the loss of virginity and the "coming of age" of prostitutes: once they lose virginity, *ah ku* are given a red robe. Moreover, the desire of every good *ah ku* is to have a cubicle of her own, similar to the nun's cell. Chat Mui also dreams of being promoted as a concubine. According to Ah Choi, a prostitute's life has some space for freedom, in contrast to other Chinese women whose feet and lives are bound:

> Poor Ah Fong. She might have the beautiful feet and the rich husband, but I have a much nicer face. Sweet and full of good-luck features. Ah Fong's life probably revolves around the whims of her husband. Having to fry the pork fat to just the right crispness. To bring him tea and slippers the moment he enters the house. Mincing about with excessively dainty steps. Aiyah! If only my sister can see me now, walking the streets with the surety of unbound feet. (53)

Chat Mui also treasures a dream of telling stories. Combined with her love for Ah Choi, this dream transmits the notion of desire: "How to speak the unspeakable? This desire for her. Without language to name it, it is not fixed like the window frame. Free like the wind, not a willow rooted to the ground, dependent on earth for its fate. This is my secret and my power" (55–56). Lesbianism, portrayed as a forbidden relationship, stands for the "unspeakable," both in the nineteenth and twentieth centuries. Chat Mui wants to give it existence by putting it into words.

Finally, Chat Mui describes women's lives in *This Place Called Absence* as always being at risk: "Women risk their livelihoods when they get pregnant. Then they risk their lives if they try to expel their accidents" (91). Furthermore, Kwa emphasizes the value of children in both plots. Wu Lan feels the absence of children, even when deciding not to have them; for the nineteenth-century prostitutes in the novel, having children may be the key to respectability and social insertion. However, the risk of venereal disease, which may make them barren, is ever present (137). As in other societies, children are the key to respectability and social acceptance for *ah ku*, but they also amount to a source of difference and prejudice among women.

The association of femininity and power is one of the central issues in *The Walking Boy*. Kwa refers to the historical figure of Empress Nü Huang in order to dramatize her search for immortality and her thirst for power. She asks, "Is it so shocking that women would yearn for power and immortality? That we might wish to pursue and conquer rather than be caught in a web spun by others?" (69) Since her time as a concubine, her life has been devoted both to the attainment of power and pleasure. On one hand she is sexually free, taking those she likes as her lovers, as she does with the Zhang brothers. On the other hand, she does not hesitate to destroy anyone hindering her way to the throne, as when she orders the execution of Empress Wang and the Pure Concubine (170, 256).

Kwa also presents the figure of Wan'er, descendant of the legitimate royal line—Nü Huang had killed both Wan'er's father and grandfather and usurped the throne of her son Li Zhe—and turned merely into a slave for the Empress, who gave her an education and appointed her Imperial Secretary. Though Wan'er has been kept aloof of the details of her family's ill fortune, she has accepted her subordinate position and her vital dependence on Nü Huang.

Wan'er's experiences are parallel to those of a woman poet she admires, Cai Yan. Intertwining both stories, the author associates writing and (female) survival in the face of difficulties:

A woman's plight is subject to a dynasty's whims
What gave you courage to dare accuse Heaven and Earth
Of inhumanity? Seeing yourself caught in their conflicts
You say: a woman belongs to the chaos of her time,
Belongs yet is lost in the wretched devastation of war
Although yourself uncommon
How could you have escaped the ravages of destruction? (156)

Later, Wan'er also traces the ties between Cai Yan and the Empress: "One woman only too aware of her captivity, while the other refuses to admit much else other than self-justification and sovereign power, yet they do share one thing in common. Their words resound with bitterness" (198). In drawing this comparison, Wan'er levels all women's lives, no matter the social strata to which they belong. *The Walking Boy* illustrates the lives of women at a fracture: Wan'er, Lady Zhen, Ling, the Empress Wu Zhao, and her two victims. Furthermore, women's lives are disconnected from men's. Male characters are related to governmental power, political intrigue and sexuality, while the Empress is the only woman who exceptionally departs from traditional gender patterns.

3. Sex and the Body

The body stands at the centre of discourse in the three books under analysis. The sexed body and the inevitable reference to power inhabit the pages of Lau's and Kwa's fiction. For both writers, the (woman's) body is the object of exchange in the marketplace (sex, ethnicity, science). Women are subjected to their bodies and often occupy an unfavourable position because of it, as evidenced by the figures of the prostitute, concubine, and female lover. In particular, ethnicity plays an important role in the appraisal of the body. In Lai's *When Fox is a Thousand*, Artemis is presented as an exotic object, as are some female characters in Lau's narrations. From that consideration stems the many representations of abject bodies and the topics of disease and suicide in both Lau and Kwa's fiction. Mutation and change alter the body—for example, the cyborg body and tattooing in Lai's novels.

Sexuality and body responses are inextricably connected in Lau's stories. Her female characters are sexually active; some practice a "deviant" sexuality according to normative standards and in many cases manifest their insecurities and dissatisfaction through their bodies. The source of this conflict may be sought again in Lau's personal experience as a former prostitute and a bulimic. The woman's body "speaks" in Lau's texts through the drives of "deviant" sexuality and eating disorders, and sometimes drug consumption. The association of pain and pleasure, recurrent in her fiction, can be traced in all three instances.

In contrast to Kwa and Lai, Lau's heterosexuality is a fact in her writing, which endlessly reproduces the male/female relationship, including father/daughter, client/prostitute, and old man/young girl. The body is central to most of these relationships: the use of the body, the selling of the body, the physical pleasure and pain that are extracted from both acts. As Hodgson-Blackburn suggests, especially in relation to *Other Girls*, the body also becomes an object of mourning and melancholia. The lover's body, for example, is remembered and desired more strongly when absent. Moreover, Lau's experience as a prostitute and a drug addict has inevitably changed the ways in which she views sex—"as a transaction, a relationship as a trap" (*Inside Out* 8)—and accepts her body.

Pleasure and pain collide in the stories of *Fresh Girls*. The title story invokes the idea of the freshness, newness, and even "virginity" of the new prostitutes, like Carol, from the perspective of an experienced one. "Pleasure," on the other hand, pays a great deal of attention to sadomasochistic sexual relationships through objects such as leather, cuffs, blindfolds, and chains. Sex and violence seem to go hand-in-hand, once more fulfilling a male fantasy. "Fetish Night" centres on sexual practices taking place behind the walls of a night club, where the clients play the role of dominatrix or slave, though remaining ordinary men and women in their everyday lives. The body in pain also appears in "Roses," in which the unnamed protagonist is promised a rose garden by her psychiatrist, who is later her lover. The bed of roses that her life would be turns into the "stain of roses" on her skin as he hits her and her blood runs: "I understood that when I did not bleed at the first blow, his love turned into hatred. I saw that if I was indeed precious and fragile I would have broken, I would have burst open like a thin shell and discharged the rich sweet stain of roses" (38).

Other Women also reflects on the association of pain and pleasure in relation to the body. For example, Fiona thinks about "leaving a mark" on her lover's body to imprint on him a sign of herself:

What he does not know is that any pain she gives him is not out of her rising excitement, but because she is trying to leave a mark upon him. That is why she bites his mouth as if to draw blood, to break the skin's elastic surface and taste his opened flesh. That is why she buries her face, her breasts in his hair, leaving it scented and unruly. She wants only to leave some mark of her passing on his body, so she can point to it later in a photograph and say, I did that, I was part of this man's life. (74)

Fiona also refers to the body in pain while remembering the feelings of nausea and relief associated with her bulimia (75).[64] Her relationship with sex is problematic, "a measure of power or abuse before we met, a way of hurting myself and, sometimes, my mother" (160). In the end, all this pain inflicted on her own body and Raymond's—and at times Helen's—can be explained as a need to look for protection, true love, and the home she has left behind.

Metamorphosis and abjection are two key terms to analyze Lai's novels. Fox's mutations, taking women's corpses in an incarnating fashion, transgress human and animal boundaries: ". . . Lai uses Fox as a metaphorical figure for constant transformations of ethnic and sexual subjectivity, affirming both difference and resistance" (Fu 158). Fox's mutability, her fluidity, her inhabiting the liminal spaces between life and death associates her with the abject—the unhomely, the uncanny, the haunting (159).[65]

Similarly, *Salt Fish Girl* discourses about the hybrid body, the cyborg, embodied by the Sonias. In response to Donna Haraway's definition of the cyborg, Rosi Braidotti comments:

> As a hybrid, or body-machine, the cyborg is a connection-making entity, a figure of inter-relationality, receptivity and global communication that deliberately blurs categorical distinctions (human and machine; nature and culture; male and female; Oedipal and non-Oedipal . . . The cyborg is Haraway's representation of a generic feminist humanity, thus answering the question of how femininity reconcile the radical historical specificity of women with the insistence on constructing new values that can benefit humanity as a whole, by redefining it radically. (Braidotti 240–41)[66]

Through genetic experimentation and mutation, Dr Flowers fathers the Sonias, and they answer by further mutation: eating from the durian and procreating. Their initiative radically expands the boundaries of the body in an enactment of hybridity. The Sonias plan to start a new society in a reaction to the generalized infertility and to the homogeneity imposed by medical research.[67] *Salt Fish Girl* is about bodies that consistently undermine order and capitalism's politics, bodies that try to be visible by all means: nauseous (and thus abject) bodies, diseased bodies, affected by the different varieties of the dreaming disease,[68] and finally the body as implicated in original reproductive policies. Critic Tara Lee explains,

> Lai writes of the need to combat capitalism's drive to control reproduction by creating a new sense of the body emerging out of and beyond late capitalism. This new body might then unmask capitalism's hidden fragmentation, using the union between nature and technology that shaped it to mutate into something variant from a capitalist will. Ultimately, Lai proposes a fertility where commodities can produce autonomously, not just be reproduced, and in doing so, reveals the body's continued capability to claim a 'home' for itself. The body thus becomes the tool of resistance. (Lee, "Mutant Bodies" 95)

In the end, the body becomes the site of difference in Lai's fiction. She also poses questions about the distinction between the natural and the constructed. Lai further reinforces the association of women with their bodies, though especially in *Salt Fish Girl* the body remains the object of subversion. In Tara Lee's words, "[o]ne might question whether agency is possible for a body so entrapped in a system of commodification and consumption, but I would argue . . . that the body can break out of its passivity by claiming agency through self-metamorphosis" (94).

Miranda's stance throughout *Salt Fish Girl* is interesting, since she is always resistant to acknowledge and thus to accept her "syndrome," her foul smell, clues of her Chinese ancestry.[69] History, body, and memory become one. The dreaming disease and the putrid odour of the durian represent the body crying for recognition.

Lai suggests how the sense of smell is invariably connected to memory and to "history that has been largely unwritten and is in the process of being forgotten" ("Future Asians" 172). She also plays with the salt fish girl and the odour of the female sex.[70] Mansbridge proposes a reading of the foulness of the body—female and racialized—as "otherness," and thus as abject. In its negotiation of inside and outside spaces, the abject is the leitmotif of the nation.

Lai and Kwa share many concerns in their appraisal of the body, among them the notion of transformation and cross-dressing as empowering strategies. Kwa's *The Walking Boy* provides some of the most significant scenes in both senses. Wan'er's forehead is tattooed with the *hua* character, which materializes in the two symbols for transformation (130). These symbols are variously interpreted in the novel as weakness: "Two identical symbols side by side, with their curved yet forked shapes, reminding her of the vulnerability of two humans lying together" (130)—and, in the Empress's eyes, transformation: "My greatest hope in choosing this symbol was to create a spell that would transform Wan'er from the unruly, disobedient self into a more restrained yet creative person. Transformation, magic, civilizing influence—what a wonderful combination of meanings!" (138). Wan'er's tattoo exposes her to public shame at the same time that it proclaims her subjection to the Empress.

Body politics are explored further through the images of the hermaphrodite and the transvestite. Baoshi's hermaphroditism becomes a very productive symbol in Kwa's story. In encompassing the "both/and" categories, Baoshi's body is an illustration of the yin yang principles, of maleness and femaleness at the same time. His hermaphroditism turns out to be an enriching condition and he is variously described as the emblem of judgment and common sense. His name, Precious Stone, is meant to stand for the uniqueness of his body and also for those innate values. The Empress herself will follow his counsel.

Kwa focuses on the diseased body in *This Place Called Absence* in relation to the life of prostitutes. She also explores the links between body and mind, adopting in her first novel the role of the psychologist, Wu Lan, and in *The Walking Boy,* that of the exorcist, Abbess Ling. It is worth mentioning the way Ling's body becomes a vehicle for spiritual expression in the latter case; for a time she is "inhabited" by the demon that plagued Empress Wu Zhao. She explains to Wan'er after the rituals, "Knowing the demon soul intimately in this way grants me the power to exorcise. There's the paradox of being possessed in order to exorcise" (274).

As in Lau's works, the body can be read in Kwa's fiction in terms of sex and pain. Firstly, it becomes the object of desire: the prostitute's body is bought and sold in an exchange between woman and client, but in intimacy it is granted for free, as in Ah Choi and Chat Mui's relationship. When she is working Ah Choi feels "absent," empty, rigid, like wood (59). At other times, her friend longs for

Choi's bodily presence:

> If only I could reach her across the absence, touch with a gentleness that could reassure her, that could soothe those scars.
>
> Her body lives in my cells, the unseen and the unspoken wounds. My lips open to air, gasp for longing for solidity. Where is she that I can't feel her under my hands any longer? That my mouth can't find hers?
>
> Tonight, hovering between worlds, I clutch her body in my mind, breathing a window into another universe. (*This Place Called Absence* 154–55)

Sex also means power vested over others in *The Walking Boy*. The secret of Baoshi's sex is a power he holds for his own sake. Ironically, his moral authority is granted over Wan'er and Nü Huang only when he is discovered (249). He shows a deeper understanding and more intuition than the rest, and knows instinctly that the Empress has been poisoned for years by drinking the Jin Dan elixir. Secondly, the (female) body is the recipient of pain. The lotus feet associated with female beauty in Chinese culture, the venereal diseases and the effects of opium in the case of the prostitues, and the paradox behind Nü Huang's futile search for immortality, are appropriate examples. Particularly in the last case, the Empress's disease demonstrates the ways in which power can be overturned through the body.

4. Addressing Race, Reading Ethnicity:
New Assessments of Exoticism and Hybridity

Whether by means of detachment or adherence, Chinese Canadian women authors of the late 1990s and early 2000s continually address the trope of race. In an essay comparing the development of Asian American and Asian Canadian literary studies, Guy Beauregard identifies race as a challenging topic in the field's future (219). Beauregard argues that contemporary politics of "colour-blindness" (223) mask a new racial discrimination in multicultural Canadian society.[71] The end of the 1990s saw, in Roy Miki's words, the reactivation of the "yellow-peril blues" (Beauregard 230).

The writers studied here answer to the theoretical challenges of race and ethnicity in quite different ways. For example, Evelyn Lau rejects the labels "Asian" and "Chinese" while she prefers to be included in the group of Canadian writers. In contrast, Larissa Lai and Lydia Kwa are more explicit about the workings of race in contemporary Canada through a number of situations in which second-generation immigrants are not even conscious. We intuit that Lau's inhibition from discussions of ethnicity could be due to several reasons, such as her biographical background or the pressures of the literary market with which, it seems, she is ultimately complicit.

In "An Interview with Evelyn Lau," Mary Condé elaborates on Lau's inability to meet her parents' high expectations—for example, that she become a doctor (107–108). As a reaction against these strict standards, Lau chose a life that would embarrass her parents. Sturgess contends further that "Lau has been constructed as 'unruly' daughter through the discourse of 'proper' Canadian-Asiancy just as she has been constructed as exotic 'Other' within normative discourse" (78–79).

Rita Wong argues that Lau rejects classification as an ethnic writer working for an ethnic community because an implied Caucasian audience leads to a larger reading public. Lau's stance can be interpreted in two distinct ways:

> The general tendency to disavow or avoid race in Lau's writing yields a number of possible readings: one is a refusal to be pigeonholed as an "ethnic" writer, and another is to consider this work as a yearning for acceptance that translates into assimilation, which is then accordingly validated and rewarded. In the absence of racialized characters, the normalized power relations at work tend to default her characters into whiteness. ("Market Forces and Powerful Desires" 136)

This normalization is only apparent, since there are different forms in which Lau obliquely marks ethnicity in her texts. It follows that the implications of whiteness will be rather different as well. In particular, Charlotte Sturgess offers an instructive interpretation of Lau's treatment of ethnicity:

> Her non-adherence to a legible script of ethnicity, for which she has been taken to task, does not therefore mean that *"ethnos"* is absent from her writing. It emerges precisely in the difficulty of locating a coherent site from which to speak, within the tensions of positioning in the encounter with the Law of the cultural, social hegemony. (88)

Sneja Gunew suggests that it is necessary to reconsider the theories that try to understand how minorities apprehend themselves:

> This refusal forces those of us who for several decades have attempted to deconstruct totalizing cultural narratives and their attendant regulatory institutional regimes in the name of women, of anti-imperialism, and even multiculturalism . . . to revisit theories and questions about how to situate the authority to speak and write for those designated as minority cultural players, and how to set up interpretative strategies that move beyond the thematization of cultural difference. (257)

Moreover, Gunew values highly Lau's effort to dissociate her intellectual production from what she considers a reductionist practice, that of identity politics. Lau's perspective is not so much that of the racial other as that of the other in Freudian psychoanalysis: the "other" woman of her title.

In *Inside Out* Lau reveals how she dealt with her ethnicity in the past. In the essay "Father Figures," for example, she elaborates on her childhood reaction (stemming from her parents' beliefs) to racist attitudes:

> When I was a child my parents instilled in me the belief that because I am Chinese, and they are immigrants, I would always be inferior to other Canadians; I would have to work twice as hard, be twice as respectable, just to be accepted by this society. Their beliefs were reinforced by the occasional, always shocking, racial taunt in the schoolyard, on the bus, from a stranger passing on the street. A powerful mix of longing and shame roiled in me. I always felt I was an outsider, pressing my face against the glass, yearning to join those people fortunate enough to be in the light and the warmth inside. Perhaps that is partly why I was drawn from the beginning to men whose lives

appeared unblemished and enviable on the surface; I wanted to be accepted by them, to find myself safe inside their houses. (64–65)[72]

In "The Dream of the Purpledresser," she goes back to the neighbourhood of her childhood and dreams of reuniting with her parents as if the last decade had never taken place (183–84). The purpledresser is the material connection with her former life, "a baggage from the past" (187) that intrudes into her present: "Once again I was left standing there, looking at the past. It had followed me into the present and it would be there in the days and dreams that stretched ahead" (212). The purpledresser calls forth long lost bonds with her parents, especially her father, representing both attachment and disconnection.

The mark of ethnicity is revealed in the collection *Fresh Girls*. In the title story Carol's first client is a Chinese man. In most of Lau's stories, however, men are white, whereas women represent the racialized other. The client in "The Session" asks Mary, "You will let me do more, won't you? You'll treat me like . . . like white trash, won't you? You'll spit on me and treat me like garbage?" (23). White stands as a symbol of its own. In "The Apartments" and "The Old Man," Lau designates the colour white with a touch of irony as the representation of cleanliness and purity. Jane imagines her boyfriend sleeping placidly in "his white bed" ("The Apartments 103) while she waits for him. White is also the colour of old age, as in the case of most male lovers in the collection; therefore, the old man's face looks "white and retired" (108).

Subtleties of a different kind appear in "Marriages," where we know that the protagonist is Asian because she recognizes the sneer behind the Japanese waiter's smile, while it goes unnoticed by her white lover (57). The chasm that separates male and female characters, however, cannot be explained as a difference of race or colour, but sphere of life—public or private, sex "within the family" or illicit sex outside of it. Yet Lau hints sometimes at the figure of the exotic Oriental woman, who is all the more exotic when she is a prostitute. In "Fetish Night," for example, "an Oriental woman stands against the wall, a latex sheath outlining her curves, plucking with a red fingernail at the juncture where stocking and garter belt meet" (76). The anonymous narrator in "Roses" becomes as well the representation of the racialized other, since she is described as young and mysterious with straight hair.

At first sight the author seems to take pains to "erase" racial marks from the text, as she rejects being pigeonholed as an Asian Canadian committed to write to an implied audience of other Asian Canadians. However, a close reading of these stories and essays foregrounds the references hidden in the texts, many of which stem from Lau's traumatic childhood and adolescence. Others correspond to a traditional representation of the prostitute as a marginal woman, the more exotic as she is Asian, with implications of submission and docility of the feminized East.[73] By evoking these troubling images Lau both enacts and rejects the two stereotypes of prostitution and exoticism as two companion forms of exploitation. Her stance is exemplified by Dhruvarajan as that of "people of colour [who] resist racism and marginalisation" (171).[74]

In contrast to Lau, the topic of ethnicity is ever present in Lai's fiction. Like that of many other women writers of her generation, her experience makes her adopt a different approach to race and ethnicity and, therefore, community, to that of other well-known and fully established Chinese Canadian writers. In an interview with Chen, Lai explains,

> People like Sky Lee and Wayson Choy and Paul Yee are all descendants of the genera-
> tion that came for the railway or the mining, where[as] my parents are recent immi-
> grants. So I think my concern with history is different from theirs . . . I don't have that
> kind of experience, in my family or otherwise, of old Vancouver Chinatown . . . It was-
> n't part of our experience of immigration or of establishing roots in North America.
> (Hilf 119)[75]

Lai's view of the immigrant plight relies on secondhand experiences. She strongly believes in the power of history as a configurative and constructive force, especially in the case of immigrants and in the narrative potential of history writing to foster a sense of community. Her perception of history evades any traditional linear understanding; she considers further the possibilities that the exercise of history offers to improve (politically and socially) the conditions and the imaginary of the immigrant, and more generally the displaced.[76]

In spite of being a second generation immigrant, Lai is conscious of belonging to what she terms a "diasporized" community; in fact, she defines herself as a "dias- porized subject": "How do we diasporized types make a homespace for ourselves given all the disjunctures and discontinuities of our histories, and for that matter, the co-temporalities of some of them?" ("Political Animals and the Body of His- tory" 149) Most crucially, she also identifies with the image of the hybrid, as char- acters in her two novels evince. The fox, for example, would be a major example of a hybrid figure in *When Fox is A Thousand*. Lai claims to inhabit a racialized space, as some of her characters also realize, namely Miranda in *Salt Fish Girl* and Artemis Wong in *When Fox is a Thousand*. In this light, one of her main concerns is to find new strategies for people of colour and minorities to empower themselves, a proj- ect that she tries to effect through writing. As in Lau's writing, Lai plays with the binary self/other, which she also applies to the non-immigrant/immigrant pair. She likes to think of herself as an immigrant because she considers that there is no way to escape this condition, unless one is aboriginal.[77]

Naming is an important symptom of this definition of identity in *When Fox is a Thousand*. For instance, there is a whole discussion about Artemis's name, and a clear contrast between herself and Diane Wong—the English rendering of the Latin name (24). They share names and look similar to white Canadians, but are in fact diametrically opposite, as Artemis realizes. At the beginning of the book, the fox highlights the importance of naming and the messages it encodes:

> You say: A funny name for a Chinese girl [Artemis]. I will correct you. Chinese-Canadian. Make no mistake, because her name is a name that marks a generation of immigrant children whose parents loved the idea of the Enlightenment and thought they would find it blooming in the full heat of its rational fragrance right here in North America. (10)

Later, we will see how Artemis's friend, Mercy, changes her name to Ming—a more Chinese-sounding name—after a journey to the country of her parents.

Lai's fictions represent present-day Chinatowns in detail, especially in *When Fox is a Thousand*. As Chao comments, Chinatown is described primarily as a commercial and tourist district in which life is busy with restaurants attended by people from every racial background (*Beyond Silence* 13). Artemis meets some of her women lovers at these places. In *Salt Fish Girl*, life in the Unregulated Zone is likely modelled after the early Chinatown communities in late-nineteenth and early-twentieth century Canada. Rita Wong analyzes Lai's exploration of the idea of the Canadian nation as home, especially concerning the immigrant experience. By foregrounding the exile of Miranda Ching's family, Lai is exploring "the immense gap between the discourses of acceptance and compassion that circulate in the name of the nation and the systemic violence of incarceration that meets those who are extra-legal—that is, who may be undocumented or structurally unable to gain access to the privileges required to enter through the nation's front door" ("Troubling Domestic Limits" 111).

Lai launches her most decisive critique against the crisis in the contemporary appraisal of the Canadian nation, which obviously affects the configuration of ethnic identity. Roy Miki's assessment of this crisis applies perfectly to Lai's denouncement in *Salt Fish Girl*: "Do we not yearn for the stability of 'identities' to close the gaps—or even produce us as accomplices in transactions with the seductive discourses of commodities offering us a future language of brands and marks to subsume the nation?" ("Altered States" 43) Lai, as Miki, is conscious of this process of denationalization in favour of globalization and capitalism that is invading Canadian society, and thus depicts Serendipity in the twenty-first century as dominated by corporations like Pallas Shoes that are actually replacing the nation state. Lai also suggests that the notion of progress that this new state of affairs brings about is merely a fantasy. In the midst of sci-fi biotechnology Miranda's basic search is for identity, in an effort to understand where she comes from. The scene that Miki describes in his article is very similar to the one that Lai reproduces in her dystopian novel:

'We' are washed in the proliferation of images that present the dissemination of newly forming subjects in global scenarios of capital expansions, of bodies undergoing forced movements and expulsions as 'refugees' in flight from homelands, and of 'immigrants' whose displacements and passages across borders have become central narratives of our time. (44)

In Lai's narrative, Miranda Ching's family has been "degraded" to the state of non-citizenship and expelled from Serendipity into the Unregulated Zone, which represents the city of the excluded, the renegade, and the "other" in the futuristic society of *Salt Fish Girl*. In this way, the Unregulated Zone becomes a metaphor for the long history of degradation of the Chinese in Canada.

In *Salt Fish Girl*, as Miki also intuits in his essay, biotechnology is at the service of global capitalism. Dr Flowers's genetic experiments, though apparently uncontrolled by the state, work in favour of racial and gender homogenization:

"Who needs the identity of the nation's time, their voices say, when there are commodities about to be born with the potential to overtake time—the ultimate, perhaps, in the not so bizarre image of the deceased body in technological suspension, awaiting the moment of its arrival on biotechnological shores—in a post-ethnic, post-historical, post-contemporary, post-future, post-whatever time" (46).

The bodies of the hybrid Sonias become illegitimate, especially as they make the most of their hybridity and try to establish a separate community, making their own produce and reproducing among themselves.[78] Lai seems to warn readers against the danger of unconscious assimilation and pledging to the dictates of global economies. This representation of the Canadian state incorporates both a view of the past and an insight into the future. In this light, the figure of the cyborg might also be instrumental in the representation and the function of the Sonias. Jenny Wolmark's definition provides clarification:

The cyborg metaphor emphasises the increasingly fluid borders between reality and simulation as definitions of the human as cyborg and the cyborg as human become blurred ... The cyborg embodies the notion of transgression against the limits and controls of the cybernetic systems within which it is situated. Within the context of the unstable boundaries between the real and the simulated, human and cyborg, the question of identity becomes highly charged, because it can become a crucial means of contesting what Bill Nichols describes as the 'reification, the commodification, the patterns of mastery and control' that are at the heart of contemporary cybernetic systems. (Wolmark 127)

The example of Evie and the rest of the Sonias points at this idea of transgression and renovation that has even altered the "natural" dictates of reproduction. Lai's project is one of appropriation by means of literary genre. As will be seen later on in the chapter, the freedom that science fiction provides is used at times like this to argue for the need of more inclusive readings of ethnicity and the body.[79]

Lai deconstructs the idea of history as progress as she presents the situation of immigrants in the future. *Salt Fish Girl* also dramatizes the plight of people living in policed borders (and therefore the risks they run when crossing those frontiers, as in the case of *When Fox is a Thousand*). Nu Wa's stay at the Island of Mist and Forgetfulness provides a wonderful metaphor for the plight of the immigrant. On the island, associated with the Pacific Rim Coast, Nu Wa feels like a complete stranger: she has to learn a new language, "forgetfullian," and at one point she is considered a criminal and goes to prison for five years. When she returns to China, things have changed and the situation is no better: the salt fish girl is an old woman, and she cannot remember Cantonese as Edwina had predicted, two signs of the lack of ties with her place of origin. More than one century later Miranda sells the rights of her mother's songs, her only legacy, to the omnipotent Pallas Shoes Corporation.

Another addition to the ethnic difference debate is the discussion about belief in "the authenticity of the original." When participating in a shooting that Eden proposes to Artemis and Ming in *When Fox is a Thousand,* the former thinks that she is only a fake posing as an Asian woman, but that is very far from the original. She scorns all things Chinese, at least at the beginning of the narrative: "The smell of mothballs was the smell of China. The smell of the small wooden trunk her biological mother had passed on to her adoptive mother the week after the papers were signed . . . [The Chinese smocks] reeked of mothballs and called to her from a distant past that she pushed away with distaste" (21). Both of her adoptive parents are white Canadians, a university professor of Asian Studies and a museum curator specialist in Asian art. When her father was at work, her mother would take her to a Chinese goods store. These are moments of exposure that Artemis feels as alien, but at the same time congenial to her: "She knew somehow that all these creepy things had something to do with her, and that she would have to eat them later. Her mother took the child's quietness for reverence or the exercising of collective memory and decided not to interfere" (*When Fox is a Thousand* 21). Japanese Canadian artist and writer Kyo Mclear comments on the burden of the "original" evoked in this novel: "Intrinsic to the practice of cultural appropriation is the possession and monopolization of the process of defining art and what is valuable. The status and power that comes with being white (male) curator, museologist or professor, institutional power, makes what they say authoritative and persuasive. They have the ability to form and disseminate cultural canons" (Mclear 27).

Artemis's search for self is a search for both personal and ethnic identity. In spite of her inspiring name, which seems to encompass the best of European and Asian ancestry (ven Leuven 45), Lai suggests that there is much more to identity than a name. Artemis is lost for most of the novel; she needs to come to grips with a past of which she is not even aware. As in other well-known examples of Asian North American fiction, such as *The Joy Luck Club* by Amy Tan, Lai's protagonist journeys "home" to China, though that barely amounts to an encounter with the past. Her friend Mercy's journey to China utterly transforms her—she even changes her name and reinscribes ethnicity artificially by tattooing her body: "There were tattoos on her arms, tattoos that revealed her road to her reinvention of herself—a dragon and phoenix, a yin-yang symbol, a lotus flower in full colour, delicate pink and yellow. Tattoos that American sailors docking at Tsim Sha Tsui for the first time would get, Artemis thought" (*Salt Fish Girl* 139). In Artemis's case, only her relationship with the fox will reconstruct her fractured identity.

In an interview, Lai develops her theory about the articulation of sites of difference, declaring that she is thinking of a particular audience to address her novels:

My own generation of younger Asian Canadians, women, maybe lesbians, maybe feminists, maybe not, but those who feel like outsiders for whatever reason. It's a kind of contingent essentialism of the moment, in which I centralize 'likeness', whatever that means to the reader in the moment. I want to recognize that none of these things are fixed. (Morris, "Sites of Articulation" 22)

This implied audience is in tune with her project of "girlhood" in *Salt Fish Girl*. Lai claims further in her essay "Future Asians":

I wanted to create a myth of origins for girls that travel, girls who come from many places at once . . . It seemed to me that to write a founding myth about travel and dislocation could be a liberating thing because it denies racial purity and denies the primacy of the citizen tied to the land. (173–74)

Salt Fish Girl (as much as *When Fox*) is full of young women on the run. Nu Wa renounces to her immortality for love and curiosity by returning to her body shape in an enactment of the mermaid-into-woman myth (Brydon and Schagerl 36). Miranda and Evie abandon society in each other's company. In *When Fox is a Thousand,* characters inhabit the shapes of others, like Fox, or Artemis herself, in a constant search for reconnection.

Furthermore, and considering her mixed-race origins, Artemis also relies on a "collective memory," also called "emotional memory," which preserves the lives and experiences of past generations:

Not that something disastrous couldn't occur, only it might not happen here the way it does in China. Was that where the melancholy she felt sometimes came from? The possibility that she might not recognize an act of repression when it struck? Or did it come from tapping into a collective memory of all the deaths, abandonments, and slow stresses of war that have gone unspoken through the generations? Perhaps the precise stories and politics had been lost, but the emotional memory might move from one generation to the next as surely as any genetic trait. (*When Fox is a Thousand* 85)

Lydia Kwa enacts a similar concept of "emotional" or "collective" memory. She plays with the notions of home and exile, the latter imposed by the hardships of immigration. The ancestors and the dead are ever present and help other characters to return to the places and the countries left behind in *This Place Called Absence*. It has been twenty years since Wu Lan left her home in Singapore; now in Canada, where she feels alone, her connection with the past comes through memory. Her task is twofold: to recover after her father's sudden death by suicide, and to reconstruct the story of Ah Choi and Chat Mui. Theirs are experiences of immigration, leaving sad stories behind. Wu Lan manages to recover the history of her family as well as that of many other Chinese immigrants, mostly unknown to her but sharing similar experiences. There is an intrinsic connection between migration and sexual subjection, as the stories of Ah Choi and Chat Mui evince, and as Wu Lan discovers in her research on prostitution: "It concerned women who had left Mainland China and Japan from the late 1800s to the mid twentieth-century, women who landed in Singapore and were indentured to the sex trade to pay off debts" (31). The case studies of late nineteenth-century prostitutes uncover stories of marginalization and suicide: "Nothing much has changed, these means of eliminating oneself. *Suicide due to*. The true causes buried beneath the means, hidden from outsiders' eyes" (47). These violent deaths help Wu Lan to see her father's suicide in a similar light.

Especially in this first novel, Kwa focuses on the association between migration and absence. Significantly, the distance between mother and daughter is enhanced by the geographical distance imposed by diaspora (20–21). On the other hand, the absence of grandmother Neo was the demon that haunted Wu Lan's father (65). Connections like this one are already lost to Wu Lan, who feels alien to her family past (and has lost her "Chineseness"). As they migrated to Singapore, Wu Lan's ancestors claimed their "purity" as an identity mark. Mahmee is in charge of presenting this information to the reader; she becomes the only link between generations and Wu Lan's bridge to her past, her connection to home and Singapore: "But we are pure, we belong here, come from China" (81). Mahmee also emphasizes the importance of ancestors, as symbols of belonging and origins, especially in the case of immigrants:

I tell Lan-Lan, good you take Chinese medicine to help you, you can go far, far away to Canada, but you still your kong-kong's granddaughter, still must do it our old way, brew with herbs, drink, good for you. Swallow, don't spit out, swallow bitterness, and you will be cured. (120)

There is a close connection between gender and race as ways of representing otherness in *The Walking Boy*. The image of immigration is replaced with that of pilgrimage, as Baoshi journeys to the city in search of his master's former lover, and as Wan'er and Baoshi perform their individual searches for meaning and identity. Furthermore, the hermaphrodite and the slave become companion images of marginalization, the former as it threatens homogeneity and exclusion politics, the latter as it counteracts the absolute power of the Empress. In this way, Baoshi and Wan'er are identified as related characters, hence their mutual attraction in the novel. In this light as well, race is represented by means of body marks, so that the body becomes once more the site of difference: tattoos and the hermaphrodite body substitute skin colour. Ling enlightens Wan'er about the meaning and the implications of her tattoo:

'Your mark is disquieting because it bears witness to the enormity of what had happened, even before its existence. Your mark is a sign of the burden of others. You may have been taken in as a slave of the court, but what does that say about those who demand your unswerving allegiance? As for your opinion about the tattoo's ugliness, I am saddened by your distress. A mark, indeed, is not just a mark on the skin.' (131)

As in *This Place Called Absence,* the sense of "home" expands to encompass a variety of notions, such as "absence," "exile," "past," and "memory." For Baoshi, home means Harelip, and the mountains: "[W]hen I started out on my pilgrimage to Chang'an, I was walking away from that secure love into a world of unknowns. Since being in Chang'an, I've struggled once again with fears of being shamed and rejected. This city is another kind of wilderness, as my Master has put it" (205–06). For Wan'er, the term acquires an added dimension; "home" is the neglected story of her family, the death of her father and grandfather at Empress Wu Zhao's hands that her mother had silenced. The recovery of her past amounts to a return home for her, as she explains:

Eternal wandering, trapped in the hidden ruins
Your songs, all the sounds your throat can permit
Now that you are returned home, a lost pilgrim.
Subtle are the nuances of a woman's longing, stirring
   Sighs
While the body sits placidly, wrists still bound
Unseen, your spirit wanders beyond limits
Plucking at the instruments,

That never fully capture the wild haunting melody
Of your isolation and mine joined
Can men understand why such songs bring tears to their
Hearts?
(287–88)

Through this love poem dedicated to Abbess Ling, Kwa reveals once more the connection between ethnic and gender issues in the novel.

5. Exploring Genre and Aesthetics: Autobiography, History, Fantasy

Lau, Lai, and Kwa share a high degree of experimentation in terms of literary form and genre. From different perspectives and often supporting opposing ideologies, the three authors break boundaries, the former exploring autobiography while the other two play with historical and science fiction conventions. Additionally, Kwa makes use of the ghost story convention. All three manage to renew their chosen forms; Lau's choice of subject matter and confessional voice, Lai's decisive attempt to merge history and myth as well as use of science fiction *topoi* with a historical insight, and Kwa's study of narrative voice seem to prove this point.

Though Lau does not rely on autobiographical material alone, it is true that as a writer she situates herself very close to this form of writing. From *Runaway: Diary of a Street Kid* to *Inside Out*, she adopts the autobiographical voice as a form of therapy. Though hardly represented as the "survivor of trauma," Lau explores the genre as an escape from her many frustrations and difficult experiences as an adolescent and young woman. Many of the female voices in her stories display similar frustrations. Apart from that, the fact that Lau advocates the position of women telling the truth also represents a political stance. She seems to claim that women have lives worth telling; her choice of women prostitutes and women lovers, who have been traditionally classified as the "other," is especially interesting.[80] The choice to use autobiography is highly charged and a decisive step towards new definitions of identity, as Leigh Gilmore argues:

> Texts that are concerned with self-representation and trauma offer a strong case for seeing that in the very condition of autobiography (and not the obstacles it offers for us to overcome) there is no transparent language of identity despite the demand to produce one. As controversial as any evidence of shaping may be in a trauma text—and what text is not shaped?—part of what we must call healing lives in the assertion of creativity. (24)

Questions of reception take an important place in Evelyn Lau's work. She first became well-known not only in the literary market, but also in Canadian society after her publication of *Runaway: Diary of a Street Kid* in 1989, in which she collects her experiences as a prostitute between 1986 and 1988. As mentioned above, her name became publicly exposed ten years later with the highly publicized libel lawsuit filed against her in 1998. In both cases, the use of the author's autobiographical data is at the heart of the polemics. Charlotte Sturgess addresses the issue of Lau's autobiographical turn, interpreting her disruption of the limits between the public and the private in her writing as an attempt to break with notions of ethnic appropriateness:

> [T]he types of self-representation which Lau projects through her work into the public domain, seem to have discredited her in terms of implicit rules of 'ethnic correctness': a somewhat ironic turning of the tables of discourses of exclusion when those often relegated to the position of the 'Other' in turn relegate to the margins. (78)

Kristeva's definition of the abject, as delineated above, is exemplified perfectly in Lau's narratives. In her desire for expression through written words, Lau, as well as Lai and Kwa, represents the figure of the writer as an image of abjection: "The writer is a phobic who succeeds in metaphorizing in order to keep from being frightened to death; instead he comes to life again in signs" (*Powers of Horror* 38). Lau's use of the autobiographical uncovers a desire not only to be recognized as writer, but also a need to be accepted as individual (Sturgess 78). When studied in relation to other women writers of her generation and context, namely Lai and Kwa, the topics proposed by Lau do not only not interfere with the goals of Canadian Asiancy, they also bring to the fore crucial questions at the level of representation. One such question is that of writing and responsibility for one's own words or towards one's own community (whether the community is one of writers in general, women, or Asian Canadian women in particular).[81]

We must remember, though, that Lau is reluctant to see her own work addressed to a specific audience of Asian Canadians. In this sense, Wong comments that "[Lau] has set her own standards for writing; her aesthetic is one with a wider appeal. Whether or not this internalizes white standards, it seems to be empowering for Lau as an individual" ("Jumping on Hyphens" 124). Lau often assumes the role of the writer of colour who argues against using that as a means to an end, but who takes a stance by way of rejection and detachment. Similar to Sturgess, Wong suggests that Lau's work has been trivialized, perhaps due to its autobiographical drive. Ironically, and in spite of her efforts at self-exclusion, she plays her part as an exotic referent:

Sometimes I have the disturbing feeling that, if Lau had not come along, the machine would have found someone else because it needs to have a bit of "colour" (but not too much) mirroring or serving the symbolic order so that it can disavow its historical and systemic racist tendencies. ("Market Forces and Powerful Desires" 123)

Lau's view of writing and of the writer's profession goes hand-in-hand with the form of autobiography. She draws on autobiographical material that she includes in her stories, a practice that she started back in 1989. In the autobiographical essays of *Inside Out* (2001), she discusses genre and the extent to which she draws on her life for inspiration. This is both a narcissistic exercise and the only way in which she understands the work of the writer, as a telling about oneself. In "The Country of Depression," for example, she describes where inspiration comes from: "For it is in the compulsions, the obsessions, the seemingly fathomless emotional experiences, that some of that writing is born. It is in that ability to go so deeply into a subject that it is like dropping down a hole into the heart of the known world" (44–45).

Sturgess addresses the question of identity and explores how it is connected to Lau's particular use of language: "Female identity as a problem explicitly centred within language and the symbolic relation of 'self' to 'Other' within representation" (77). Language is what mediates between life (dim, morbid, disgusting) and self in Lau's writing. At the same time, language is for her the sign of otherness: her devotion to writing since early childhood was instrumental in her development; this inclination for the written word became in her case the only true means of communication, as well as the trait that made her different, an "other." She idealizes the writer's profession, which for her inevitably brings about immortality: "It is jolting to discover that I rarely want to pray for inspiration, even when the muse hides for months behind a cloud. Instead I speak to him sternly, demanding an end to our bargain. I will exchange all the written words left in my lifetime, hand them over in a bursting sack, if he will give me the other thing I currently want" (89–90). This thing was none other than the schizophrenic dissociation between herself and the writer, to take herself as a suitable object of study, and to gain the distance needed to write about her life.

As mentioned above, Lau's conflict has always been to bridge the gap between the public and the private, which for her amount to the same thing. Art, in particular literary art, means telling truths, and disguising the real referents in a text is closer to lying than to anything else (91–92). Writing provides precisely the connection between the two spheres: "I suppose I don't understand the notion of privacy very well. There has always been this strange urgent need in me to make the private public, *to turn things inside out so that what typically lives hidden in darkness is exposed to the light*" (100; my emphasis). The innovation of the writer lies somewhere else, in the choice of the words and in the perspective adopted: "It is a strangely journalistic approach to literature, this fierce desire to record rather than to create. This satisfaction at finding the phrases that describe people and events as they are, and not always asking, 'What if?' Why is it that imagination is valued over recorded experience?" (102–03).

Literature is seen in a different light when tested against law in "Anatomy of a Libel Lawsuit," a chapter about the lawsuit that the Canadian writer and Lau's former lover WP Kinsella filed against her in 1998, after the publication of the article "Me and WP" in a Vancouver magazine.[82] Lau turns this difficult experience into a topic to write about: "The power of language started to take on a whole new meaning—in the eyes of the law, where an author's intentions were considered irrelevant, words were examined as carefully as jewels under a microscope" (114). This confrontation highlights the question of a writer's freedom to decide over the material fit for writing, or as Lau understands it, the conflict between the right to tell and the right to privacy: "As a writer I was both fascinated and repelled by that division, the tension between those two selves. On some level I deplored people who maintained this duplicity; it reminded me too much of the men who came down to the streets to buy sex from girls the age of their daughters . . ." (130). Lau enacts this conflict quite often in her stories; "The Old Man" in *Fresh Girls* provides a good example. Going back to the "Anatomy," Lau considers writing to be her only possession, the only place she belonged that has been taken from her violently, transporting her back to the time when she was a child in her parents' house (138). In this essay she discusses the distinction between a reality show and autobiography, trying to establish the limits between one and the other. Ironically, her depression and writer's block following the lawsuit began to disappear once she began to look at it as a writer, and not merely as a participant (158).

The rest of her narrative draws profusely on autobiographical material, including obsessive father/daughter relationships, surrogate father and mother figures, sex workers and other marginal women, the weight of the past, the uneasy relationship between the individual and the community. In this sense, and in the particular way in which she understands autobiography, silences, gaps, and omissions become powerful narrative strategies as much as the words that are said.

As genre is concerned, and as suggested above, Lai experiments with "other" ways of seeing history—what she sometimes calls an "artificial" history—but her understanding of the discipline is entwined with her use of dystopic elements, as she does in *Salt Fish Girl* (2002), or myth, as in both her novels. She explores the limits of history, both as a discipline and as a subjective experience with a clear social component ("Future Asians" 172). Lai does not rely on the idea of progress; on the contrary, she deconstructs it by imagining in her second novel a futuristic dystopian society that entails a way back to an old economics. The topic of hybridity and multiplicity of forms is also important in relation to Lai's view of genre and aesthetics. Lai makes use of several genres, including history, myth, dystopia, fable, and fairy tale. Accordingly, she explores the nature of truth in her fiction, a search that is compatible not only with the musts of postmodernism but also with some of the movements emanating from the margins. The understanding of a multifaceted truth has a political concern: "Politically, what I was interested in when I was writing *Fox* was exploring the multiplicity and instability of the notion of truth while also producing a subjectivity that doesn't seem to have a stable site of articulation" (Lai quoted in Morris, "Sites of Articulation" 25). The subject character is at odds: the fractured self of Artemis needs to heal and she will do so with Fox's help at the novel's close, but also by means of her gradual reconciliation with the past. There is no clear positive reading of the past as origins, but rather a message about how disarticulation works across time and space, as in the case of Fox.

When *Fox is a Thousand* is a remarkable account of "generic hybridity" (Morris 76), since it fuses the historical figure of the ninth-century poet with the mythical tale of the fox. To Robyn Morris, "This melding of ancient spirits and ancient bodies with contemporary student life emphasizes not only the historical continuity of the female story, but also the importance of the past in the formation of a bicultural identity in a specifically mono-Canadian present" ("Revisioning Representations of Difference" 71). Literary hybridity matches in Lai's case the hybrid nature of her characters. Hybridity, mutation, and change are commonplace in both novels under study. Genres flow, as do subjects, not only in *When Fox*, where the protagonist's time travels allow for her own and Artemis's admittance of lesbianism and personal acceptance, but also in *Salt Fish Girl*, in which the distinction between human, animal, and machine is never clear. The figure of the clone and the cyborg are two examples. As this concern for genre demonstrates, Lai is aware of the power of fiction as a strategy for transformation:

> "I am conscious of my choice to write fiction as a strategy chosen because it reaches people. On the other hand, in this age of steroid-enhanced capitalism, the tension between engaging those technologies, which enable one to reach large numbers of people, of opening oneself and one's work to quick fix consumption, is no easy thing to resolve." ("Political Animals and the Body of History" 148)

Lai's choice of the science fiction genre marks a new reading of *Salt Fish Girl*. As mentioned earlier, this form purports a higher degree of freedom to the novelist, especially when gender issues are at stake. Clearly, her position is a feminist one, and that means a great addition to the genre, as Wolmark argues:

> Feminist appropriations are inevitably partial because they remain embedded within the conventional narrative structures of the genre, but they can nevertheless alter the

focus of the narratives to reveal the equally embedded nature of the power relations within which the subject is constructed, and which defines the relations between self and other. (55)

These science fiction narratives written by women from a feminist standpoint necessarily inhabit a slippery ground, which Jameson calls "generic discontinuities"; solutions are always incomplete, and sexual and social revolution can never be taken for granted:

> The ambivalence and ambiguity of these narratives introduces elements of instability and uncertainty, a reminder that the reconstruction of gender can take place only in de Lauretis's 'elsewhere,' where such partial perspectives are a means of resisting the totalising tendencies of hegemonic discourse. (Wolmark 55)

Miranda and Evie's attempt at a relationship must remain hidden, as well as the all-women community of the Sonias at the novel's close, even though the door remains open at the end and a more hopeful future is hinted at.

If *When Fox* was about the past, *Salt Fish Girl* deals with the future (Morris, "Sites of Articulation" 25). This a novel both relies on and resents tomorrow. Hope lies in the future, as the controvertible example of the Sonias makes clear. Though generally read as a dystopia, their case seems to point in another direction: in the face of state and scientific manipulation, the Sonias represent a single-sex society that manages to evade reproductive state or medical intervention. Lai creates a scientific fable that goes beyond the limits of technology, and the Sonias subplot helps to renovate the conventions of the genre by expanding its limits.

Like Lai preceding her, Lydia Kwa relies on the use of history as an integrating force; for her it is a means of reconciliation with the past: of crossing timelines and borders, of looking for the common thread among women belonging to different generations and inhabiting diverse places. In her novels, she engages in similar projects of historical visibility. *This Place Called Absence* calls forth a sense of poetic *cum* historical justice, while she endeavours to rescue and study the stories of these nineteenth-century Chinese prostitutes in Singapore and also manages to recompose the history of her own country while in absence. The writer questions the validity of official accounts of history in controvertible stories like those of *ah ku*; it is difficult to believe in the true causes of events. Like Lai, Kwa explores the meaning of truth and the validity of its representations. She hints, for example, at the recalling of the official list of *ah ku* who committed suicide and at guessing their reasons for doing it (47). Kwa offers stories about disempowered women who look desperately for ways of empowering themselves: *ah ku* use sex to exert their scant authority over wives and prospective lovers, for instance. This is also, and by extension, a story about the untold: homosexuality, which is never spoken overtly and publicly; prostitution; suicide; the pains of diaspora and immigration; and finally, the pains of "visibility."

The Walking Boy problematizes the notions of official and unofficial history. In a world dominated by men, Wu Zhao leaves her mark by making sure her version of events will survive:

> It is not just for myself that I am doing this. As a woman, an unconventional woman, do you not recognize the worth of this document of mine? The men will be writing their own version of my reign in the Veritable Record when I am gone. It matters greatly to me that this Palace Diary exits as a statement in support of women like us, women who face immense obstacles against gaining power in the world of men. (182)

Wan'er and the reader's ironic account of Wu Zhao's purposes contribute to changing our view about the objectivity of the historical document. Furthermore, the role of the historian, Wan'er, the one who collects information, selects it, and construes the historical text, is also analyzed: how can we account for her outward complacency and complicity? Moved by circumstance, she finally appears as a survivor who outlives even the Empress.

Kwa further explores the trope of visibility in *The Walking Boy*. The symbol of hermaphroditism, embodied by Baoshi, remains hidden—his nature is kept secret as a means of survival. Like *This Place Called Absence, The Walking Boy* plays with different plot lines and narrative perspectives, and once more we are subdued by the voices of the enslaved and the abandoned, people like Wan'er, the Imperial secretary kept in a state of submission by the Empress, and Baoshi, rejected by his parents. The author herself defines her work as a "trans-historical novel," "because it's a quirky and queer novel set in early-eighth-century China, during the Tang dynasty" ("The Walking Boy"). As Kwa points out, she chose to write the whole novel in the present tense as a strategy for communicating a sense of immediacy, "as if it's happening in your imagination as you read/create." In different ways, her novel is a "ghost story," and Kwa manages to "feed" those ghosts coming from the past—most clearly the two female opposers murdered by Wu Zhao, but also Wan'er's own ghosts, her family history, and Baoshi, who is reconciled with his bodily experiences.

In both novels Kwa recreates the world of ghosts, fostering the reading of the supernatural in the novel. On one hand, the ghost plot reproduces part of the Chinese tradition of respect for ancestors and their spiritual manifestations after death. On the other hand, Kwa also revises the basic conventions of the fantastic genre and the gothic form, including uncanny appearances, the use of the *doppël-ganger*, or the presence of the supernatural. Starting from groundbreaking works like Todorov's *The Fantastic* (1973), this genre has been associated with the act of reading: "The fantastic implies, then, not only the existence of an uncanny event, which provokes a hesitation in the reader and the hero; but also a kind of reading, which we may for the moment define negatively: it must be neither 'poetic' nor 'allegorical'" (Todorov 32). Like Todorov, Von Mucke also foregrounds the three-sided bond of text-hero-reader. She suggests that the fantastic offers new light on the reader's own subjectivity: "The strange psychology of the fantastic tale further-more questions rationalist assumptions of agency as well as commonly held assumptions about the relationship between cause and effect" (3). Other voices like Rosemary Jackson's privilege the subversive nature of the genre, which is said to elicit the stories of those who stand outside the cultural order, usually in oppo-sition to capitalist or patriarchal structures (in Von Mucke 14).

In Kwa's fiction, the ghost plot brings conflicts to the surface. In *This Place Called Absence*, Wu Lan's father becomes an unwelcome presence. His spirit haunts both his wife and daughter in their dreams, but his ghost, together with the fact that he died by committing suicide, makes Wu Lan relate him to the silenced sto-ries of nineteenth-century *ah ku* who died in similar circumstances. The ghosts in *The Walking Boy* also haunt Empress Wu Zhao, not only in her dreams. If Wu Lan's and Mahmee's dreams of the defunct father and husband could be read as exam-ples of post-traumatic stress, in the Empress's case, the presence of these uncanny apparitions can be explained as the hallucinations of a woman who has been grad-ually poisoned through the years, paradoxically by drinking the Jin Dan Elixir. As these two examples reveal, the ghost embodies and represents the Freudian "return of the repressed."

Kwa relies on polyvocal narratives. *This Place Called Absence* is woven by the dif-ferent voices of Wu Lan, Mahmee, Lee Ah Choi, and Chow Chat Mui. The notion of memory comprehends different meanings: it is related to an intellectual exercise (to bring back the past), but also to the body (as it is related to the senses), and is, therefore, a subjective act. As a writer Kwa reflects on the power of language to encode meaning and on its importance as the medium of telling. In doing so, she spins a discourse on storytelling: how to make the invisible visible, to speak the unspeakable.[83] That is further connected to both Chat Mui's power with words and Wu Lan's profession as a clinical psychologist. Like Abbess Ling in *The Walking Boy,* Wu Lan acts as an exorcist, liberating and saying good-bye to her father, using the power of words: "What does Father want to tell me? What he didn't get to say before he died? I feel some kind of urgency has infected me as never before, and I keep thinking of eggs, of blood, of the water in our bodies, and the fragility of boundaries" (57). Wu Lan learns that her name is connected to the casting of demons. Both Wu Lan and Chat Mui try to calm the dead, to "feed" them. The lat-ter visits Ah Choi's burial place; the former defines "this place called absence" as the place of the psychologist in front of the clients.

I'm returning to this place called absence, where in front of me, a stranger talks. Stringing words together. Two strangers who sit across from each other in a small, soundproofed room. Face to face? Truths or lies?

A torrent of words, like a seasonal monsoon, underneath which lies the deepest pain. Aren't all stories true? To intuit the meaning of what is left unsaid.

I am Wu Lan, an exorcist of hidden demons.

I am the discoverer of secrets.

I stir fire into the bones of the dead.

I prepare the dead for release.

Bending into the porcelain whiteness of the bathtub, I lean very close to his embalmed body and whisper one last time.

Goodbye, Father. (208)

The influence of psychology and the inner world of characters is commonplace in *The Walking Boy*. In an interview Kwa admitted that, as a clinical psychologist, it is very important for her to draw on the workings of the mind: "How the external world affects the internal, and how the internal world of the psyche is enacted and replicated in the external" ("Singapore on My Mind" 24). The character of Wan'er provides a wonderful example of this interest. Her particular reading of Cai Yan's poems favours the overflowing of thoughts and feelings. The reader's perception and assessment of the text is highly complex and multifaceted, while Cai Yan's texts, and Wan'er's answers to them, are simultaneously disposed in layers. Moreover, Cai Yan's vital experiences help to heal and exorcise Wan'er's demons, and there comes a moment when their voices are fused—from the external to the internal and way back:

Did each poem relieve your torment?
A captive lotus, voicing crisis of dislocation.
Bitterness rooted you
With the breath of your brooding, the gamble of
    anguish
Pain's hard, fragile carapace insisting you alone were
    dealt a unique fate.
Embattled, sheltered.
Questions separate us, disjunction of meaning.
(*The Walking Boy* 197–98)

Cai Yan's poems constitute, finally, the means for Wan'er to "speak" her mind, to unfetter her memory.

6. Conclusion

It is no easy task to find a common thread that identifies an incipient generation of Canadian women writers of Chinese origin, or to recognize a single pattern in their fiction. Voices like Judy Fong Bates choose to follow well-known precedents such as Sky Lee and represent the hardships of first generation immigrants, focusing in her case on the study of masculine types, as she does, for example, in her 2004 novel. Others depart from this model, and though acknowledging the guidance and merit of "foremothers," they prefer to focus on the here and now, on other pressing issues including a great deal of political commitment, sexual politics, and a critical view of class and world economics. In this apparently neat panorama, Evelyn Lau is seen by other Chinese Canadian women writers as the "black sheep" of their generation. She defies any further association with her "Chineseness," a part of her identity that she has publicly abhorred, and in that sense she is considered snobbish, proud, a traitor to her people. In spite of not sharing similar experiences, Lai and Kwa's agendas coincide in many respects. Against Lau's individuality they stress the importance of the social and the communal; both believe as well in the power of radical and marginal communities like the *jokappas* or the Sonias, as models of survival against odds. All three authors explore the topic of difference from the points of view of ethnicity and gender, and their works exemplify how these two questions are inextricably linked. The figures of the Asian prostitute in Lau and the *ah ku* in Kwa epitomize extreme representations of otherness, encompassing femininity, race, deviant sexuality, and youth. Evelyn Lau's work in particular foregrounds difference through binaries or dualisms: self/other, absence/presence, displacement/embodiment, mind/body, and integration/disintegration.

The worlds that the three writers portray are bleak, whether eighth-century China or the over-technological society of mid-twenty-first century Canada. There is almost no place for the individual, whose integrity is under threat by the currents of global economy and social exclusion. Lau's work is a cry for personal recognition as the unruly daughter of a whole generation of Chinese immigrants working for social acceptance in Canada. In contrast, Lai's stance is militant: she is an activist who does not rebel against her Chinese origin but against the complacency of the daughters who have experienced a backlash and do not wonder anymore about who they are. Kwa's view adds new light. As an immigrant into contemporary Canada her experience is both radically different and strikingly similar to those of the first Chinese sojourners: historically speaking, she has not shared their experience of exclusion, yet she has in common with them the pains of invisibility and living in exile. In different ways, they pose questions about what is true and about the limits of believability. Their conclusions are also multifaceted and varied. Their proposals share, though, the search for agency, which Roy Miki explains as follows:

> What is important for a culture to thrive is a renewed belief in the viability of agency, so that writers from a diversity of subject-positions can develop the conditions in which social justice can be achieved through a language free from the tyranny of hegemonies of all kinds. It may be an impossible end but the movement towards that "across cultural" end can initiate those heterogeneous and indeterminate spaces (potentialities) where writers of colour, including Asian Canadian writers, can negotiate their (non-totalizable) specificities—without looking over their shoulders for the coercive gaze of homogenizing discourses. (*Broken Entries* 123)

III.
BEYOND REDRESS:
JAPANESE CANADIAN WOMEN'S FICTION

1. Introduction

As World War Two broke out, the Canadian government started to look with suspicion on the Japanese Canadian communities living along the Pacific coast of Canada. Such suspicion evolved into frightened alarm upon the Japanese attack of Pearl Harbor in December 1941. The following year, the Canadian government implemented a series of wartime measures against Japanese Canadians, regardless of whether or not they were Canadian born or Canadian citizens. Their possessions were confiscated and they were transported into the interior of British Columbia, where internment camps were built. Families were often split up in the process, with many Japanese Canadian men being put to work separately on road building projects.

After the war, the interned Japanese Canadians were given the option of being "repatriated" to Japan (though many of them had no previous contact with that country) or dispersing across Canada. Returning to British Columbia was forbidden. Those who attempted to recover part of their lost property immediately after the war met with little success and even open hostility. As McAllister points out, "public discourse justified the internment of Japanese Canadians either in the name of national security or as a means of assimilating a supposedly inward-looking ethnic minority into mainstream society" (30). The relocated Japanese Canadians were subjected to supervision and surveillance until 1949. They had to carry identification cards and their freedom of movement was restricted.[84] As a consequence, Japanese Canadians retreated into invisibility and assimilation in the post-war period: "Racism, the uprooting and resettlement, the loss of all goods and properties, and the stripping of their citizenship provided a strong subconscious determination for them to disperse first and foremost as sparsely and thinly as possible" (Makabe 28).

The reawakening of self-awareness among Japanese Canadians and the recuperation of their memories is masterfully described in Joy Kogawa's novel *Obasan*

(1981). Similarly, in *Itsuka* (1992), Kogawa portrays the obstacle-ridden development of the Redress Movement in which she herself closely participated. There she emphasizes the disunity of a community that has lived under the weight of dispersal and silence for decades. Nevertheless, the Redress Movement emerged victorious in 1988 with Prime Minister Brian Mulroney's public acknowledgement of the racist treatment to which the Japanese Canadians had been subjected in the 1940s, and with the negotiation of an agreement with the National Association of Japanese Canadians (NAJC) to compensate the surviving victims, although such compensation could only be more symbolic than real.

2. In the Shadow of *Obasan:* The Trauma of Internment

Kogawa's work became the forerunner of a new generation of Japanese Canadian writers who shunned invisibility in order to narrate their experiences in the context of a multicultural society. Roy Miki asserts that "to the late 1960s, the concept of a Japanese Canadian writer or artist had no public body, even though, of course, a few JCs were writing and producing art" (31). However, in the 1990s men and women of Japanese ancestry, both Japanese- and Canadian-born, published a variety of works, including Hiromi Goto's *Chorus of Mushrooms* (1994), Gerry Shikatani's *Lake and Other Stories* (1996), Terry Watada's *Daruma Days* (1997), Tamai Kobayashi's *Exile and the Lesbian Heart* (1998), Sally Ito's *Floating Shore* (1998), and Kerri Sakamoto's *The Electrical Field* (1998). These examples attest to the growing vitality and prominence of Japanese Canadian writing in the wider context of Canadian Literature.[85] This chapter will trace the politics and poetics of Japanese Canadian women writers of the 1990s, particularly through the novels of Hiromi Goto and Kerri Sakamoto with the occasional turn to the short stories of Sally Ito and Tamai Kobayashi, and attend to contrasts with their forerunner in the 1980s, Joy Kogawa.

It is worth mentioning that Japanese Canadian women writers published in the 1990s and later have had to cope with the shadow cast on their accomplishments by those of their predecessor, Joy Kogawa. Kogawa's visibility in the 1980s was paramount, perhaps because this decade was characterized by the awakening of academia to the distinctive value and make-up of Asian North American writing.[87] The rediscovery of pioneers like Sui Sin Far by such US academics as Amy Ling or Sau-ling Cynthia Wong roughly coincided with the publication of Kogawa's *Obasan* (1981), *Itsuka* (1992), and *The Rain Ascends* (1995).[88] At the same time, one must acknowledge how empowering her example has been for the next generation, who felt that it lacked a tradition in English, as the Sansei[89] writer Mona Oikawa remarks:

As a Japanese Canadian woman, I have sought writings that depict what it was like for my parents and my grandparents during and after their internment in World War II. The works of Tsukiye Muriel Kitagawa and Joy Kogawa have helped to paint part of that picture. Muriel Kitagawa, who protested the actions of the government, did not live to complete her story of the wartime injustices. But her papers testify to her outspoken determination to challenge the Canadian government and the citizens of this country. And reading Joy Kogawa's book, *Obasan*, was like restoring memory of my past, giving me threads of connection to a community shattered through imprisonment and dispersal. (101)

Yet this new generation of Japanese Canadian women writers often offers new perspectives on the wartime experiences of Japanese Canadians, although the subject matter is similar to Kogawa's. For instance, Sakamoto's *One Hundred Million Hearts* (2003) portrays the participation in the war of those Nisei men stranded in Japan. Such a topic evinces the writer's courage, as Goossen remarks,

To focus on this group during the time of the Redress Movement (successfully concluded in 1988), when Japanese Canadians and their supporters were struggling to obtain official apology and compensation, would have been regarded as counterproductive. Not a single act of sabotage or treason had been committed in Canada by a Japanese Canadian; the expropriation of property and the dispersal of the community to internment camps had been both unjust and strategically unnecessary. But at the time of the Redress Movement, maintaining this position . . . required that experiences and individuals who might compromise the "official narrative" had to be excluded. (63)

Sakamoto's novel fills that gap and addresses the complexity of the Japanese Canadian experience, problematizing the binary opposition of Japanese/Canadian, and displaying instead a cast of characters where both identities exist in a variety of shades and degrees, grounding identity in several locations, times, and generations.

Other Japanese Canadian writers of this younger generation introduce new themes, charting experiences that are not so intimately related to the events unfolding during World War Two. Such is the case of Hiromi Goto, whose family came to Japan after the war, and whose work only occasionally opens up to a legacy that is not truly hers. Instead, her novels[90] *Chorus of Mushrooms* (1994) and *The Kappa Child* (2001) trace the efforts of newly arrived immigrants to fit into Canada's mainstream society in plots that closely resemble her own experience. Goto's work also differs from that of other Canadian Nikkei writers in refusing to give way to nostalgia for an essentialized, unproblematic Japanese identity while acknowledging such ancestry, offering instead shifting patterns of identity and belonging.[91] However, on occasion she too discloses silenced cultural experiences of the Japanese during World War Two. Thus Naoe, the grandmother in *Chorus of*

Mushrooms, remembers her time in China during the Japanese occupation with pangs of guilt. Forced into a loveless arranged marriage, her bitterness blinded her to everything and everyone around her, including her daughter Keiko. Only in her eighties, with the benefit of hindsight, does she come to understand and feel guilty about those events. As she dwells on the complex web of inter-Asian relations in the period, she expresses her pain at having colluded in the exploitation and suffering of others:

> Makoto [Naoe's husband] building bridges across rivers and chasms. He even convinced himself that he was working for the betterment of the Chinese people. To aid in their development. Stupid fool. The bridges were for the Japanese soldiers to march across to kill their inland cousins. And I was the stupidest fool of all. I never questioned why the schools were made separate, why Chinese and Japanese were not taught together. Why Chinese children had to learn Japanese, but Japanese children were not taught the words of the land they lived in. Why there were servants in our modest homes while there were people starving outside the walls of the city. The words of one woman would not have turned the marching boots of men, but the pain of not having spoken, of not bothering to ask questions, still aches inside me now. (*Chorus of Mushrooms* 45–46)

Naoe's words point to the conflicting issues of silence and alienation, of self and community that recur in the writing of Japanese Canadian women of the 1990s, despite contrasting with the portrayal of Japanese women of her generation that Joy Kogawa painted in *Obasan*. As Beauregard has remarked, "The older women form a compelling pair, with Goto's increasingly mobile and incessantly talking Naoe functioning as an assertive and noisy response to Kogawa's silent and housebound Aya Obasan" ("Hiromi Goto's *Chorus of Mushrooms*" 52). For Beauregard, Goto is "writing back" to Kogawa, producing a remarkably different picture of a Japanese Canadian family in rural Alberta while engaging in similar topics and experiences. Libin, too, perceives Naoe as writing back to another canonical Canadian work, Margaret Laurence's *The Stone Angel* (1964): "*Chorus of Mushrooms* draws on *The Stone Angel* as a literary antecedent, as Naoe, like Hagar before her, abandons her house and her family. But unlike Hagar, who is limited in physical capacity and whose forays into the past are viewed as delusional, Naoe is equipped for her journey and is lucid and uncanny throughout" ("Some of My Best Friends" 107). Naoe is an unusual character for a woman of her generation. Rather than being crippled by the memories of a traumatic past, she is so empowered that she comes to symbolize a wealth of future possibilities. Thus, when asked about the whereabouts of her grandmother, Muriel gives whimsical explanations, from a hypothetical return to Japan to her being a succubus in the shape of a woman. Naoe embodies the power of the tale and the storyteller to create new life and endow the current one with new meanings.

3. An Absent Community: Dispersal, Isolation, and Assimilation

Sally Ito believes that, as a writer, she is responsible for telling her community's stories. She says,

> The notion of a story being one's own is particular to Western culture; in other cultures, stories are a collective possession and the story-teller is a voice for the people, and not a voice for him/herself. The writer of colour must see him/herself in that light—as a voice of the community. The writer must therefore be "obedient" and accountable to that community. ("Issues for the Writer of Colour" 172)

This notion of accountability to the community is also evident in the work of Sansei writers such as Kerri Sakamoto, who feels obligated to portray the current situation of Japanese Canadians and to cancel out the past decades of silence. In *The Canadian Sansei*, Tomoko Makabe has collected valuable information about the third generation of Canadians with Japanese ancestry. According to Makabe, Japanese Canadians constitute one of the smallest and most fragmented ethnic communities in Canada because of the dispersal policies enforced by the federal authorities in the post-war period. These policies were exceptional in the context of Canadian history; no other ethnic community has been subjected to the same degree. But these policies can also be considered unexceptional within the history of Japanese Canadians, since they were the target of many racist policies from the first recorded arrival of a Japanese immigrant in 1877.

Fragmentation and dispersal also resulted from Japanese Canadians' conscious need to protect themselves from further persecution. The Canadian Nisei began to actively seek invisibility and assimilation:

> Nisei parents chose to live in communities in which ideally they would be the only Japanese family, and thus, they thought, less conspicuous . . . A lot of Nisei, if not all of them, purposely avoided joining any Japanese group or association. They did not

speak the language, they did not send their children to Japanese language school, they did not even use chopsticks, and most gave their children Anglo-Saxon names. Rejecting and abandoning their ethnicity meant Anglo conformity (Gordon 1964) on the part of the Japanese Canadians, who completely renounced the immigrants' ancestral culture in favour of the behaviour and values of the Anglo-Canadian core group. (Makabe 68–69)

The acculturation that Makabe describes is closely related to the disruption of family life caused by the war measures and their long-lasting effects. Assimilation often means marrying outside the Nikkei community, to such an extent that Omatsu identifies herself as belonging to "a genetically disappearing people" (39). As Tourino points out, the protagonist of *Obasan* observes that Japanese Canadian women either did not marry or did not have children.

Kogawa suggests that the childlessness of the women in *Obasan* is not the result of a celebrated and free choice but is related to trauma, and that alternative families created through surrogacy and adoption are not ways to circumvent patriarchal families but are responses to tragedy. Naomi *worries,* in her oblique way, over her family pattern of childlessness as she contemplates a photo of her own small family: "Some families grow on and on through the centuries, hardy and visible and procreative. Others disappear from the earth without a whimper" (25). (Tourino 136)

Like Naomi, the protagonist of Kerri Sakamoto's first novel is unmarried and childless. Asako Saito belongs to a small community of Japanese Canadians living close to an electrical field in the period before Redress. Because they are still living in relative isolation in the 1970s, Asako is surprised at the arrival of a third family in the neighbourhood (*The Electrical Field* 68), demonstrating the extreme dispersal of the Japanese Canadians at the time. The choice of location is far from innocent, as Peepre has perceptively noted:

Living under an electrical tower is known to blight human life and cause cancer and death. By placing her Japanese protagonists under the shadow of these towers Sakamoto intensifies her message about the emotional blight left on the lives of all Japanese Canadians who were subjected to the injustice and inhumanity of the Wartime Measures Act. The image of these monstrous towers gives metaphorical significance to the events of the novel and the very real human tragedies that are enacted in the blighted field beneath them. (61)

Thus, the electrical field becomes a metaphor for the "failed acculturation" of the Japanese Canadians, who have become stranded in "a barren wasteland between cultures" (55–56). Asako represents this state of frozenness; according to Peepre, she is trapped between the past (embodied in her neighbour Yano and his efforts for the Redress Movement) and the future (embodied in her neighbour's Japanese-born wife Chisako and her struggle to join the Western mainstream culture). Peepre's views are fairly convincing, though she takes into account only the community outside and does not analyze the pattern of relations within the Saito family itself.

Howells interprets the character of Asako as bearing the author's reflections on "a specific cultural moment of deep demoralization for Japanese Canadians, a time now thirty years in the past in that wilderness period, thirty years after the end of World War II and before the Redress movement had attained any momentum" (126–27). After exploring Asako's web of relationships within and without her family circle, Howells concludes that the trauma caused by the legacy of silence and shame surfaces indirectly, by means of three characters that she considers Asako's "uncanny doubles" (132): the young teenager Sachi Nakamura and the two neighbours, Chisako and her husband Yano. Howells adds to Peepre's insights an analysis of Asako's thwarted sexuality, repression being only the extreme manifestation of physical and emotional alienation deriving from her wartime trauma (132–42). In Howells's view, what makes the novel so impressive is its portrayal of the violent trauma involving this community, and this is where she establishes the metaphoric meaning of the electrical field:

> That strip of barren ground has a dual existence in the text, for not only is it a real place in a rather dreary landscape ... but it is also a space where violent psychic energies are unleashed. In physics an "electrical field" is a field of force between two highly charged bodies, one positive and one negative, where patterns of movement might be diagrammed as a series of concentric circles. This is the image that haunts Asako ... (138–39)

However, the electrical field is not the only feature of this barren landscape. Asako and her friend Yano often walk together to the Mackenzie Hill, named after the Prime Minister who, Yano reminds Asako, "put us in the camps" (*The Electrical Field* 157). The hill looming in the distance as an inescapable memento of the state's power over the individual: "Living in sight of the hill made his wounds fester. It was an ugly hill anyway, a mound of garbage that had filled in a green field. They said the garbage would make a natural fertilizer, but the grasses and trees they'd planted on it years ago were still patchy, ashen, and frail" (*The Electrical Field* 157). The garbage on the hill reflects the shame Japanese Canadians feel because they were once found wanting in Canadianness, lesser citizens than the rest, as well as the weight of self-loathing that the Canadian government deposited on their shoulders. The hill is therefore one more important symbol of the Japanese Canadian community's stunted growth, and attests to their fear that history may repeat itself. "We hide away, afraid that they'll lock us up again," says Yano in another momentous conversation with Asako. In this hopeless situation, these characters neither expect support from others nor provide it. Even when she a

faces complete nervous breakdown, Asako rejects the possibility that she may find
healing and nurture among those who underwent the same trauma:

> Those Nisei women who stood in line in front of me at the Japanese grocery store
> downtown? Who barely remembered me from old camp days? Who had chased after
> my Eiji? Whose mothers had tsk-tsked about Mama being too old to be pregnant
> there? Now all they could do was politely ignore me. Perhaps they called me ki-chigai
> baa-chan behind my back, crazy old woman. But I wasn't an old woman yet, even
> though I wore the clothes of one. One who was already dead. (*The Electrical Field* 202)

In Sakamoto's second novel, *One Hundred Million Hearts*, the Japanese Canadian community is reduced to two people, father and daughter, one completely
absorbed in the other. Growing up in Toronto under the strict supervision of her
deeply caring father, Miyo Mori is deprived of a sense of communal belonging.
Here too the girl's alienation is the result of her family's determination to cut itself
off from all things Japanese and instead assimilate to white mainstream culture.
Miyo remembers a Japanese family living nearby years earlier:

> Miyo's father shunned them when they passed with their timid glances and tentative
> smiles. Once they came to the door, but he refused to answer. I'm not one of them, he
> said, and she peeked out the window after they'd left. As a child, she'd seen a few other
> Japanese faces in the neighbourhood—though she couldn't always tell if they weren't
> Chinese or Korean, except if she heard a snippet of their talk and recognized the
> accent. (*One Hundred Million Hearts* 28)

Miyo's physical disability also sets her apart. She is totally dependent on her
father. The protagonist's isolation becomes extreme at the death of her father,
which sets her on a quest to understand her roots and heritage. Miyo must face her
father's hidden past, which features a second family in Japan. Interestingly, "community" here includes only the biological links of family relatives. This is probably
because by the end of the twentieth century, the dispersal of Japanese Canadians
had reached such an extent that their "imagined community" had trouble reaching
outside the family circle. Thus, in Sakamoto's second novel issues of belonging and
community need to be discussed in the context of ancestral ties to the homeland,
rather than the country of birth, and this in turn also involves coming to terms
with World War Two events and of the Japanese and the Nikkei.

As Miyo arrives in Japan, she reaches out to her half-sister Hana. Hana and
Miyo are twinned characters, brought together by blood but separated by culture.
Through them Sakamoto attempts to solve issues of similarity and difference in
people of her own ancestry who come from diverse social and cultural backgrounds. She also bravely conveys the difficult balance between both, suggesting
that the Japanese look down on the diasporic Japanese, whom they consider

rough, unpolished, and inferior. They are puzzled when they come across someone who, like Miyo, does not speak the language although she looks Japanese. She is embarrassed to find herself helpless in Japan, identified as "a foreigner," strikingly at home yet utterly displaced. Purity of ancestry becomes a focal point of Sakamoto's narrative, not just conveyed through looks but also in more elusive items, such as manners, verbal and body language, taste, and so forth.

Miyo's other twin character is her white lover David, left behind in Toronto. The Canadian city's familiar skyline and subway system mirrors the foreign skyline and subway system of the unfamiliar Tokyo. Interestingly, David sends Miyo a map of Toronto to remind her of their intimate link and of her home:

> There was a letter inside. *Come home soon,* it said on the first white sheet . . . Miyo unfolded the second sheet. It was a map he'd sketched of the Toronto subway. On it he'd marked three X's as Where we Met, Home, and Where We Said Goodbye. Beside the last X, he'd drawn an airplane. On another page he'd taped a subway token and a quarter for the telephone. (*One Hundred Million Hearts* 97)

It is to Toronto, and to a white community where she may not fit in completely but feels she belongs, that Miyo eventually returns. David's embrace of the scarred body of his Japanese Canadian lover, with descriptions of the way they fit together, like "a puzzle corked together" (*One Hundred Million Hearts* 15; see also 77), powerfully suggests the integration of the Canadian Nikkei in the larger white population.[92] In so doing, the character of Miyo simply sanctions the racial isolation of the Japanese Canadians that is by now irreversible. But more importantly, she leaves behind a Japanese past to look forward to a Canadian future.

Put together, Sakamoto's two novels map out the difficult destinies of her diasporic community since World War Two. In both cases, Sakamoto uses the female body to convey the far-reaching effects of this trauma. In *The Electrical Field* she deploys the repressed and barren body of Asako, while in *One Hundred Million Hearts* Miyo's physical disability embodies communal trauma. The narratives chart the discrimination the Canadian Nikkei have encountered in both countries. In neither have they been treated fairly. In order to survive, Japanese Canadians have sought the veil of invisibility and assimilation in their land of birth, although even now they seem unable to experience unproblematic Canadian citizenship.

Miyo's isolation also resembles the loneliness of Japanese immigrant families in Hiromi Goto's novels. In *Chorus of Mushrooms* (1994), Japanese Canadians inhabit what Sasano defines as a kind of border territory:

> The Tonkatsu family in *Chorus of Mushrooms* inhabits Bhabha's 'liminal space' within the nation, performing a different, acceptable, yet subversive Canadian identity. Goto's characters experience marginalization, but ultimately dissolve the centre/mar-

gin dichotomy upon which it relies, resisting the prescribed notions of Canadianness and Japaneseness in the Canadian context through the performative act of writing themselves into the nation. (39)

A story of three generations told from the point of view of three women, the focus shifts from one to the other, although Goto's poetics deploy a bilingual dialogue between the Japanese-speaking grandmother Naoe and the English-speaking granddaughter Murasaki. The latter feels alienated from her Japanese ancestry, having been raised according to strict Western mainstream rules, even though they are not the only Asians in the small southern Alberta town where they live. Murasaki's isolation is underlined in her relationships with other Asians, such as her Chinese Canadian classmate Shane Wu:

> And I never talked with him in my entire life. He never talked with me. Instinct born of fear, I knew that being seen with him would lessen my chances of being in the popular crowd. That Oriental people in single doses were well enough, but any hint of a group and it was all over. I thought I was proud of being Japanese-Canadian, but I was actually a coward. I don't know what Shane's reasons were for never talking with me. I never asked. (*Chorus of Mushrooms* 125)

Likely for the same reason, Murasaki did not learn a word of Vietnamese despite working for years with the Vietnamese pickers on her parents' mushroom farm (*Chorus of Mushrooms* 105). What she calls "cowardice" is perhaps connected to the many instances of white liberal racist behaviour of which she is often a target. Murasaki records people's tendency to take her for Chinese, or to assume that she can read or speak any Asian language or identify Asian vegetables, simply because she looks Asian. She irritably complains, "Let a woman choose her vegetables in peace" (91). For Ty, this kind of situation is due to the fact that

> Chinese food and Chinese names have become more widely accepted in Canadian mainstream culture than Japanese food . . . Thus, innocent signs at a supermarket are indirect, daily reminders of the tenuous position of Japanese culture in Canada in the past and today. (*Politics* 158)

Similarly, Darias Beautell identifies multiple tensions between the liberal discourse of racial equality and the colour-coding that pervades Murasaki's world. Beautell stresses the clash in a scene from Murasaki's childhood when, in order to act the main part in the school play, Murasaki discovers to her horror that she is required to wear a blonde wig. Beautell concludes, "The scene reveals the workings of the strategies of homogenization of the other within the white dominant so that difference is categorized and controlled from within, a process in which the racialized subject may even participate, as is the case of the mother's compliant attitude"

(11). Goto powerfully conveys her critique of the extent to which the liberal policies of multiculturalism continue to rely on the visual.

Part of the conflict in this novel springs from the tension between a Japanese grandmother who refuses to let go of her language and cultural habits, and a second generation of immigrants determined to fit in regardless of the cost. This second generation is represented by Muriel's parents, Keiko and Shinji, now known by the Anglicized forms of their names. Their assimilationist practices puzzle Murasaki and fill Naoe with resentment. Naoe accuses Keiko of having forsaken her identity and she feels that "a noisy silence" (48) lies between them, broken only by limited physical contact when Keiko washes her mother's hair or asks for her help cleaning her ears. Murasaki see her mother in terms of lack: lack of stories, lack of ethnic house smells as Keiko tries to "cover up [their] Oriental tracks" (62), and lack of vegetables in their relentlessly Western diet. Her parents purposefully choose invisibility, and therefore they are mere shadows of the full beings they could have been.

The border zone becomes most evident in the case of the grandmother, who remains "literally immobilized in the hallway during the first part of the novel, at the cultural crossroads between prairie wind and internal dispute with her daughter, thus metaphorically standing on the border between the East and the West" (Sturgess 22). Although she is frozen like Asako in The Electrical Field, unlike her Naoe achieves liberation when she finally leaves the "chair of incubation" (Chorus of Mushrooms 76) in the family home and embarks on a journey across Canada.

The unnamed narrator of Goto's novel The Kappa Child is a second-generation Japanese Canadian woman whose abusive father sets out to grow Japanese rice in the dry soil of the Albertan prairies. She must tease out her identity in the midst of conflicting family allegiances and with the dubious help of unsuitable role models of pioneering life in the prairies. The mother and four sisters evolve in different ways under the weight of the father's verbal and physical violence. A man whose main traits are his unpredictability and his stubbornness, he hits them all frequently and at random, and his most common term for them is "bakatare" (idiot). Throughout the girls' childhood, Emiko accepts her role of submissive wife and mother, seeking invisibility as the safest position and expressing her suffering only through repeated sighs. The eldest sister, Slither, grooms herself into the perfect image of vulnerable Asian femininity. To the narrator, Slither is weak, spineless, and only too willing to conform. The passive behaviour of the two younger sisters also fails to satisfy her. PG retreats behind a screen of words, for instance, her childhood refrains "Happy endings, sad endings" (29) and "scary things are not scary if you are not scared of them" (128). The youngest, Mice, is always frightened and often silent. The narrator resents her "collect long-distance calls, her breathing and breathing on the phone for two hours straight, just so she doesn't have to breathe alone" (108).

In the midst of such a dysfunctional family, the narrator is forced to look elsewhere for productive role models. Throughout her childhood, she finds them in the pages of her favourite book, *Little House on the Prairie,* in the character of Laura Ingalls, with whom she strongly empathizes, even though much of the book makes little sense to the girls:

> "The Ingalls family were from the east so they went west. We're from British Columbia, so we were in the west, but we moved east to get to the same place, funny, huh?" I beamed. Gapped teeth I could only bare to my family.
> "No," PG frowned with the back of her head.
> "Why don't you just read?" Slither sighed.
> "All right."
> . . .
> "I don't get it," Slither said. "Why does that Laura girl want to see a papoose so bad? I bet there were a lot of flies in that wagon. It's kinda sad that the dog got swept away in the river. Do you think salt pork is like bacon?"
> I scowled. "It's about being pioneers. See, we're like that right now, get it? It's not about salt pork!"
> "Did Laura's pa hit the ma?" PG muttered.
> "He never hit her! Ever! He played the violin!" I exclaimed. Though something gnawed inside. I hadn't noticed before, but now that I read it out loud, Ma seemed so much weaker than I'd imagined. *"Oh, Charles,"* she said. *"Whatever you think, Charles."*
> "Anyway, they all liked each other and got along. Except for Laura and her older sister who was a goody two-shoes."
> "I like Mary most of all," Slither said. "At least she was clean."
> (*The Kappa Child* 42–43)

An alternative role model is provided by the narrator's closer neighbours, the Nakamura family. Janice Nakamura is a Canadian Nisei who lives with her son Gerald, the result of a short-lived marriage with a First Nations husband. Both as a family and individually, the Nakamuras fail to meet the standards of both white and non-white society. Firstly, they do not represent the ideal of happy family life in *Little House on the Prairie.* Secondly, Janice Nakamura's behaviour is too manly, outspoken, and self-sufficient to fit into the Japanese construction of femininity. She does not speak Japanese, and neither does she strictly follow the rules of politeness, but her ways are efficient and she shows the new family where to get water while the narrator's father vainly digs a well in the dry soil. The children must learn not to pass judgment solely on grounds of appearance: Janice's rice balls may look too big to be the perfect Japanese *onigiri,* but they do taste delicious. Thirdly, Gerald Nakamura's mixed-racedness places him beyond the pale. As a person combining two racial identities, but especially as a Native person, the narrator finds him "incomprehensible" (188–89), but in a way that brings him close to her as she feels stranded among such diverse identities.

Consequently, Ty sees the unnamed protagonist of *The Kappa Child* as an outsider: "The protagonist's sense of alienation comes from a strong sense of difference and otherness that she feels, partly because of things that happened in the past in her family and partly because of her perception of her Asian body" (*Unfastened* 114). Goto eventually manages to creatively suggest ways for the narrator to come to terms with her own isolation from mother and siblings, and to bring some hopeful closure to her conflicting issues on sexuality and racialized identity.

4. A Conspiracy of Silence

For Sally Ito, silence is an aesthetic trait that is deeply rooted in Japanese culture and its rituals, like the Japanese tea ceremony:

> The aesthetics of silence has been passed on from the Japanese to the Japanese Canadian as evidenced in the work of Nisei writer Joy Kogawa. Silence is a running theme in her novel *Obasan*. Silence is a way of giving shape to things that would not be so evident if talk or noise were in the way. ("Issues" 177)

Yet silence in these novels often stems from different cultural or historical reasons. Drawing on a number of surveys conducted among the Nisei and Sansei in the United States and Canada, Makabe concludes that "conscious efforts were made by many Nisei not to talk about the past, particularly about the internment, not to congregate together, and to assimilate as completely as possible" (82). She further describes

> the very high degree of silence and concealment that has surrounded the subject of internment within most Japanese Canadian families. Communication tended to be quite limited in both frequency and length, with little substance. Consequently, the Sansei's knowledge about the event is, generally speaking, limited and fragmented." (78)

Maryka Omatsu remembers how at the death of her father in 1981, they were "virtual strangers" who had not once spoken about the family's wartime experiences (34, 36).

One of *The Electrical Field*'s earlier images presents Asako resisting Yano's endless probing into her camp internment, eluding what she considers his "taunts" (*The Electrical Field* 5). In particular, Asako tries to protect her younger brother, Stum, who was born while the family was already in the camp. Since he is free of memories of pre-war life on Vancouver Island, he is unable to see their current life as a shameful fall from grace, which is Asako's dismaying perception. He relies on his older sister for such memories, although she is brusque and often ignores him altogether:

> "Why do you keep things from me, ne-san?"
> "What things? I don't keep anything from you."
> "About our brother. About what happened. You never talk about it."
> "There's nothing to say, ototo-san." (*The Electrical Field* 180)

Asako's self-contained and uneventful life revolves around the hidden trauma of the internment camps, but her repression can only be expressed indirectly through her behaviour towards the men around her. Goldman likens Asako to Naomi in *Obasan*, contending that these characters "take up 'the challenge of loss' rather than acquiesce to mourning, which may involve an inappropriate and impossible denial of loss and a conscious or unconscious complicity with hegemonic assimilationist strategies" (368). As in Kazuo Ishiguro's novels,[93] Sakamoto's readers need to realize that Asako's words should not be trusted and that she struggles daily to pretend that nothing is wrong with her or with the world. Sakamoto's skillful narrative technique forces readers to look beyond surface appearances and seek out the ripples on the quiet waters of her Nikkei characters' lives. Only to the Sansei child Sachi does Asako open up, in rare moments of intimacy. Asako tells Sachi about her past, though she always finds it an ordeal: "It exhausted me, calling up this memory . . . I found myself unable to continue; the words and pictures in my mind had vanished, and Sachi had fallen into a deep sleep, her cheek pressed into my pillow" (*The Electrical Field* 81).

In *One Hundred Million Hearts,* Miyo's father's actions are deeply wrapped in silence. He is often described doing things "silently" or like "a silent soldier," imparting the notion of someone uncomplainingly discharging their duties, but also invoking the war, which is at the root of such bottomless silence. The only trace of Masao's past is a photo of himself and his wife taken in 1943 in a place that, to Miyo's naïve ears, appears to be "a schoolyard," while the uniform and the weapons he carries are qualified as harmless decorations meant to impress his sweetheart (*One Hundred Million Hearts* 20–21).

Foregoing the use of the Japanese language is another type of silencing, which entails a conscious effort to assimilate into white Canadian culture and to cover oneself with the cloak of invisibility that the English language provides. In *The Electrical Field,* Asako's daily routine includes reading the paper and doing the crossword to improve her English: "I went through the newspaper with my dictionary every day, and began filling in the crossword puzzles to put myself to the test. I wanted to better myself. I was petrified, in spite of the progress I was making, of sliding back" (69). The English language is Asako's only weapon against semiotic chaos, disorder, and annihilation. She fears that the world she has so carefully built within the fragile walls of her home may be disrupted again, as her sick father's moans from upstairs constantly remind her it once was. In *One Hundred Million Hearts*, the only two Japanese words Miyo grows up with are *ichi ni* (one two), used by her father as he forces her to exercise her damaged leg. By not passing on the Japanese language to her, he attempts to help her assimilate into the Anglophone culture. Similarly, in Goto's *Chorus of Mushrooms* Murasaki's father explains,

> We decided, your Mom and I, that we would put Japan behind us and fit more smoothly with the crowd. And from that day, when we decided, neither of us could speak a word of Japanese. Not a word would pass our lips. We couldn't even think it. And I was ashamed. I felt a loss so fine it pierced my heart. Made it ache . . . And I was feeling like I was half missing for a good ten years, never mixing with other Japanese folk, the communities in Calgary and Lethbridge, because it made the ache unbearable. (*Chorus of Mushrooms* 207)

Yet this sacrifice of their cultural roots as well as the effort to mix in and to pass for white heralds only silence and invisibility. Shinji/Sam becomes "a voiceless man," "a living mystery" (*Chorus of Mushrooms* 59–60), and Murasaki dismisses her parents as "Dad: the man without an opinion, and Mom hiding behind an adopted language" (98).

Critics perceive connections between the use of the Japanese language in this novel and the consumption of Japanese food. Food is another important marker of racial and cultural identity, as Murasaki highlights:

> There are people who say that eating is only a superficial means of understanding a different culture. That eating at exotic restaurants and oohing and aahing over the food is not even worth the bill paid. You haven't learned anything at all. I say that's a lie. What can be more basic than food itself? Food to begin to grow. (*Chorus of Mushrooms* 201)

Sturgess states that "to eat or not to eat Japanese is synonymous in the novel with the recognition or non-recognition of cultural heritage" (33). It is a perceptible sign of difference, and therefore conducive to either appeal or rejection. In *The Electrical Field*, Asako recognizes the scent of her own otherness when she visits another Japanese Canadian home, and "a scent filled my nostrils [with] the not unfamiliar smell of fried fish and daikon. This half-known thing disconcerted me; made me flush with shame at our shared habits, our odours. For my home was no less fragrant than Yano's" (114). Cooking can also be a comforting ritual to Asako, bringing to her the relief of repetition, routine, and order. Most importantly, it is a way to make herself and others aware of her purpose in the domestic realm, to the point of making her younger brother feel guilty. Cooking is a cultural way to include or exclude others; Asako criticizes the cooking and homemaking habits of her younger brother's girlfriend who, though Asian, is not Japanese Canadian:

> Inside the refrigerator, I found two foil-wrapped plates labelled "Papa" and "Asa" in Angel's flowery handwriting. Such a waste, I thought, smoothing out the creases and tucking the foil back in my drawer . . . Mazui, I clucked at Angel's overboiled vegetables and tasteless bits of chicken that I'd downed. Stum would not like this, I thought: it would not do. (*The Electrical Field* 290–91)

Similarly, food plays an important role in the game of antagonism and empathy between the different generations of women in *Chorus of Mushrooms*. Keiko, who has chosen the path of assimilation, feeds her family a bland Western diet of "weiners and beans. Endless evenings of tedious roast chicken and honey smoked ham and overdone rump roast" (13). Out of resentment, Naoe rebels by holding a secret post box where her Japanese family sends her packages of savoury delicacies that she consumes late at night in her room with the assistance of her granddaughter Murasaki. These late night feasts nourish the link between the two women; in chewing and smacking their lips they meet halfway, overcoming the barrier of language: "Smack, smack! (Obāchan) Smack, smack! (Me) Smack, smack! (Obāchan) Smack, Smack! (Me)" (17).

Food also has restorative powers. When Keiko has a nervous breakdown after her mother's departure and won't leave her bed for three months, a desperate Murasaki finally realizes that Western food is powerless to heal Keiko. After finding the necessary ingredients and teaching herself to cook using of a Japanese cookbook, the smells of Murasaki's cooking bring the family, even ailing Keiko, to the kitchen, and there starts a midnight feasting similar to those that Murasaki used to enjoy with her grandmother. Even though "there were no hugs or kisses or mea culpas" (153), this meal constitutes a major breakthrough. It serves, as Libin has pointed out, as "a gathering together of the family, a re-connection of community" ("Lost in Translation" 132). Keiko starts to recover and a new though fragile understanding between parents and daughter is built on the strength of Japanese food and sharing. Although Keiko eventually returns to her Western habits, she continues to enjoy Murasaki's Japanese cooking. Thus, through food the Tonkatsu family eventually reaches a less stifling and more flexible performance of their Japanese Canadian identity.

5. Alternative Communities:
(Female) Body Politics and the Challenge to Heteronormativity

Some of these Japanese Canadian women writers have challenged the idea of a community based on biology and its categories (race, ancestry, family) and turned instead towards alternative communities. This is the case of homosexual love, which is featured in the work of Hiromi Goto and Tamai Kobayashi. Iwama pinpoints the links between the collective and the individual in Canadian Nikkei women's writing of the body:

> A common theme in fiction and poetry by Nikkei writers such as Joy Kogawa, Noriko Oka, Mona Oikawa, and Tamai Kobayashi is the experience of inhabiting and inscribing bodies that do not find their counterparts in the images that society privileges. From this historical place of denial, Nikkei women have constructed selves that depend on the body as a means of knowing and communicating. While Kogawa's constructions of desire and the body are, perhaps, more subtly transgressive than the other writers mentioned, she has begun a tradition of articulating desire that several younger writers claim as formative in their own creative practice. Kogawa's poetics engage the body as a metaphor of community. (94)

Female body politics feature prominently in both of Hiromi Goto's novels. In *Chorus of Mushrooms,* the female narrators are remarkably outspoken about their sensuality.[94] Although these two women are strikingly different in terms of age, education, and language, both Naoe and Murasaki find productive ways to express their sexuality and *jouissance.* Most surprisingly, female desire is voiced by the aged grandmother, who declares herself "eighty-five years old and horny like a musk-drenched cat" (*Chorus* 39), thus challenging the stereotypical asexuality of the elderly and triggering in her watchful daughter Keiko the growing suspicion that she is finally going senile. Naoe has denied her own body for so long that she finds it difficult at first to see to its needs. While she was trapped in an arranged marriage, her anger at her husband precluded any sexual joy. She was "too bitter, too proud to fall into [her] flesh" (39). Later divorced, she lives for a time in physical isolation from others. The only exception is the weekly ritual of hair-washing, when the touch of Keiko's fingers awakens in her body a wealth of pleasant sensations.

Now in her mid-eighties after a long period of stagnation, Naoe determines that she does not want to die without "falling into" in her flesh, and she decides to leave her home to embark on a journey without destination for the sake of experiencing those things she never has. Ty remarks that Naoe's self-empowerment is conveyed with the help of insect imagery (*Politics* 163), while Goto compares her transformation to that of a silk moth like the ones Naoe grew attached to when she worked in a silk farm, as well as to the cicada, likewise associated with Naoe's early life in Japan (163–64). Naoe's sexual reawakening is conveyed in her visit to the mushroom farm where the moisture fills her dried-out body like "an aged shrimp [and h]er skin, so dry, slowly filled, cell by cell, like a starving plant, the mushroom moisture filling her hollow body" (*Chorus of Mushrooms* 84). Finally out of her dry cocoon, she experiences a complete rejuvenation. She touches this new body in wonder and climaxes with "the unheard chorus of mushrooms" (86). From then on, Naoe searches for and obtains sexual fulfilment without compunction or regret. Like the cicada, which after seven years of obscurity must "find a mate in seven days and complete their cycle" (*Chorus of Mushrooms* 157), Naoe pushes herself to new limits, "transgressing traditional expectations that come with her age, with her racialized and gendered body" (Ty, *Politics* 165).

Like her grandmother, Murasaki's early relation with her own sexuality is troubled. She finds her racialized body stifling. As a child, she detested the Orientalized Valentine cards she received every year, and she abruptly left her first boyfriend—to her friends' and family's dismay—because he asked her for "Oriental" sex. Murasaki painfully comes to understand, "The shape of my face, my eyes, the colour of my hair affected how people treated me" (175), and even more so when it comes to sexuality, a field in which the stereotypical representation of the submissive Asian woman is ever present.

Yet, like Naoe, Murasaki finds an appropriate partner with whom she experiences sexual fulfillment. Both relationships involve physical closeness as well as sharing of food and stories. In both cases, this intimate dialogue transcends the barriers of language. Naoe meets a truck driver she calls Tengu; as they drive, they exchange stories about Japan. Although at first Tengu speaks English with a drawl and Naoe does not speak a word of English, they have no trouble understanding each other. Later they stop in Calgary's Chinatown where they enjoy a feast of long-missed flavours, and finally they share a bath and a bed. In this relationship, words become the first step that leads to the partaking of other, equally intimate, physical joys. Similarly, Murasaki meets a stranger at the airport, a newly arrived Japanese man with whom she experiences immediate rapport. In the italicized sections of the novel, the narrator and the unnamed lover share a bed for days on end, experiencing pleasure in multiple forms: sex, food, and stories. The connection between these activities is seamless. In fact, their multi-faceted love-making transforms their world:

> We lie on our giant futon, so big that it covers completely the floor of our bedroom. It is a decadent pleasure. There is no frame beneath us, just the futon, and our naked bodies on top. We move in our sleep, all over the expanse of the floor, then meet each other in surprise when we wake up. (87)

Awake and asleep, they share bodies, words, and food in a deeply satisfying exercise that transcends all hierarchies. Once more in *Chorus of Mushrooms*, the strong link between discourse and body politics is highlighted.[95]

Women's bodies are again featured prominently in *The Kappa Child* as the narrator's identity crisis revolves around issues not just of personal and racial identity, but specifically around her sexuality. Goto brings all these elements to bear on the narrator's psychological conflict through a supernatural figure drawn from Japanese myth, the Kappa, a green creature of water and water places.[96] The narrator reaches a crisis when she suspects she is pregnant after an odd encounter with an extraordinary Kappa-like female character during a lunar eclipse. Her increased awareness of her body, which she has always thought of as ugly, as well as her doubtful pregnancy convey her psychological voyage. As Ty rightly comments, in the wonder of her pregnancy the narrator overcomes the self-hatred that characterizes most of her statements: "Comparing herself to the ideal of Western figure [or, one could add, the exoticized Asian female body], the protagonist finds her body lacking. In her description of herself she uses food imagery—the pomegranate, daikon, bratwurst" (*Unfastened* 115).[97] Almeida sees the pregnancy itself as the symbol of the narrator's alienation, and the alien creature within the womb as the experience of abjection: "This abject body, significantly a gendered and maternal body—the locus of the abject *per se*—hosts a stranger, an outsider, in other words, an alien, a kappa child" (56). As will be discussed below, Goto consistently portrays the maternal body in terms of abjection.

The Kappa embodies the narrator's tensions regarding her sexuality. Although sexually attracted to two female friends, Genevieve and Midori, the narrator represses her feelings and maintains a strict celibacy and emotional aloofness that takes its toll on her. When her two friends become lovers, she feels excluded to the point of utter loneliness until her encounter with the Kappa leads her to confront her fears and inadequacies. Her crisis coincides with her mother's unexpectedly walking out on her husband and departing on her own voyage of self-discovery with a new partner, her long-time neighbour Janice Nakamura. This becomes a source of wonder for the narrator, who never dared to expect that such liberation could take place. A final confrontation with her father allows the narrator to move away from her childhood and to accept herself and her siblings as full-fledged adults who may still have a chance for happiness. Fretting over her mother's whereabouts, the narrator visits her elder sister Slither and is forced to come to terms with her sisters' adult lives rather than the picture of them she has held since their traumatic childhoods.

In *The Kappa Child* the dialectics of sameness and difference play out in the realm of the biological. The four siblings are depicted simultaneously as similar in racial background and upbringing, yet markedly different in their personalities and lifestyles. Further complicating the matter is the issue of same-sex love, which is also solved when the narrator embarks on a relationship with a Korean Canadian character, Bernie. The novel's final scene displays the two lesbian couples enjoy a night out under the stars and are symbolically blessed by the Kappa when the rain starts to fall:

> The wind feels good, the stars glitter. And somewhere, planets align.
> Then, a raindrop falls. Full and round, as big as a Muscat grape, I look up but there's not a cloud. Where has it come from? A perfect orb drops on my lips, seeps to my tongue. Sweet. Then more droplets fall, plump, warm, soft as kisses, they rain down on us. We turn to each other, eyes wide with wonder. (*The Kappa Child* 274–75)

Nature and nurture are finally in harmony. The human-made links between the four friends and lovers are at least as strong, if not more so, than those between the four biological sisters. A sisterhood of the heart displaces a sisterhood of the body by the novel's end.

Hiromi Goto's 2004 short-story collection *Hopeful Monsters* continues to delve into the psychological and physiological experiences of motherhood, particularly in the stories "Hopeful Monsters" and "Tales from the Breast." They are joined by the theme of the bodily process of motherhood, including pregnancy, giving birth, and breastfeeding, as well as the underlying experience of pain and its multiple manifestations. Moreover, they can be read as companion stories because they convey a clash between the scientific, normative discourse on the maternal and the ongoing experience of the narrator. Such dialogical clash can be read once more with the assistance of Kristevan texts such as "Stabat Mater," in which the theoretical examination of the Christian embodiment of motherhood, the Virgin Mary, combines with the description of Kristeva's own experience of pregnancy and childbirth. The split page in that essay powerfully conveys Kristeva's notion of the maternal body as "a thoroughfare, a threshold where 'nature' confronts 'culture'" (Kristeva, "Motherhood according to Giovanni Bellini" 302).

For Kristeva, scientific discourse on motherhood fails to address "the mother as site of her proceedings" ("Motherhood" 301). "Tales from the Breast" exemplifies the split between the prescriptive account of breastfeeding and the new mother's subjectivity by starting each section with a heading from a self-help book entitled *Your Child's First Journey*. Milk is described as raw and fresh, but the narrator discovers to her horror that hers is instead blood-flavoured, and when the milk comes in, her breasts become "the stuff of horror movies . . . expanded to the point of blood splatter explosion" (*Hopeful Monsters* 59). The narrator talks back to the textbook's supposedly objective discourse that is silencing her own experience. This is the case too when the textbook attempts to describe the affective bonding between mother and child: "*The hormone prolactin, which causes the secretion of milk, helps you to feel 'motherly.'* Just how long can the pain last, you ask yourself. It is the eleventh day of nipple torture and maternal hell" (*Hopeful Monsters* 61).

While well-meaning and superficially benevolent, the practice of health care proves to be far from helpful, and in Goto's story it even betrays a racist tinge. The nurse who looks after her in the first few hours after giving birth nicely warns her not to leave valuables around because the hospital has been having some problems with theft, and she knows that "you people have nice cameras." Later, when the narrator's Japanese mother-in-law visits her, the nurse asks "Are you people from Tibet?" (*Hopeful Monsters* 57). Goto draws the reader's attention to what she calls elsewhere the "daily small erosions" of unacknowledged racism and how these acts racialize the experience of motherhood for Asian Canadian women.[98] For Libin, this is one of the most striking features of Goto's writing:

> Her writing of racialized difference delivers pointed reminders to the white reader that, even assuming a self-professed benevolence towards the otherness of the text, reading practices might still suppress or appropriate this inescapable difference. Reading Goto's texts, I am repeatedly asked to remember that I read from within the space of whiteness. ("Some of My Best Friends" 94)

Science is not the only voice imposing silence on the new mother. Neither her husband nor her mother-in-law lends a sympathetic ear to her complaints on the constant pain, or to her faint attempts to give up breastfeeding and feed the baby formula instead. While the husband lectures her on how this is just something "natural" that the narrator is needlessly complicating, the mother-in-law offers her food day and night in a vain attempt to soothe her pain. "Tales from the Breast" provocatively deconstructs the scientific discourse on motherhood.

"Hopeful Monsters" gives a detailed account of pregnancy and childbirth. Here too the scientific discourse on motherhood stands out from the very beginning through an opening quote apparently taken from a genetics textbook. The quote clarifies the meaning of the title, for biology allegedly classifies as "hopeful monsters" those mutations that may have beneficial effects on an organism by providing traits that help it survive and prosper. In describing a "mutation" as beneficial, the term suggests a redefinition of the very concepts of normality and abnormality, surely one of the main topics in the story.

The protagonist is thirty-one-year-old Japanese Canadian Hisa who is having her first child. The story develops simultaneously with her pregnancy, following her earliest symptoms and focusing on the young mother's mounting bodily distress as the moment of birth approaches. Not surprisingly, the text abounds in those references to polluting bodily fluids that Kristeva associates with abjection. But this is not the only way in which Kristevan concepts can be put to use here:

> By giving birth, the woman enters into contact with her mother; she becomes, she is her own mother; they are the same continuity differentiating itself. She thus actualizes the homosexual facet of motherhood, through which a woman is simultaneously closer to her instinctual memory, more open to her own psychosis, and consequently, more negatory of the social, symbolic bond. ("Motherhood" 303)

This is the kind of reunion with one's own mother that the story performs. At first, Hisa and her partner Bobby appear to be a team, while Hisa keeps her own mother at arm's length. While the mother claims she feels a powerful connection to all her children, thus being able to tell immediately when Hisa is having her first contractions, Hisa herself refuses to acknowledge that this is so, and is even slightly repelled by the thought. But later, as she goes into labour and the pains start to come closer together, Bobby's role as partner and father-to-be retreats, and it is her mother that Hisa yells for.

The substitution is completed after the birth, when Hisa's baby daughter is found to be slightly "abnormal." She has been born with a caudal appendage, a little tail that can be easily amputated. Although Hisa is at first in favour of the procedure, like Bobby and the doctors, she later changes her mind and decides to preserve her daughter's difference. The shift occurs after her mother reveals that all of her children, including Hisa, were born with the same abnormality. While her first three children were stillborn, Hisa survived. In both cases the father, Hisa's father and now her partner Bobby, rejects the child's abnormality and endorses its suppression. As a result, they are excluded from the experience of fatherhood.

Instead of the nuclear father-mother-child family, "Hopeful Monsters" constructs a female genealogy, bonding mother to daughter through the powerful symbol of the baby's tail that, to Hisa's wonder, circles her wrist and creates a connection beyond words. In fact, the baby remains unnamed, existing outside the logocentric order. Her tail can also be read as racial difference, for Hisa associates the tail with a Japanese folk tail and her own Japanese ancestry is clear in the novel, setting the women apart from their partners.

When Hisa embraces the semiotic and rejects the symbolic, another relevant connection is made with other "abnormal" subjects, for Hisa's plans to steal away from her partner are supported by a lesbian couple she became acquainted with during her prenatal class. Despite a superficial acquaintance, Hisa's troubled thoughts turn to them because "what did she know about being abnormal, living as abnormals?" (*Hopeful Monsters* 165). Just as Hisa needs to revise her conceptualization of physiological difference, so does she need to overcome her value judgements regarding sexual orientation. The affirmation of a female genealogy seems to go hand-in-hand with the affirmation of a homosexual orientation, as well as with a rejection of mainstream society's exclusionary practices, despite the protagonist's conservative attitudes. Commenting on the hopeful tone of the ending, Pearson remarks, "Creating wholeness and balance through the revaluation of monstrosity and abjection is a recurrent theme in Goto's work, which resists hegemonic discourses of sexual and bodily shame, racial and cultural 'difference' (read: inferiority), and the hierarchies of linguistic competence (English counts, Japanese does not)" (81).

Like Goto, other Japanese Canadian women writers place their work in the political context of lesbian women writers of colour:

> I believe my ability to consider myself a writer is due to the fact that there are communities of women writing around the world. I am particularly indebted to women of colour, and even more so, to lesbians of colour who have taken great risks in writing the truths of their lives. Writers such as Gloria Anzaldúa, Beth Brant, Chrystos, Audre Lorde, Pat Parker, Barbara Smith, and Merle Woo have challenged white male heterosexual history. Their powerful works have carved out deep paths in the forest of feminist literature, providing lesbians of colour with safer routes by which to travel and move forward. (Oikawa 101)

Closest to this position is Tamai Kobayashi,[99] who has admitted to being influenced most of all by lesbian theorists such as Audre Lorde, and by US Japanese authors like Hitsaye Yamamoto and Mitsuye Yamada in an interview with Chinese-Canadian writer Larissa Lai. A founding member of the association "Asian Lesbians of Toronto" (ALOT) and well known as a local activist, Kobayashi's stories are deeply rooted in the everyday life of the lesbian community of Toronto. Tamai Kobayashi's short-story collection *Exile and the Heart* (1998) traces the lives of Asian Canadian lesbians in Toronto through the voices of four young Japanese Canadian women: Kathy Nakashima, Naomi Chiba, Gen Tanaka, and Setsuko Nozoe. Central to the twelve stories in the collection is the characters' loneliness and their efforts to build up lasting love relationships, which Kobayashi brings to the fore by interweaving situations and characters from one story to the next. By appropriating the form of the short-story cycle, Kobayashi inserts her work in the wider frame of Canadian literature, because, as Martín Lucas among others has claimed, this form has had a long tradition and a remarkable popularity in Canada.[100]

With the subtitle "Lesbian Fiction," Kobayashi also positions herself outside the economy that defines Asian women as commodities, objects of male heterosexual desire. Specifically in the case of women of Japanese ancestry, this commodification involves the geisha stereotype. Kobayashi's work resists this paradigm and contributes to make visible "woman-loving" women (to use Larissa Lai's term).

The stories feature the four Japanese Canadian protagonists and their lovers who come from diverse ethnic and racial backgrounds, from First Nations to South American. For these lesbian characters, the biological notion of "family" stands out as particularly difficult, not just because of the inherent instability of any love relationship, but because their sexual orientation remains either unacknowledged or rejected by their parents and relatives. Kobayashi successfully juxtaposes two different instances of silencing and repression in the related stories "Given Names" and "Driftwood," which focus on two generations of women, Kathy Nakashima and her mother Norma. The former story centres on the daughter and the blanket of silence that hides her sexual orientation. Partly out of cowardice, partly out of habit, Kathy has never opened up to her mother about her lesbian identity. In "Given Names," Kathy finally visits her mother after an absence of three years, and she brings over her "friend" Gen under false pretences. Kathy lives in constant fear that her mother will discover that Gen is more than just a friend: "Kathy shivers. Does her mother know? That she is a lesbian, that Gen is her lover? No, god, it would kill her" (Exile and the Heart 42). Ironically, her mother does know, although she respects her daughter's silence.

The mother-daughter relationship is made more complex in "Driftwood," in which Norma Nakashima returns to Vancouver after an absence of fifty years since her family was interned. The reason lies in a wedding invitation from her former friend Michiko, for whom she experienced but suppressed a strong attraction in her youth. The reunion with friend and city leads her to regain a sense of her long-lost self, "still Harumi Watanabe, before the journey, the boxes and departures, before the war" (Exile and the Heart 98). The overlapping repressions of sexual orientation and racial heritage find a moving expression in Harumi and Norma's relationship. In these stories, Kobayashi powerfully transmits how complex the notions of family and home may be for Japanese Canadian women, and she explores their many nuances from a historically grounded perspective.

As a result, the stories in Exile and the Heart engage in the politics of Asian Canadian women's lives by describing an alternative community, a different kind of family made up of an international group of women who are deeply committed to activism at many levels. In the final story, "Stone Heart," Gen Tanaka remembers her involvement in anti-war campaigns while she is on her way to a meeting of the Toronto Coalition Against Racist Policing: "She pushes through the crow, into the auditorium. Her gaze sweeps over the seats, to the banners hanging on the walls:

Freedom for Peltier, Garment Workers for Justice, Women Working Against Violence. Memorial: November 11, 1992 and Audre Lorde is dead" (*Exile and the Heart* 100). Meanwhile, Naomi Chiba decides to join her lover Clara in Mexico, where she works in the refugee camps. Like Larissa Lai's *Salt Fish Girl*, Kobayashi's collection revisits the concept of family in order to assert bonds linking women across the policed borders of nation and race. At the same time, Kobayashi's stories attempt to correct what Iwama perceives as the underrepresentation of lesbian relations in Canadian Nikkei women:

> In spite of their real and common existence in Nikkei social life, Nikkei women whose desire transgresses the boundaries of faithful, monogamous heterosexuality have thus been un(der)represented in Nikkei discourse, appearing mainly in textual shadows. A recent challenge in the critical approach to texts by Canadian Nikkei is that Nikkei women have begun writing frankly about transgressive desire in the constructions of lesbian sexualities. (np)

6. Enemy Aliens:
Japanese Canadian Masculinities

Unlike other Asian North American writers, Japanese Canadian author Kerri Sakamoto has displayed no interest so far in establishing a female genealogy or delving into matrilineal connections. On the contrary, Sakamoto declared in an interview that the absence of mothers in her fiction is related to the fact that she saw eye-to-eye with her mother, while it was more difficult for her to empathize with her father. Where there was no conflict, she argued, there could hardly spring the impulse for fiction writing (Cuder-Domínguez 141–42). Instead, her novels feature male characters from the perspective of female narrators. Her position runs counter to much North American Nikkei writing, where the absence of the maternal can be read, as Traise Yamamoto says, as a trope that "subtly foregrounds interpretive strategies that privilege the daughter's subjectivity and suggests the need to read simultaneously from the mother's point of view" (*Masking Selves* 6).

Little work on Japanese North American masculinity has been undertaken to date, although John Okada's *No-No Boy* (1957) and Joy Kogawa's *Obasan* (1981), two paradigmatic novels of the new Asian American canon, offer tantalizing examples of Japanese North American men in the aftermath of World War Two. *Obasan* has received more attention for its depiction of female characters than male.[101] However, this novel traces the reactions of two different generations of men. The protagonist's meek uncle resignedly accepts his fate and tries to move on despite his many losses. Naomi's most poignant memory of him is of how this former British Columbian fisherman misses the sea terribly and strives to recapture it by looking at the sea of grass of the Albertan prairie. This memory opens and closes the novel, with Uncle Isamo's words "umi yo no" ("it's like the sea") bringing the reader full circle to the Japanese Canadian experience of unspeakable loss (*Obasan* 1, 247). On the contrary, Naomi's brother Stephen devotes his strongest efforts to pretend that the war and the subsequent internment and relocation never happened. As Cheng Lok Chua has remarked, "Stephen's experience with

Canadian racism leaves him uneasy with his own ethnic identity" (101). In this novel and in its sequel, *Itsuka* (1992), Naomi accuses her brother of retreating into the supposedly race-free world of music and blames him for the heartache his aloofness brings to the rest of the family, most pointedly their aunt and adoptive mother, who dies while waiting vainly for his visit.[102]

Kogawa's novels highlights the fact that the experiences of men of Japanese ancestry in North America have been shaped to date by the long-reaching events of World War Two. The Nikkei internment in the US and Canada, the community dispersal, and the success of the Redress Movement in the 1980s have all left their imprint on the lives of several generations of Nikkei, and perhaps more particularly on men, because they enjoyed higher visibility than women at the time. That is Kerri Sakamoto's opinion:

> When I think about the experiences of my father or my grandfather, I think how very difficult it was for them to be interned and then to have to make their way in the public world, how they were emasculated by the system. They still had to go out there and "be the man" and provide for the family and show this public face that has been reviled as "the enemy" or as "the yellow monkey" while still retaining some dignity. And in that generation they didn't have the tools, the language to deal with the emotional cost of that kind of experience. It's so much easier for our generation, there's a vocabulary and a knowledge of human psychology that wasn't there then. I am really interested and really moved by that struggle, by the toughness also that has been visited upon the family, they had to grow a "thick skin" to be out in the world. Then they didn't know how to be soft and loving with their families. I've always been interested in that, and tried to work it through and understand it. (Cuder-Domínguez 141)

Sakamoto's struggle to understand the plight of previous generations of Japanese Canadian men underlies her novels *The Electrical Field* and *One Hundred Million Hearts*. World War Two projects its shadow on her plots and characters. Though both novels are "about men," women are the narrative focus, which results in a comprehensive view of how historical events impinge on the lives of both genders. As seen above, in *The Electrical Field* Sakamoto explores the legacy of displacement and internment from the unjust treatment of Japanese Canadians during and after the war through the memories of a Nisei or second-generation narrator, Asako. In *One Hundred Million Hearts*, a young Sansei (third-generation) narrator suddenly uncovers her father's direct participation in the war after he has passed away, and she is compelled to revise the past in view of these revelations.

The conduit of Sakamoto's lessons in Japanese Canadian history is a woman in both novels. In *The Electrical Field* it is Asako Saito, an unmarried middle-aged woman living in 1970s Ontario, who is completely devoted to the care of her elderly father and her younger brother Stum. Asako's life is thrown off-balance by the sudden double murder of Mrs Yano, one of her Nikkei neighbours, and the woman's lover when the husband discovers her love affair with her Caucasian boss. Over the next few days, after Mr Yano flees town, the uncertainty shocks Asako into rehearsing their shared history, both of the neighbourhood and of the larger Japanese Canadian community. These events also awaken unwelcome memories of internment and dispersal to the point that she suffers a nervous breakdown, letting go of her routine and forgetting about her father's needs and her own. Only the news that Mr Yano has also killed his children and himself releases her tension, and in her grief she finally faces the memories she has tried the hardest to forget, those of her beloved older brother's death in the camps.

The female narrator's subjectivity is deeply entangled with the men in her life so that the narrative unveils the extent to which masculinity is constructed within a web of personal and communal relationships. Asako's self-contained and uneventful life turns around the hidden trauma of the internment camps, but her repression can only be expressed indirectly through her behaviour towards the men around her, as we will see below. Like *Obasan, The Electrical Field* has attracted a number of critical approaches centering on its narrator to some neglect of other stylistic features, and several of these readings emphasize her psychological shortcomings. Asako can be seen as exhibiting the characteristics of Sigmund Freud's hysteric, suggesting that "the social wounds of the internment have yet to be resolved and remain an ongoing reality" (Visvis 74).[103] Similarly, Stone perceptively uses a psychoanalytical approach to point out the ways in which Asako's body is "dislocated physically and temporally as a result of internment [and to] investigate how the narrator's simultaneous phsyiological regression to a pre-pubescent stage and her progression to a menopausal stage represent her body's separation from traditional processes of aging" (37). Compelling as these views are, they should not obscure the way in which Sakamoto masterfully uses her narrator to filter the account of the past, to build suspense, and to delay her traumatic revelations.

In her second novel, Sakamoto replaces the repressed narrator with one that is missing crucial information. Miyo Mori in *One Hundred Million Hearts* is also flawed and unreliable. Although psychologically average, Miyo suffers a physical disability that isolates her from her peers. In the absence of her deceased mother, Miyo's father Masao contributes to this isolation by his protecting care and withholding sensitive information about himself. As the focus of the novel, Miyo is not inherently unreliable; she simply lacks information. When her father dies, she discovers that he married again (although the marriage failed) and has another daughter, Hana, living in Japan. It finally dawns on Miyo that her father is a different person from the one she grew up believing in, and that throughout her life he fed her half-truths and silences. She embarks on a journey of self-knowledge that entails a revision of the collective past as she travels to Japan in search of her half-sister.

Unlike *The Electrical Field, One Hundred Million Hearts* is partly set in Japan. In this ancestral land Miyo may find the key to understanding the lives of the previous generation of Japanese Canadians. The alienating landscape of Tokyo, where her half-sister lives, provides a powerful symbol of the surface sameness and underlying difference that links the Nikkei to the Japanese, for it feels like an unreadable labyrinth to her, with her complete ignorance of the language and customs. With the assistance of several local guides, Miyo's quest to uncover her father's past meets with success. The main stops on Miyo's and the reader's quest for knowledge are Hiroshima, her mother's hometown, with its visible nuclear-bomb scars, and Yasukuni Shrine in Tokyo, with its controversial idealization of the war. By inserting Japanese Canadians in this context, Sakamoto bravely opens to resignification the role of her community in World War Two and foregrounds the experiences of returnees that fought for the Japanese. This may explain why her second novel is less popular both with critics and the general public.

Although Sakamoto's fiction displays a wide range of male characters, three main types can be identified: the emasculated male standing for abjection and bearing the mark of shame, the idealized hero marked by sublimated desire, and the survivor who occupies the interstitial spaces between abjection and sublimation while participating in both.

Asako's father, known simply as Papa in the novel, is the most obvious example of abjection. He leads a muted existence in an upstairs bedroom, tucked away from view. However, his presence makes itself known by an occasional smell or sound drifting down from upstairs. The decay of his body also haunts the narrative, surfacing again and again:

> I looked down at my father lying there so pitifully, and somehow I was stunned yet unmoved by what I saw: the spreading stains across the sheet, where he had overflowed his diapers; the vomit crusted around his mouth; his eyes, lolling and then locking on me . . . He was trembling too—ice-cold, soaked in his day-old shikko. (*The Electrical Field* 191)

In Kristeva's formulation of abjection, "polluting objects fall, schematically, into two types: excremental and menstrual . . . Excrement and its equivalents (decay, infection, disease, corpse, etc.) stand for the danger to identity that comes from without: the ego threatened by the non-ego, society threatened by its outside, life by death" (71).

Asako's memories of her father hint at the origin of his degradation in the war internment. Before the war, when the Saitos lived on Vancouver Island, he was a strong man who worked at a mill and often came home drunk in the evening. At camp, he became more subdued and caring. Asako unexpectedly remembers that it was him, and not her mother, who looked after her when she was sick with grief on her brother's death. As they left camp and moved east, Asako found herself promoted to head of the family. Her father retreated from an outside world that he was too old and humiliated to face again:

> "On-ta-ri-o," Papa kept saying with his pitiful accent. He'd wanted to come east to the city but all he could do was huddle behind me with Mama and Stum. With Eiji gone and Stum just a baby, I was the first-born, born here; they pushed me out to the big city, to the world, thrusting my homely face to it when they were afraid. (*The Electrical Field* 51)

Although fragmented, Asako's memories allow readers to piece together the progress of Papa's emasculation. Shame and fear worked on him day after day. A first stroke left him semi-paralyzed in a wheelchair. A second turned him into what Asako coldly describes as "less than an infant" (*The Electrical Field* 102). His emasculation and powerlessness are then complete:

> He closed his eyes and I moved in, all shameful efficiency: I yanked back the sheet from his shrunken body, I hitched down his pyjama bottoms without flinching at the sight or the smell, unpinned, wiped, and changed him. He gave a thread-fine shudder at my final movement: tucking the cooled sheet back over him. His mystery, power, gone. (*The Electrical Field* 10–11)

As a representative of the Issei, Papa stands for ancestral Japaneseness and thus for the stigma that can never be cleansed, no matter how often or how thoroughly Asako changes him. She tries to combat his lack of coherent speech in either Japanese or English with the order of educated, phonetically precise English in order to combat being swallowed by his black hole. In Kristeva's words,

> What is abject . . . is radically excluded and draws me towards the place where meaning collapses . . . A weight of meaninglessness, about which there is nothing significant, and which crushes me. On the edge of non-existence and hallucination, of a reality that, if I acknowledge it, annihilates me. (2)

Asako fears that the world that she has so carefully made for herself within the walls of her home may be disrupted again, as the moans from upstairs remind her it once was.

Such disruption comes hand-in-hand with the Yanos. Masashi Yano was, like Asako, a second-generation Japanese Canadian. He was put to work on a road crew during the war and later chose to go to Japan instead of moving east like the Saitos. Yano is bitterly angry for his treatment by the Canadian authorities and his loss of home, country, and family. Although Yano is not as completely emasculated as Asako's Papa, he has also been defiled by his war experiences, and he too is closely associated with the abject, evidenced by repeated mention of his rank, "unwashed" smell, his unkempt hair, and his filthy fingernails. His speech also bears the sign of his shame, for Asako notices the awkward accent of the Nisei of which she works so hard to rid herself (*The Electrical Field* 67). Shame has psychologically crippled Yano in ways that he believes make him less of a man and that, in his mind, explain his wife's need for an extramarital affair: "We're so full of shame, aren't we, Asako? We hide away, afraid that they'll lock us up again . . . Chisako saw it in me . . . It isn't attractive, Asako. Especially in a man. I don't blame her" (*The Electrical Field* 231). Moreover, Yano is linked explicitly to death by the murder of his family and his own suicide. In fact, from the beginning of the novel Stum's nickname for him, "the kamikaze," marks him as a suicide case, a bomb waiting to explode.

Another character known as "the kamikaze" and as full of anger as Yano is Koji "Buddy" Kuroda in *One Hundred Million Hearts*. A Nisei who grew up in Vancouver before the war, Koji experienced anti-Asian racism every day in his early life: "Back home, *yellow skibby* someone once called him on the street. It was forever one ugly name or another, even in the neighbourhood around Powell Street. Yellow skibby stuck, no escaping it" (*One Hundred Million Hearts* 139). He seeks and finds his self-esteem in the intoxicating redefinition of Japanese identity stemming from the Imperial propaganda in Japanese newspapers, which includes the notion of a new, utopian land where "Asians" (a term hiding the imperialistic designs of the Japanese over continental Asians) could be masters and not servant. Still a young boy, Buddy relocates in Manchuria, assuming the more advantageous identity of the "pure" Japanese. From then on, he becomes Koji and never again speaks a word of English. Shame weighs heavily on Koji throughout his life. First, as an Asian boy in Canada; later, as a Nikkei in Japanese Manchuria; and finally, after the war, as a war criminal convicted for torturing prisoners. He is always found wanting by himself and others because he lives a lie. Although his Japanese is excellent, there is some clumsiness in him even sixty years later, a visible though elusive sign of his difference. Another Nisei is able to spot him because of "the broken, wayward pride in his step, the unease of trying to be what he thought a man should be; the bitterness that could turn ruthless" (*One Hundred Million Hearts* 251). To this Nisei's eyes, he was a traitor to the Japanese Canadian community, his family's skeleton in the closet.

Sakamoto's novels also feature a sublimated or idealized male hero who by virtue of an early death is saved from the war's degradation, and who lives on as an object of the female narrator's unfulfilled desire. In *The Electrical Field*, such is the case of Asako's older brother Eiji, who died during the internment. The framed photo of Eiji is Asako's most valued possession. Eiji is the representative of perfect

Japanese Canadian masculinity, the man that could never do wrong, and the role model to whom Stum constantly feels inferior. Asako has frozen Eiji into an icon in the photo and an idol in the stories about his accomplishments that she passes on first to Stum and then to her young neighbour Sachi Nakamura. In these stories, he is young, handsome, strong, selfless, and brave. He inhabits the idyllic world of pre-war British Columbia and presides over Asako's happy childhood, playing on the beach, teaching her to swim, and taking her on all his errands. Asako's recurrent dreams about Eiji exhibit a quality of joy and rapture that suggest incestuous desire while recalling Kristeva's description of how the sublime object

> ... dissolves in the raptures of a bottomless memory ... I then forget the point of departure and find myself removed to a secondary universe, set off from the one where 'I' am—delight and loss. Not at all short of but always with and through perception and words, the sublime is a *something added* that expands us, overstrains us, and causes us to be both *here*, as dejects, and *there*, as others and sparkling. A divergence, an impossible bounding. Everything missed, joy—fascination. (12)

However, Asako never touches on the subject of death. Only under the stress of the Yanos's tragedy can she eventually face her dire memories of life in the camp. She remembers her small-child jealousy at her adolescent brother's flirting with girls his age, and how she went to the river and jumped into it one night, fully expecting her older brother to follow her and rescue her, which he did. What she had not expected was his ensuing death from pneumonia. This is Asako's most private shame and guilt, which she has never overcome. Her physical contact with her older brother constituted her awakening to sexual desire, and she has tried to repress both her memories of this incestuous drive and the jealousy deriving from it. The role she played in Eiji's demise as well as her own feelings of guilt and loss have devastated her, turning her into an unloving and unloved woman.[104]

But Asako is not the only one to remember and cherish Eiji. While their father is in good health, a memorial is held for the elder son every year where other Japanese Canadians who had lived on the same camp pay homage to the young man. Thus, Eiji's untimely death transcends the domestic circle of Asako's shame to become a symbol of the stunted growth of the Japanese Canadian community. Such symbolism is most evident in one of Asako's recurring memories of how Eiji illustrated the meaning of the Japanese word "utsukushii" by pointing to the blossoms on an apple tree in the camp: "He was showing me the kind of pretty glimpsed at a certain time, in a certain light—a special light. A pretty that can't last; a pretty that can even turn ugly" (*The Electrical Field* 218). Like those flowers, Eiji stands for the poignant beauty that will soon fade. Unlike them, death protects him from becoming ugly and defiled. This male character stands for the values of honour and dignity that the Japanese Canadian community cherishes, but, significantly, only after his death. However, by describing Asako's feelings of guilt and her self-blame, the author hints at the complicity of Japanese Canadians in their wartime victimization.

In *One Hundred Million Hearts* the sublimated hero is Hajime, a young member of the elite Special Attack Forces *(tokkotai)*. As a pilot, he is expected to fight to the death. His survival would signify his failure, for on his final mission he is expected to collide against his target, giving up his life in order to cause maximum damage. His sacrifice would be recompensed, according to the official creed, by his rebirth in the cherry blossoms of Yasukuni Shrine. As he leaves on his final mission, he dreams that "when I crash into my target and sink a great American battleship, I will be a fiery blossom lighting the sky" (*One Hundred Million Hearts* 266).

Hajime lives and perishes by this code of duty to the Emperor, and so his untimely death turns him into a symbol of perfection and generosity. Like Eiji, he is made into an icon by the woman who loves him most, his fiancée Kiku, who every year for six decades visits Yasukuni Shrine in cherry blossom season and faithfully mourns him, together with other war widows and mothers. Against this landscape of nostalgia Sakamoto posits the more critical viewpoint of the younger generation. Hana's art includes looking back on the lives of the kamikaze without the adoring eyes of the ones left behind. She has created a wall mural representing a huge cherry blossom out of whose stamens grow the old photographs of young kamikaze pilots, among them Hajime. To Miyo's eyes, Hana's mural is at the same time "exquisite and hideous" (*One Hundred Million Hearts* 75). Such waste of young lives may well be an aberration, while the idealism and selflessness of the pilots themselves should be admired.

The third and final kind of male characters in Sakamoto's fiction is that of a survivor who is relatively untouched either by abjection or sublimation. Living under the shadow of the internment but fairly untainted by it is Asako's younger brother Stum in *The Electrical Field*, who is born while the family is already in the camp. She sees him as spineless, and though he is an adult, he remains for her a helpless and needy child:

> The sound of him, his voice when we first moved here after Mama died. So high it made you grit your teeth at its girlish softness; no edge, no bottom. He was not the slightest bit like Eiji; not handsome at all, not strong. He was a boy of twelve or thirteen, miserable at first, missing his mama who'd always kept him close, missing his Chinese friends in the city. His face was shapeless, shy to show itself. (*The Electrical Field* 56)

Stum leads an invisible life, going from his job to his home alone and without friends. However, Asako's nervous breakdown empowers him, and in establishing a relationship with a Philippino woman he starts to move outside Asako's crippling domestic environment, changing the balance of power in the home.

Stum represents the adjustments that the Japanese Canadian community had to make after the war. Although somewhat tainted, he has escaped total emasculation, instead choosing assimilation and isolation as a means to survive. But through this character, the narrative offers hope and the possibility of renewal. As Howells remarks, "the story is told as an exorcism of ghosts and Asako's narrative manages to gesture, however tentatively, beyond loss and trauma into wider social spaces, which the 'sansei' of Sakamoto's third generation of Japanese Canadians now occupy in their native land of Canada" (142).[105]

Perhaps the most ambiguous male character in Sakamoto's fiction is Miyo's father, Masao Mori, in *One Hundred Million Hearts*. As a Nisei sent to Japan to improve his education, he is safe from the war at the Tokyo university where he studies until conscription reaches him near its end. He appears to believe in the honour and duty code enforced by war propaganda, to the extent that he hides information that might deprive him of his opportunity for a "final mission." For example, the fact that he is foreign-born might have made his superiors consider him unworthy. However, as time goes on, Hajime's letters record Masao's growing doubts about his mission as well as the fact that "he can't bring himself to believe that he will flourish in the afterlife" (*One Hundred Million Hearts* 265). This lack of faith makes Hajime take pity on him and offer to trade places with him.

Masao survives but has to live with the shame of not completing his assigned mission. After he returning to Toronto and starting a new life, he imposes on himself a strict code of silence and isolation, avoiding other Nikkei and never speaking Japanese. Yet, his second wife Setsuko reports that his guilt weighed very heavily on him, to the extent that he thought his daughter Miyo's disability was a punishment for his fault. Most of Miyo's memories are of a man devoted to his duty and exhibiting the kind of stoic qualities of endurance and self-denial with the military. Although in appearance he may be leading a normal life in Toronto, at heart Masao seems to be paying his dues for what he considers a past act of cowardice. As he lay dying in hospital, his parting words to his daughter were no other than the motto of the *tokkotai*, "Endure the unendurable" (*One Hundred Million Hearts* 42).

As a result, Masao is a man of two faces, a Janus-like figure of two worlds and two countries, each of them represented by one woman. As Setsuko remarks,

> He never fit in . . . Nowhere. He was sure the nisei didn't like him because he had fought for the Japanese, but they didn't have anything against him. He wasn't in the internment camps back home, and he wasn't a repat in Japan. In Japan he saw all the Japanese pouring in from Taiwan, China, the Philippines, Malaya, all those dirty places that got dirtier after the Japanese left. He wasn't one of them either. (*One Hundred Million Hearts* 123)

Miyo and Setsuko hold contesting views of the man they both loved and for whose attention they competed. For Miyo, Masao was simply a Toronto mechanic. For Setsuko, he was a true hero deserving recognition and gratitude. Much of the novel's suspense lies in discovering who the true man was, and accordingly where his ashes should be laid to rest. By the end of the novel, however, Setsuko understands that Masao's place (like her own) is in Canada, the country where, as Miyo never ceases to point out, Masao had chosen to live out his life.

Sakamoto's relentless exploration of the Japanese Canadian male psyche in her fiction is built on the perceptions and experiences of its female narrator, but it is by no means imbued with a spirit of gender antagonism. Rather, it appears to be an honest attempt to empathize with the male characters and understand their plight, as the author tenderly unveils the multi-layered legacy of ethnic and communal trauma and (inter)national strife in all its complexity. Howells has intelligently described the sophisticated political awareness of Sakamoto's work:

> Sakamoto is taking the debate about Japanese Canadian identity forward in original ways that could only be undertaken from the relatively detached position of a writer belonging to a later generation, as she strikes a precarious balance between the otherness resulting from white prejudice against the Japanese Canadians and the Japanese Canadians' deliberate othering of themselves. (138)

This task is by no means easy. As the analysis of the male characters in Sakamoto's novels reveals, the legacy of World War Two on the North American Nikkei is extremely complex and exhibits different nuances in each generation. The focus of *The Electrical Field* is on the Nisei in the period before the success of the Redress Movement. Through the figures of Asako, her brothers Eiji and Stum, and her neighbour Yano, the author discloses the underlying pain and guilt of members within the same generation. Her later novel shifts its interest to how the Sansei have been deprived of knowledge and been kept in the dark about their community's recent past. To that purpose, Sakamoto brilliantly deploys the figure of Miyo and her quest for information, crossing her path with three conflicted male characters of the Nisei generation.

Through a daring narrative technique that displays the multifaceted male and female psyches, and that sometimes leads her to reverse the conventional hierarchies of outside/inside, symbolic/semiotic, community/personal, and white/non-white, in her fiction Kerri Sakamoto goes beyond and problematizes the representation of Japanese North American masculinity in previous seminal works, such as Joy Kogawa's.

7. Japan, or the Attempt to Fix Identity

Sally Ito describes her writing as being characterized by the impulse "to make bridges, to create points of identification, and to create feelings of empathy and understanding for [her] characters" ("Issues" 178). This is certainly true regarding the settings and characters in *Floating Shore;* many of the stories feature people either recently arrived from Japan or travelling there. The immigrant and the tourist mingle freely with the native-born or the older resident. In that context, the stories convey a fascination with Japanese identity and Japanese ancestry, which, though remarkable, is not unusual. As a writer, Ito explores her own affinities with Japanese aesthetics:

> The more I read and studied about Japanese literature, the more I realized how much Japanese aesthetics and ways of thinking informed my writing. The writer of colour has access to other traditions in forms and aesthetics, and the challenge is to incorporate and synthesize these elements to create new writings in English. ("Issues" 177)

However, as a Nikkei woman, Ito is also bound to feel an interest in all things Japanese, which reveals an attempt to ground and fix identity. Other Japanese Canadians have recorded their reactions and attitudes towards Japan,[106] such as Roy Miki, who says,

> In 1969, Slavia [Miki's wife] and I went to live in Japan, naively intending to live, work and study there for at least five years. We bought one-way tickets with only visitors' visas, with no means of support there. Luckily we found jobs in Tokyo, teaching English. We lived in Japan for only sixteen months. I soon discovered I would never become "Japanese" . . . It struck home that the attempt to reclaim my "roots" (in the lingo of the day) was fraught with contradictions, and even a diversion from the more inevitable job of understanding "Japanese Canadian identity," whatever the term could come to signify. (23–24)

Omatsu travelled to Japan in the same period and describes her conflicting feelings of sameness and difference, belonging and unbelonging:

> ... when I visited Japan in the early 1970s I felt very Canadian. I found their male chauvinism and rigid behavioural social codes oppressive and restricting. At the same time, in Japan I delighted in my ability to disappear in a crowd, to look like everyone else and not to stick out. Once, when I was arranging by telephone to meet a stranger at a Kyoto metro station, I described myself as a Japanese Canadian woman. At home that would have been all the identification I needed. In Japan my caller, puzzled, said, "But what will you be wearing?" Still, I knew I did not belong in Japan. (41)

Ito's own reflections on Japanese roots come through in her story "Furyo," which charts the psychological quest of a Canadian Sansei narrator who spends a year in Japan with her relatives: "Kyoto, they told me, had been the ancient capital of Japan and there was a lot to see and do. It was a good place to find my true identity—my true Japanese self" (*Floating Shore* 187). There she meets another Sansei, Peter Arawaka, a US citizen who functions as a twin character/*doppelgänger* in the story. He too has set out on a voyage of discovery, although he pretends he is in Japan just to drink and enjoy himself while supporting himself with English lessons, probably to hide the embarrassing truth that his quest for identity is metaphysical. In the process, he also becomes a teacher figure for the narrator. From him she learns to re-examine many of her unquestioned notions about Asian identity and affiliation, like her uncritical use of the term "Oriental" (*Floating Shore* 188) and about Asian North American writers like John Okada, and she is encouraged to write about her family's fortunes and misfortunes throughout the twentieth century in both Japan and Canada.

Ito's story delves further into the complexity of those experiences through the figure of the narrator's grandmother. Though born in Canada, the grandmother spent much of her life in Japan—first for several years of education as a girl, then returning as a married woman after her husband signed up for repatriation following the war. Now in her seventies, she feels that she is too old to return to Canada. Ito's tale maps out this intricate web of relations, locations, and identity positions while at the same time she worries that such stories may be used to further the western world's consumption of Orientalist artifacts, and that they may become "the kind I'd seen occasionally in the drugstore—the long immigrant saga of a family trying to survive against cruelty and prejudice in the new world . . . The story would be so far from the truth it would be laughable. *No thanks*, I thought, I had other plans for my writing" (*Floating Shore* 196).

Japan is the focus of the two characters' search for identity as they try to unpack their feelings towards a country that both accepts them and rejects them, where they are both at home and permanent foreigners. Ito is also careful to suggest that such quests for an essentialized identity may be deceitful, in the words of a Japanese uncle:

> "You Nikkei. You come here to find your roots and you end up being more Japanese than the Japanese."
> "You think?" I said rather absently. I looked at the figure in the mirror. She seems so Japanese, I thought, hardly recognizing her—a woman in a white dress. I twisted a loose strand of hair around my finger and then let it drop, watching the reflection to see if it would do the same thing. (*Floating Shore* 206)

The conflicting feelings of sameness and difference, belonging and unbelonging that Ito portrays here are echoed in Kerri Sakamoto's account of her own visit to Japan. Sakamoto spent three months there on a fellowship granted by the Japan Foundation. Part of her experiences went into the writing of her second novel, *One Hundred Million Hearts* (2003), which is set in Tokyo and Toronto. She describes her more personal reactions in an article for the *National Post*:

> It's a shock. The shock of self-recognition. As a third-generation Japanese-Canadian growing up in the suburbs of Toronto in the 1970s, the sight of another black-haired Asian was rare; even my own reflection in the high school washroom mirror could be jarring. Now the experience of racial sameness for the first time in my life—coupled with simultaneous cultural and linguistic difference—is a potent mix of intimacy and alienation. (1999, 6)

Sakamoto is painfully aware of her own attitudes towards race and culture. She describes herself as a "cultural pauper" because the forced internment of Japanese Canadians deprived her of those family heirlooms that were legitimately her own, and feels that, like other Sansei, "this history has turned me into a collector, a fetishist of my own cultural heritage" (1999, 6). Yet she is also critical of Japan, and in her second novel she raises questions about intra-Asian racism by means of Japanese characters that look down on the Koreans or on the Nikkei. In the same article she points out,

> In the post-war years, according to one nisei who "returned" to Japan after being pressured to "repatriate" by the Canadian government following his release from an internment camp, nikkei (foreign-born Japanese) were labelled *kimim*—throwaways. (1999, 6)

Like Ito, Sakamoto deploys a Japanese Canadian female narrator who visits Japan on a quest, though roots are not what she is actually searching for. Miyo Mori is deprived of her past and her heritage by a silent father who cuts her off from all things Japanese in order to protect her from the unsavoury parts of his own troublesome past. In Kobayashi's story "Rabbit Moon," Gen Tanaka travels to Japan to take her father's ashes back to the ancestral home. For her too, this journey entails a kind of reconciliation with her roots. This involves a physical recognition of racial similarity as she enters the country of the kind Sakamoto described above: "Faces, faces. Japanese faces. Homecoming" (*Exile and the Heart* 73). But Kobayashi's story also displays a biological link to the past through the figure of her Bachan, or grandmother, very much like Ito's story.

All three are telling examples of attempts to unravel the web of affiliations and the conflicting emotions of sameness and difference by which the Japanese Canadian subject is bound to be beset, while discursively engaging in the historical events that have come into its construction. Japan figures prominently in such a construction. It stands as the object of a love/hate relationship as well as the source of answers for the characters' many questions concerning the lives of previous generations of Japanese Canadians that have been surrounded by silence. Setting the record straight about those past troubles, for better or for worse, has become a task for a new generation of Japanese Canadian writers.

8. Politics and Poetics: Innovations in Genre and Aesthetics

Although the Japanese Canadian writers examined in this chapter display distinctive individual features, they all share an innovative approach to narrative. Kerri Sakamoto's deployment of unreliable narrators destabilizes essentialized notions of identity and challenges racialization from multiple perspectives. Likewise, her fiction re-introduces neglected topics and forces readers to face untold experiences, particularly those of World War Two.

Hiromi Goto partakes of this interest in the workings of subjectivity, particularly in her metafictional work *Chorus of Mushrooms*. As Ty remarks, "The multiple narrators and the fictional documents create a multilayered perspective, which has the effect . . . of what Mikhail Bakhtin calls 'heteroglossia'" (154). In the italicized sections of the novel, the narrator becomes an unidentified storytelling "I" swiftly responding to the reactions and interests of a listening "you." In those sections, Goto explores the structure and tests the limits of fiction at its most basic level of interaction. Similarly, the boundaries between truth and fiction often become blurry, with storyteller and audience inhabiting a liminal space where anything can happen. In contrast, the non-italicized sections are variously identified as Naoe's or Murasaki's, but they occasionally weave their stories together so that at times it is hard to say who is doing what. For example, in the telling of the traditional Japanese story "Uba-Sute Yama" about a society in which elderly people are taken to the mountain and abandoned, Murasaki's role becomes increasingly more active. Beauregard remarks that this joint storytelling transforms "Uba-Sute Yama" from "a place where people are abandoned" into "a place of abandonment" ("Hiromi Goto's *Chorus of Mushrooms*" 51). By the end of the story, an intrigued Murasaki exclaims in wonder: "Good gracious me and my tits! Where in mackerel did that story come from? I can't tell where Obāchan ends and I begin, or if I made the whole thing up or if it was all Obāchan" (*Chorus of Mushrooms* 68). Such intimate collaboration is only possible, as McCullough says, when there is deep trust between both members: "In *Chorus of Mushrooms,* narrative is revealed as an encounter in which teller and listener are mutually at risk, and where trust is responsible for the unique experience of each and for the relation between words and worlds" (151).

Interest in all kinds of texts, not just verbal ones, pervades these works. In Sakamoto's *One Hundred Million Hearts* World War II letters are introduced, subtly enhancing the impact of the tale. Miyo receives maps and tokens from her lover in Toronto that intertextually recall the seventeenth-century Map of Tenderness inspired by Madame de Scudéry's fiction, which graphically showed the obstacles lovers had to overcome on their path to fulfillment. These devices indicate the use of hypertextual techniques as defined by Beeler, i.e., a combination of

> the textual and the visual by incorporating actual photographs or paintings, descriptions of photographs, or various scripts and fonts into their 'texts'. This layering of visual/textual images allows these authors to contain or document certain images temporarily while also conveying the resistance of a particular culture. (182–83)

Visual elements act as a hypertext in Sakamoto's second novel. Several images anchor the narrative in the fraught waters of World War Two: the photograph of Miyo's father in uniform and the red-stitched mural produced by Hana as she tries to come to terms with her father's life and that of his generation. Both acquire a haunting quality. As Goossen suggests, Hana's art conveys the violence of the war:

> Until the final sections of the novel, the war's brutality is conveyed indirectly, through art and snatches of memory. Hana obsessively superimposes small photos of kamikaze pilots and tiny bundles of yarn over a wall-sized picture of her father's face and then over a picture of the emperor. Wartime atrocities emerge from the mist, are briefly confessed, then disappear again. Old women dance beneath the cherry blossoms for lovers now too young to be their children. Like Hana's art, *Hearts* presents the Pacific War in montage form as a succession of shifting images set against an ideologically charged historical backdrop. (65)

Similarly, the description of the annual rituals held at Yasukuni Shrine in memory of the fallen helps readers reconstruct the war in their imaginations and envision its far-reaching effects.

These writers are keenly aware of the nuances of languages and codes in the widest sense. For Sally Ito, language is one of the most important issues a writer of colour must tackle. She has examined how biculturalism and bilingualism affects the writer of colour's use of language as concerns several aspects: tone in characterization, dialogue, and idiom. In describing the techniques that can be used, and in critiquing the white critic's take on language, she says,

> The issue at stake for writers of colour is that when they choose to write in that particular idiom, they are open to the criticism that their works are poorly written in

"bad English." Yet no one will say that James Joyce's writings were written in "bad English" . . . Critics, therefore, must understand that a new idiom is being created (admittedly with its attendant fits and starts) and that that idiom is as legitimate as any other English idiom. ("Issues for the Writer of Colour" 175)

Goto's approach to language is particularly interesting because she inserts long sections of untranslated Japanese words or Japanese script, which disrupts "the reading experience, especially for the reader not familiar with Japanese" (Beeler 188). Sturgess also draws attention to code-mixing in Goto's first novel:

> The linguistic migrancy at work in *Chorus of Mushrooms* foregrounds cultural differ-
> ence, and also underlines the dilemma of subjective erasure to the ends of "fitting in":
> the necessary adoption of unified world views where personal and the public percep-
> tions do not necessarily coincide. Yet, such yuxtaposition of Japanese and English sites
> of speech—the displacing from one linguistic system to another—not only under-
> lines difference but establishes "a bridge" (56), a relationship between two distinct sys-
> tems which could be seen as a revisionary possibility. This hybridity combines two
> distinct cultural discourses and histories and thus creates a third possibility. (29)

As Libin explains, this linguistic strategy departs from the choice made by both Kogawa and Sakamoto, who usually insert Japanese terms but provide their translation into English ("Lost in Translation" 123). Each choice determines a politics of inclusion/exclusion for potential readers. For Sasano, this can be explained as Goto's "refusal always to cater to those who are in the majority" (45), i.e., a white mainstream readership.[107] Sakamoto is more inclusive (or, as Sasano would have it, more geared towards the mainstream), but she also finds strategies that allow her to transmit the contrast between the characters' regular use of Japanese and their occasional use of English for communication even while using standard English throughout the novel:

> Although [Asako] has always made great effort to improve her English and still does
> the newspaper crossword every day, she preserves a sense of cultural identity in her
> narrative by scattering Japanese words and phrases throughout. While reminding
> readers of the narrator's otherness (or perhaps of the reader's otherness to Japanese
> culture) these linguistic signs of difference need not exclude non-Japanese readers.
> Most words are translated within the same or the following sentence . . . Asako's
> ambivalence over the language question suggests a chosen othering on her part,
> related not only to her internment experience but also to her Japanese conservatism
> and what has been called "the strong exclusionary strain in the Japanese psyche."
> (Howells 131–32)

As mentioned above, translation is a key issue in Goto's first novel. At times it becomes oddly unnecessary between people speaking different languages, thus intimating true communication beyond words, whereas at other times translation allows for metamorphosis, change, and progress, resulting in a fluid, unfixed subjectivity. Most of all, this applies to names. Naoe gives her granddaughter Muriel the Japanese name "Murasaki," meaning "Purple," but also alluding to the Japanese author of *Tales of Genji*, the novel's main intertext. Murasaki appropriates the name and plays with it, for example by choosing to buy a purple futon (a device that once more links language and body politics). Yet, later in the novel, a renewed Naoe will give herself the name "Purple." These acts of naming make Naoe and Murasaki virtually interchangeable. In fact, Murasaki briefly becomes Naoe at one point when she sits in her grandmother's chair. Her mother Keiko addresses her as "Obāchan," and the young woman replies in Japanese, just as Naoe would have. In the subsequent italicized section, Murasaki comments, "It wasn't a thing of taking over—more of a coming together. Or a returning. I don't know" (169). Similarly, the truck driver Tengu willingly adopts the nickname he was given by Japanese children due to his reddened face (110–11), and the Tonkatsu family is identified by the only word that Sam remembered in his native language (208–09), even though it is a hybrid word consisting of the root "ton" ("pork" in Japanese) and "cutlet" (of uncertain origin). Rather than grounding identity, names in *Chorus of Mushrooms* are facilitators of change and reminders of the transitoriness of being.

For Sasano, the novel's attitude towards language reveals that "language and culture are not inherent; they can be learned and unlearned" (45), while its approach to names might be less than unique, for it is "fairly common for Japanese Canadians to be given or to adopt an English name as well as a Japanese name" (52). But race is not the only force that may lead one to accept or reject a name. *Chorus of Mushrooms* also highlights the impact of gender, especially in Naoe's remarks about the patriarchal transmission of family names, so that her name Kiyokawa is to end with her brother because he had no children. She also makes clear that a family name that has been forced upon a woman can be as deadening as the marriage it comes with:

> I had to put the Kiyokawa aside, the name to flow through my brother's blood, to the child they never conceived. Dai Naoe. The words written on the marriage document made it so. Lucky for me I changed my name before I came to English. The spelling different, but the weight of the word in sound would have been burden enough to plague me. Naoe die. (38)

The innovative use of genre conventions also sets apart the writing of these Japanese Canadian authors. Intertextuality is perhaps most prominent in Goto's *Chorus of Mushrooms*, which variously draws from *The Tales of Genji*, *Richard III*, and *Alice in Wonderland*. Ty points out,

By playing with the genres of myth, fantasy, and the novel, she makes us aware of the importance of voice and perspective. Whose myths and values are being reproduced in society depends on who is doing the telling and who is in control. (155)

The novel's "Acknowledgements" and "Postcript" sections point the reader towards the peculiar combination of background material. On one hand, Goto alludes to taking liberties with autobiographical materials such as her grandmother's history, and departing "from 'historical' facts into the realms of contemporary folk legend" (np), while also listing three collections of Japanese tales that "influenced" her writing: *Folk Legends of Japan, Japanese Mythology,* and *The Tale of Genji.* Throughout the novel, grandmother and grandchild bond as they weave together the old tales in new forms, starting with the time-honoured formula "Mukāshi, mukāshi, ōmukashi." Beauregard compares this treatment of the folk tale with Maxine Hong Kingston's in her popular novel *The Woman Warrior,* concluding that Goto's revisionist agenda reveals an ongoing effort to resist tradition as a fixed script:

> By explicitly adopting and adapting "impure" myths and legends, Goto refuses to accept the "fixed tablet of tradition" offered to her by hegemonic groups; she refuses their imperative to reproduce "Japanese culture." ("Hiromi Goto's *Chorus of Mushrooms*" 51)

Narrative turn-taking between Naoe and Murasaki of the kind described at the beginning of this section as well as the repetitive but ever-changing nature of folk storytelling produce a kind of circularity, one story feeding into the next so that it is hard to tell beginnings from endings. This imparts a timelessness that makes Goto's immigrant saga at the same time strikingly current and traditional.

In her second novel, Hiromi Goto chooses again an Asian myth to challenge the one-sidedness of the realist script. *The Kappa Child* has been widely read as science fiction,[108] even winning the 2001 James Tiptree Jr Award "for works that expand and explore gender roles in SF and fantasy." The main fantastic element is the presence of the Kappa, a mythical water creature that, according to Iwamoto, became popular in late-1920s Japanese writing. It is described as a small green figure with webbed fingers and a bowl-shaped head containing the water from which it draws power. Further, an entry from *Kenkyusha's New Japanese-English Dictionary* helpfully annexed to the novel describes the Kappa's fondness for cucumbers and interest in sumo wrestling.

As a trickster, the Kappa serves a variety of functions in Goto's novel. First, because it is a water creature, it sets off the displacedness and isolation of the Japanese characters in the dry landscape of the Canadian prairies. It is a mark of their race and ethnicity, and one of many symbols of the East-West encounter in the novel. Its timeless voice interacts with the contemporary plot of the narrator and her family. Second, its connection with water awakens Freudian associations with human sexuality, and thus the Kappa appears as a sexually attractive female Stranger, met on the night of the last total lunar eclipse of the twentieth century in Calgary's Chinatown:

> The Stranger was leaning against the wall of the hallway. Wearing a silk red wedding dress, snug on her slender body, and slightly worn on the curve of a middle-aged belly. A black beret covered an oddly shaped head, strands of thin hair hanging long and limp. A heavy leather jacket. In the strange glow of the streetlight, the Stranger's complexion looked almost olive. (*The Kappa Child* 88)

The Stranger suggests they watch the eclipse, and they end up sumo-wrestling naked on the grounds of the international airport.[109] As the narrator wakes up alone the next morning, she feels an unusual craving for Japanese cucumbers that signals the onset of an even more unusual pregnancy. As the narrative unfolds, it becomes evident that the narrator's pregnancy is psychological, and that she is bound to give birth only to a renewed self. Once more, the motif of rebirth that first appeared in *Chorus of Mushrooms* recurs. This time, instead of an elderly woman looking to make up for lost time and to live out her life in full, the narrator must overcome her childhood traumas and accept her own body and sexual orientation.

Goto provides happy endings for the protagonists in both novels, even while rejecting complete closure. This has led Libin to describe Goto as an optimist in contrast to the "melancholy" tone of Kogawa and Sakamoto:

> One factor that has led to the enthusiastic critical reception of *Chorus of Mushrooms* is the whimsical tone with which Muriel and Naoe relate their stories. Although the narrative clearly articulates the obstacles that a Japanese Canadian woman faces in a homogeneously white culture, it is distinctly more affirmative in its plot and characterization than other recent texts by Japanese Canadians, such as Joy Kogawa's *Obasan* and Kerri Sakamoto's *The Electrical Field*. In the face of such novels, in which the effects of white Canadian racism are recounted in a melancholy tone, *Chorus of Mushrooms*, with its rejoicing in storytelling and a variety of sensual pleasures, including food and sex, may seem to the white Canadian reader like narrative absolution from a legacy of national shame. ("Some of My Best Friends" 93)

Libin's comments aptly remind us of the differences in tone between these writers, but fail to take into account the distinctive subject matter of each. One can hardly be other than "melancholy" when dealing directly with World War Two's "legacy of national shame," as both Kogawa and Sakamoto do, whereas it is comparatively easier to sound "affirmative" if touching on the subject in passing, as Goto does. These superficial differences should not hide the deep connections that have come up in this chapter regarding their politics. Both Goto and Sakamoto—and, in their stories, Ito and Kobayashi as well—reject the more traditional family saga as the form to voice the lives of the Japanese Canadian community. Instead, they engage in creatively challenging examinations of racialized experience in Canada from the perspective of gender and sexual orientation.

9. Conclusion

This section has attempted to complete the map of Asian Canadian women's literature drafted in the earlier chapters on South Asian and Chinese Canadian women's writing by describing the multifaceted fiction of Japanese Canadian authors that attests to how far we have moved beyond the situation in previous decades. Miki has remarked that the Japanese Canadian community of the 1950s and 1960s had no writers until Roy Kiyooka's first published work in 1964; he would be a lonely and invisible voice until Joy Kogawa's *Obasan*. But even then, Miki argues, Japanese Canadians were being spoken for, instead of speaking out (*Broken Entries* 117). Through the experience of racial targeting, mass uprooting, and dispersal during and after World War Two, this community learned the self-defensive practices of muteness and invisibility that have persisted to this very day.

However, the generation of Nikkei writers emerging in the last few years of the twentieth century has provided a voice for this disempowered group. As seen above, the fiction of Goto, Sakamoto, Ito, and Kobayashi depicts a rich and complex community that has been racialized in a number of different ways. Many characters and situations continue to delve into the heritage of World War Two, but even then they have challenged the more traditional representation of Japanese Canadians as victims and disclosed a variety of subject positions, probing into how racialized subjects may collude with such victimization. Other works involve more recent waves of immigrants from Japan and their specific plights. These writers stress fluidity, mobility, and multiple passages rather than fixed and stable racial identities. Homes and selves are often many rather than one, constructed by history but also by geography, class, and sexual orientation. Such nuanced pictures are built by innovative narrative strategies that, as seen above, stress the power of language as communication rather than as a barrier, and fuse genre conventions in order to create new, hybrid spaces for self-growth and community development.

NOTES

1. The references embedded in this quote come from: Edward Said, "Representing the Colonized: Anthropology's Interlocutors" (Critical Inquiry 15, 1989), and Kwame Anthony Appiah, "Is the Post- in Postmodernism the Post- in Postcolonial?" (Critical Inquiry 17, 1991).

2. For example, Kenneth McGoogan wrote in his review for Books in Canada: "Such a Long Journey is not a Canadian novel" (12), and he quoted Robertson Davies on the novel: "Such a Long Journey may well be the best novel written in Canada in 1991. That doesn't make it a Canadian novel. Because in no way does that novel reflect this place, Canada" (12). Contrary to this opinion, Malashri Lal sustains in her article "Politics of Self-Definition: Mapping Asian-Indians in Canada" that "Canada, most subtly but significantly, permeates the text" (64) and that although "Canada does not play any part in the book if one goes solely by plot or character . . . a vital connection in the theoretical uses of space in the novel may point otherwise" (64). Shyam Salvadurai has offered the following illuminating reflection on the disputed Canadianness of diasporic texts: "It is from this space in-between, represented by the hyphen, that I have written what I consider Canadian novels set exclusively in Sri Lanka. For though the material may be Sri Lankan, the shaping of that material and the inclusion, for example, of themes of gay liberation or feminism are drawn from the life I have lived in Canada . . . My thoughts and attitudes, indeed my craft as a writer, have been shaped by my life here in Canada" (2).

3. Amita Handa defines "South Asian" as a "diasporic" term that "refers to people who have a historical and cultural connection to the South Asian subcontinent," pointing out that "its construction as an indentity (as opposed to geographical description) is in some ways relevant only in the Canadian context. One is not South Asian in Trinidad (one is Indian), Britain (Black or Asian), or the United States (Asian), for example" (173).

4. I am using here Gwladys Downes's term in "Contrasts in Psychic Space," where she deals with the sense of displacement of migrant writers in Canada and the gap between psychic and geographical space. Parameswaran has also written in similar terms: "though the landscape around me is spruce and maple, the landscape of memory is treed with mangoes and banyan, and the contribution of South Asian Canadians is that we bring Ganga to the Assiniboine not only for ourselves but for our fellow Canadians" (1996: 147). I have analyzed elsewhere this contrast in Jamaican Canadian short-story cycles (see Martín-Lucas 1998).

5. Farida Karodi, Yasmin Ladha, Shani Mootoo, and Ramabai Espinet are clear exponents of the multi-diasporic nature of this "South Asian" category, having migrated to Canada from Africa or the Caribbean.

6. Mootoo insists frequently in her short stories on the expectations raised by skin color and this idea of the "failed" Indian. For example, in "Out on Main Street" she writes, "[W]e is watered-down Indians—we ain't good grade A Indians. We skin brown, is true, but we doh even think 'bout India unless something happen over dere and it come on de news" (45); and in "Upside-downness of the World as it Unfolds" the narrator says, "The only Indian words I know are those on the menus in Indian restaurants and in my very own *Indian Cookery by Mrs Balbir Singh*. From the first day I arrived in Canada people would say, 'Oh, great! You can teach me to cook Indian food, and that tea, what is it called? Masala tea? chai? You know, the one with the spices.' But I didn't know, hadn't heard of such a tea unitl I came up here" (117).

7. María Reimóndez has more recently translated Erín Moure's *Little Theatres (teatriños)* into Galician (*Teatriños ou Auturuxos Calados*, Editorial Galaxia, 2007).

8. See, for instance, Gita Mehta's *Karma Cola: Marketing the Mystic East*, Graham Huggan's "Consuming India" in *The Postcolonial Exotic*, or Sarah Brouillette's "South Asian Literature and Global Publishing."

9. Niessen, Leshkowich, and Jones analyze this phenomenon in *Re-Orienting Fashion: The Globalization of Asian Dress* (2003).

10. There has been an ongoing controversy in India around Salman Rushdie's assertion that Indian writing in English is stronger and more important than any other vernacular literature from India (see for example Krishna Sarbadhikary's essay "Indian English Literature at the Turn of the Century"). Despite the recent increase in translations from other Indian languages, there is no question that the Indian literature predominant in Western markets is written in English, and translated into other languages from English.

11. Before them, Anita Desai and Bharati Mukherjee. In 1992 Yasmin Ladha complained about the exclusion of women from the fashionable elite of "Diasporic" writers in her fiction-essay "Giving Up the Company of Women," that closes her collection *Lion's Granddaughter*. Though the situation has improved in terms on the number of women authors now incorporated into the market, I find her quote unfortunately descriptive of the contemporary scene: "In mainstream literature, the celebration of Other has been encouraged in recent years: Other-texts, *gurujis*, writing workshops, funding agencies, global awakening, conferences. It is the season of the Other, 'Please, after you, after you,' I am ushered on mainstream's promenade deck. And especially these *maha* hyphenated-magicians, writing back from the Raj-*wallah*-Empire. These magicians parted the East-West sea. To call these magicians prophets would blunt their glory. Now, the immigrant can go back and forth, shamelessly collecting along the way. The parting, call it sea parting or hair parting or margin is packed too close. These *maha* hyphenated-magicians' *istyle*, superbly western but their content ground for an *asli*-authentic burp/pleasure: spicy-yellow-sour-loud, no apology. I speak of Salman Rushdie and Hanif Kureshi, the clan-*wallahs* of Other writing. But there are others and I get impatient when texts by lesser-known *pen-wallahs* are not incorporated into the school syllabi, more speedo, *fatafat, chap chapa*. I welcome established pen-wallahs like RK Narayan and Anita Desai, but I have had enough. I want Sujata Bhatt, Sara Suleri, Gita Mehta, Debjani Chatterji,

and Sky Lee" (86–87).

12. Lakshmi Gill's *During Rain I Plant Chrysanthemums* (1966) "was the first work to be published by a South Asian woman in Canada" (Rahman 99, 98). It is a poetry volume. Her only fiction text is the novel *The Third Infinitive,* published by TSAR in 1993.

13. The subject of this study is restricted to adult fiction, hence the exclusion of Gilmore's and Himani Bannerji's juvenile and children's fiction.

14. Gerald Lynch *(The One and the Many: English-Canadian Short Story Cycles)* and WH New *(Dreams of Speech and Violence)* have studied the origins and development of the Canadian short-story cycle, looking at the more canonical and traditional examples. Rocio Davis has produced a book-length study of Asian American and Asian Canadian cycles, *Transcultural Reinventions: Asian American and Asian Canadian Short Story Cycles,* which includes an analysis of Rachna Mara's *Of Customs and Excise.* My own study of the genre (Martín-Lucas 1999) looks at the short-story cycles in English by Canadian women from 1971 to 1991 under the scope of feminist and postcolonial theories; chapter four is dedicated to the cycles by diasporic women writers, including Mara's.

15. Published in the USA and the UK with the title *Tamarind Woman;* it has been translated into French and German. Although Shani Mootoo shares with these authors a common racialization as "Indian" in Canada, she has sometimes complained about this simplification of her origins and insisted on claiming her Indo-Caribbean background, questioning (white) curators's/publishers's obsession with marketing her racial and sexual identities (see, for example, her interview with Sarindar Dhaliwal).

16. *The Hero's Walk* was also chosen *The Washington Post* Best Book of 2001.

17. A quick visit to the South Asian Women's Net's (www.sawnet.org) Bookshelf section, specializing in works by South Asian women, provides plenty of examples. See also the book covers of the different editions and translations of Badami's and Baldwin's texts on their own websites:
http://www.anitaraubadami.ca and http://www.shaunasinghbaldwin.com.
It is also interesting to notice that this is not the case with most small presses in Canada: Yasmin Ladha's and Rachna Mara's books, published by NeWest, TSAR, and Second Story Press do not use the obvious woman-in-sari image.

18. Guy Beauregard has analyzed this marketing strategy in reference to Japanese Canadian women's fiction: "feminize and racialize the author to make her a suitable object of consumption" (191). Miriam Tey, chief editor of the Spanish imprint "Étnicos del Bronce" (now "Étnicos del Cobre") offers a telling comment about publishers' marketing strategies: "If an author is alive, he [sic] is the one who can tell more about his [sic] book and what works best is personal interviews. Most especially if the author is a beautiful, transgressive, perverse or lewd woman" (in Memba; my translation).

19. Shani Mootoo shows her awareness of this pressure on the feminist writer by having a female character reflecting on it in the story "Out on Main Street," in a scene set in an Indian restaurant in Vancouver: "Whoever does he [the owner] think he is! Calling me dear and touching me like that! Why do these men always think that they have permission to touch whatever and whenever they want! And you can't make a fuss about it in public, because that is exactly what those people out there want to hear about so that

they can say how sexist and uncivilized our culture is" (55).

20. Diaspora Studies have received a significant impulse in recent years with the creation of reference works such as the *Encyclopedia of Diasporas* edited by M Ember, CR Ember, and I Skoggard, the consolidation of old and new journals, conferences, workshops, etc.

21. Antonia Navarro-Tejero contends that "[m]ost expatriate writers have a weak grasp of actual conditions in contemporary India, and tend to recreate it through the lens of nostalgia, writing about 'imaginary homelands.' Alongside this, there is a considerable amount of work, which is aimed at the western audience and engages primarily with western theory written both by the expatriate and the stay at home writer. This is of varying degree, equality and authenticity, it is conflictual, experimental and also at times selectively exotic. Distancing lends objectivity, but it can also lead to the ossification of cultural constructs, and even if memory is sharp and clear, the expatriate is not directly in contact with the reality of India" (17). For an example of critical hostility within India see, for instance, Rajeshwar Mittapalli's "Global Temptations and Local Loyalties" (2004).

22. In her analysis of Asian-Indian writing in Canada, Malashri Lal concludes that "the Indo-Canadian women poets are particularly emphatic about their female identity in the new spaces of their adopted land" (64). We can make this conclusion extensive to Indo-Canadian fiction writers too. Roger Bromley defines diasporic fiction as writing by and about the excluded, and hence women's texts are more abundant and characteristic: "That the narratives are mainly produced by women is not surprising at this juncture, as the 'worlds' they are challenging are almost exclusively male dominated and designed primarily for fulfilment in terms of the human as envisaged by men occupying positions of power; the women are doubly exiled" (4). Notwithstanding, we will also look at the special attention paid to the construction of masculinity in Baldwin's *English Lessons,* Mootoo's *Cereus Blooms at Night,* or Gupta's *The Sherpa.*

23. In the story "Devika," set in Canada, Badami records such a transformation in a different male character, Ratan: "'I want to ask Pete Kendall and his wife to dinner next month. We must buy a barbecue for the balcony and by then we will have bought drapes—curtains—and maybe a new dinner set.' He took in her silk salwar kameez but all he said was, 'You need to muy some Canadian clothes, Devika. Try a skirt and blouse—it might suit you" (157).

24. Badami's *The Hero's Walk* and Mootoo's *Cereus Blooms at Night* focus on father-child relationships instead. Baldwin's "Rawalpindi 1919" and "A Pair or Ears" deal with the conflicts between mother and son.

25. The bibliography on the symbolic use of women's bodies in nationalist discourses and its effects on legislation and social customs is extensive. This is a key fundament of rape as a war instrument, as will be argued below. See, for instance, Anthias and Yuval-Davis, Giles and Hyndman, Layoun, West, or Yuval-Davis.

26. Although these patriarchists would like to think Indian women talk back only if they are influenced by white women's ways, thus attempting to preserve their power over women in the name of cultural tradition, there are in these narratives a number of Indian female rebels with acid tongues who have no contact with Western feminists, like

Saroja of the tamarind tongue, in *Tamarind Mem*, Asha in *Of Customs and Excise*, and Satya in *What the Body Remembers*, figures who continue a long-lasting tradition of Indian feminism (see Narayan 1997).

27. A similar distrust of Americans and preference for the British is expressed in Baldwin's story "Simran," where a mother is relieved her daughter "had not caught an American accent. I have always tried to teach my pupils to speak the Queen's English" (36). This woman has introduced her daughter "to great literature: Sir Walter Scott, Lord Tennyson, Oscar Wilde, Jane Austen, the Brontës and Charles Dickens. But now I felt shut out as I looked at the titles she was reading—all American sidewalk psychology and all this American liberty theory that only America with all its land and so few people can afford" (44).

28. There are plenty of examples in the short stories here commented of old women (mostly mothers and mothers-in-law) that fulfil this indoctrinating function and act as role models of proper feminine behaviour.

29. Other interracial couples appear in "Lisa," "English Lessons," and "Jassie." In all cases, there is a profound cultural misunderstanding between the white and Indian characters. On the contrary, in Rachna Mara's *Of Customs and Excise* the interracial couple formed by Mala and Jake appears as an almost idyllic one, Jake being everything Mala's father is not: understanding, supportive, good-humoured, and a caring father to their little Nina. In Mootoo's *Cereus Blooms at Night* Lavinia and Sarah's love transgresses both racial and sexual normative restrictions; although their running away together brings catastrophic consequences to Mala and Asha, their relationship is depicted as a fulfilling one.

30. Baldwin, Mootoo, and Gupta extend their scope to include innovative constructions of masculinity, heterosexual in Baldwin's works, and homosexual and/or transexual in Gupta's and Mootoo's. In Baldwin' story "The Insult," the husband newly arrived from India does not correspond to the prototype of the traditionalist Sikh man that feels superior to women discussed above, since he rejoices when his baby daughter is born: "It was a girl, and there were telegrams and letters of sympathy from relatives. 'Don't worry. By the Guru's grace, it will be a boy next time.' My husband threw the letters from him with surprising force, and he was gentle with the little one, singing her to sleep with a lori and, once in a while, a Simon and Garfunkel song" (139). The reference to the Simon and Garfunkel song may be interpreted as a sign of cultural contamination; this Sikh man is becoming "Americanized," and as in the case of the young women analyzed above, this may imply a revision of the gender codes of behaviour. Although in the story it is not explicitly associated to his lack of hair, a Sikh sign of masculinity, it can be read as an important symbol of the "feminization" of the new masculinities in their acceptance of a more nourishing parenting, as is also the case of Jake, Mala's husband, mentioned before.

31. A most interesting strategy employed by contemporary racialized lesbian writers in Canada to contest this novice trope of the motherland is the metamorphosis of the body, which I have analyzed in terms of resistance to national, racial, gender, and sexual categorizations in "Metaphors of the (M)Otherland" (2009). Among them, Shani

Mootoo provides us in *Cereus Blooms at Night* with a brilliant cast of transvestite, transsexual gay and lesbian characters that escape entrapment into any hetero-normative catalogue.

32. One more example of the anticolonialist discourse in the novel, as commented in the section on racism, that points out a finger at the West's representations of the Other as violent savages.

33. As mentioned above, the whole collection abounds in references to the torture of Sikhs along history. In the story "Simran," Amrit reminds us of the killings of the Sikh Gurus by Moghul rulers, the massacres at the hands of Muslims during the Partition war of 1947, and "the sight of Sikh women, raped and disgraced by Muslims" (37). For a detailed analysis of the trope of war rape in this story see Beerendra Pandey's essay "A Paradigm Shift in the Representation of Violence in Partition Short Stories by Women."

34. The embedded quote is from Susan Brownmiller's "Making Female Bodies the Battlefield."

35. Incest narratives always stir much debate and strong opposition within one's own cultural group, since they expose to the light secret transgressions that profoundly disturb well-established ideas of "normalcy" and of the family as a safe, nurturing group that is the founding pillar of our societies. The debate over "false memories" has polarized the discussion even more. See, for instance, the Recovered Memory Project website: http://www.brown.edu/Departments/Taubman_Center/Recovmem/, Shelley Park's "False Memory Syndrome: A Feminist Philosophical Approach" (1997), or Sue Campbell's "Women, 'False' Memory, and Personal Identity" (1997).

36. See Jodi Lundgren's "Writing 'in Sparkler Script': Incest and the Construction of Subjectivity in Contemporary Canadian Women's Autobiographical Texts" (1998).

37. Shazia Rahman offers in "Mingling Margins" a detailed analysis of colonialism in these short stories, especially embodied in the figure of the Black servant Juma (meaning Friday), whom she fruitfully compares to the colonized Friday and Caliban in Defoe's and Shakespeare's works.

38. See also the extensive sociological studies by Helen Ralston (1999), Vijay Agnew (2003), and Amita Handa (2003). Similar experiences are told by several mixed-race writers in Anne Marie Nakagawa's film *Between: Living in the Hyphen* (2006).

39. For a detailed and acute analysis of food in the construction of palatable ethnic difference see Anita Mannur's *Culinary Fictions: Food in South Asian Diasporic Culture*; discussing divergent versions of "culinary citizenship" Mannur studies, among others, Shani Mootoo's story "Out on Main Street" and *Cereus Blooms at Night*.

40. Amita Handa also expresses her disagreement with these extreme dichotomies: *"Why is it that every time I begin to speak about the tensions of home, I become a part of a backward, repressed, outdated culture? Why is it that every time I turn my attention to the issue of racism, I have to construct home as a mythical and infallible place? This is where I am caught: not between two cultures, but between omissions, between fragments of myself"* (3; italics in the original).

41. Academic circles in Canada understood the term "ethnic" as referring to the immigrant peoples of European descent, and neglected for a long time the experience of Asian

Canadians, among others, probably as part of the colour-blind multicultural politics of the 1970s and 1980s (Goellnicht 24).

42. Goellnicht quotes Richard Fung in his critique of multiculturalism: "Multiculturalism shifts the focus away from the political and social questions of race such as housing, employment, education, access to power, into a political marketing of personal identity. It champions a notion of cultural difference in which people are encouraged to preserve cultural forms of song and dance they didn't practice before they came to Canada" (9). Roy Miki considers multiculturalism, however, as one more step towards the negative construction of Asian Canadians as the "Other": "However imagined, the existence of 'Asian' in 'Canadian' has always been a disturbance—a disarticulation that had to be managed, first as the 'asiatic', as the 'oriental', then as a sign of the 'multicultural', as the 'visible minority', to sustain the figure of the 'citizen' as the 'end' of assimilation—rather than a subject position vested with privileged differences based on racialization (white), ethnicity (anglo/European), sexual orientation (hetero) and gender (male)" (56). In a still more recent study, Eleanor Ty and Donald Goellnicht subscribe David Palumbo-Liu's conviction that Asian American identities are more than ever going through a process: "The twenty-first century will undoubtedly present yet another set of manifestations that press the particularity of race against the universalities of the modern state. The subjectivities produced within such a context will, no doubt, continue to try borders and revise interiors, and in so doing leave a particular impress upon history" (in Ty and Goellnicht 2004, 9).

43. For an enlightening analysis on the empowering nature of the anthology for Chinese Canadian writers, see Chao's "Anthologizing the Collective: The Epic Struggles to Establish Chinese Canadian Literature in English" (1999). Chao stresses the importance of this format in the conformation of a collective self, especially in the case of the Chinese Canadian community. For a comprehensive scope of these efforts, see Daniel Coleman and Donald Goellnicht's Introduction to a special issue of *Essays on Canadian Writing* 75 (2002) dedicated to the question of race in contemporary Canadian writers of colour.

44. In the case of the three writers under analysis, only Lydia Kwa makes a clear effort to include Chinese characters and vocabulary, perhaps due to the fact that Chinese is her native tongue, while others, like Larissa Lai, cannot speak the language.

45. For enlightening introductions to the topic, see Chao's essay "Constituting Minority Canadian Women" as well as Chapter 1 from *Beyond Silence: Chinese Canadian Literature in English* (1997), "Rereading Chinese Canadian History" (1–16).

46. As mentioned above, a long string of memoirs covers this odd hundred years of Chinese immigration to Canada. Among them we could mention Wayson Choy's *Paper Shadows* (1999), which contains remarkable echoes of his former novel, *The Jade Peony*, and it is based on Choy's discovery of his origin as an adopted child, and Denise Chong's *The Concubine's Children* (1994).

47. For an insightful analysis on the topic of Chinatown communities in Fong Bates's short-story collection, see Cuder-Domínguez (2000).

48. Sky Lee acknowledges doing so in her second work, the short-story collection

Bellydancer (1995), in an interview with C Allyson Lee: ". . . I'm trying to do some very interesting things. I'm trying to look at what I call use of language and I think people like us who have been literally culturally marooned have a specific kind of language. And I'd like to enhance that because it's part of our reality" (394).

49. Lau's distress is a common trait in the writing of other Chinese Canadian women like Judy Fong Bates. Some of the protagonists in *China Dog and Other Tales from a Chinese Laundry* (1997) and *Midnight at the Dragon Café* (2004) speak about the uneasiness that their parents' wishes provoke in them.

50. The book's title reads as a sort of autobiography, and transmits the idea of movement in different senses, for example, in reference to the time when Lau suffered from bulimia, or in relation to her choice of the genre of fictional autobiography.

51. Lai chooses the Greek term *pallas* as an echo of the Greek goddess *Pallas Atenea*, and in due reference to the Nike company, whose translation into English is "victory."

52. Salman Rushdie declares in *Imaginary Homelands* the need for the diasporic subject to construct the image of home by way of imagination: the Indias of the mind, as he did when writing his novel *Midnight's Children* (10).

53. Wong also claims that this analysis of female roles could be extended to Lau's treatment of ethnicity, as we will see below.

54. Along these lines, Rita Wong also points out a contradiction in terms in Lau's imaginary, when she refers to her representation of family and community relations: "While collective spaces where one is loved or at least safe—be they a family, a writing community, an ethnic community, or some other configuration—are only imagined and do not exist in immutable, reliable forms in that they are always subject to internal or external forces that threaten them, the rejection of these humanly constructed spaces has interesting consequences" (136). As the critic aptly interprets, this is probably the other axis that should be taken into account to fully understand one of the constants in Lau's fiction: the desperate search for connection and a sense of belonging in the face of a rejection of traditional and conventional relations.

55. See Hodgson-Blackburn's article for a reading of surrogate motherhood in *Other Women* as the result of the search for female bonds in the face of maternal loss.

56. This is a recurrent narrative strategy in Lau's fiction, the way in which she creates "disembodied" characters—women like Fiona in her short novel, who easily turns from the subject to the object position (in her love relationship, in her self-perception) (Sturgess 86).

57. In reading Lau's fiction, one cannot help but adopting Judith Fetterley's perspective about the active role of the woman reader, who must dissociate herself from the world that the literary text represents. That is, according to Fetterley, the political purpose of literature: "To expose and question that complex of ideas and mythologies about women and men which exist in our society and are confirmed in our literature is to make the system of power embodied in the literature open not only to discussion but even to change" (xx).

58. Charlotte Sturgess refers to "asiancy" initially as the "traditional Chinese background" (77) which is considered as "proper" and desirable, especially for the sons and

daughters of Chinese immigrants. In addition, the concept implies the commitment of "the community as a whole." In *Broken Entries*, Roy Miki endows the term with the notion of agency; in his related article, he asks for the need of empowerment of minority writers of colour, and particularly Asian Canadian writers. The critic denounces that in many cases they are still *spoken for*. He uses Deleuze and Guattari's terminology, "deterritorialization," to describe "the baffled textual screen characteristic of minority writing in its interface with dominant society" (117).

59. The wearing of the smoks in *When Fox is a Thousand* can also be counted on as a case of cross-dressing, and therefore the whole episode can be read as an instance of ethnic "crossing." Lydia Kwa also works with images of cross-dressing and drag, assessing them as empowering strategies in *The Walking Boy*.

60. Miranda's mother will die very soon. Her early state of orphanhood resembles Artemis's lack of a substantial mother figure in *When Fox is a Thousand*. By looking at these examples, we observe that girls in Lai's fiction either have to do by themselves or they look for substitute guiding figures like the fox. We cannot speak of the rejection of the mother, as in Lau's writing, but of mother figures whose example is either not followed by the daughter or of no consequence for her.

61. Miranda is pointing here to a new myth of the Canadian nation state. Marginal people like her, affected by the dreaming disease, and most significantly Evie, the cyborg, represent a clear identity shift which is threatening the once neat understanding of the nation. Their characters, as much as Nu Wa's reformulation of original myth, challenge those notions considerably. See Brydon and Schagerl's enlightning essay exploring the topic in depth.

62. This topic will be retaken later in the chapter, as Kwa explores profusely the body in pain in her two novels.

63. Eleanor Ty notes how the motif of suicide links both plots in the novel: Wu Lan's feelings of remorse and guilt for her father's death are partly soothed by her search and recovery of the lives of anonymous *ah ku* like Lee Ah Choi, who ended her life in like manner (*Unfastened* 28).

64. In the essay "An Insatiable Emptiness," included in *Inside Out*, Lau reproduces as well the time in which she was a bulimic, in part to punish her mother: "What my mother didn't know was that I was already beginning to incorporate her inside me. She didn't know that she was winning, and that for the rest of my life I would contain aspects of her . . . Yet afterwards it was still there inside me. After years of vomiting, I had not purged myself of any of the things that were making me sick" (80, 84). Bulimia becomes both a way of cleaning her past, and an attempt to control her life by controlling her body.

65. The analyses of both Lau and Lai's novels benefit from Julia Kristeva's definition of abjection. In general terms, according to Kristeva the abject represents meaninglessness and is essentially primal (2). Moreover, the abject amounts to the unrepresentable, the crossing and instability of boundaries, whether they are those of the body—the corpse, the loss of the self, or of hybridity—the miscegenated body, in the transgression of boundaries it represents, stands for the abject. Quite often, Lau and Lai's representations

of the self reveal the abject: the foul body, the ageing body, the body in pain. Further-more, Lau's interpretation focuses elsewhere on the abjection of the self, based on the idea of "want" and desire "on which being, meaning, language . . . is founded" (Kristeva 5).

66. Donna Haraway's often quoted references to the cyborg may be very enlightening at this point, and in general terms they work as a metaphor of the implications of this figure in Lai's novel: "The main trouble with cyborgs, of course, is that they are the ille-gitimate offspring of militarism and patriarchal capitalism, not to mention state social-ism" (51).

67. Lai's remarkable precedent for the way in which massive pollution and genetic experimentation are responsible for general infertility might be Margaret Atwood's *The Handmaid's Tale* (1985).

68. Lee claims further that Lai's exploration of the "dreaming disease" works as another reminder of the body's capacity for subversion: the treatment of the disease reveals the way capitalism pretends to do away with difference and fragmentation. People with Miranda's condition—there is a whole variety of degrees—are considered patients and are thus studied as pathological cases, in a macabre alliance between capitalism and medical science (Lee 97–98).

69. Miranda shares this initial lack of awareness with Artemis Wong, Lai's heroine in her first novel. As the author herself argued in "Future Asians": "Artemis Wong is a prod-uct of my thinking through what happens to young Asian Canadian women in the absence of a radical community-based identity politics. She has some awareness of colo-nialism and white-privilege, and some awareness of how her body is read within main-stream white society, but she does not really have any useful tools to deal with this knowledge" (168).

70. Nu Wa freely decides to renounce to immortality and assume a human shape. This sexual goddess who reinvents the myth of origins becomes the emblem of transforma-tion.

71. Following Enoch Padolsky's 2000 essay on multiculturalism in Canada, Beaure-gard associates the term to English and French nationalisms (229).

72. Following Althusser, Nguyen describes "model minorities" as "good subjects . . . who 'work by themselves' in the vast majority of cases" (144). Historically speaking, tra-ditional model minorities such as Asian Americans were the repositories of hate and resentment by other minorities who were used to suffer continuous situations of inequity. This idea about the "model minority" is masterfully described in Asian Cana-dian novels like Wayson Choy's *The Jade Peony*. As Rita Wong accurately affirms, the claim for the right to raise their voices and speak by themselves is considered as a breach and a discordant note in their character ("Jumping on Hyphens" 119).

73. Edward Said explored in *Orientalism* (1978) the feminized representations of the Orient in colonial discourses.

74. She contends that, in general terms, people of colour in Canada strive by different means to belong to the nation, in spite of obstacles and hindrances in their way. That sense of belonging does not necessarily mean assimilation.

75. That invariably bears implications for the topics and forms selected in writing. Ty comments in this respect, that authors like Lai belong to a third generation of Asian North American writers who consciously depart from realism and explore the fantastic (2010, 89).

76. Lai is very reluctant to accept the so-called "triumphs" of a multicultural politics that were so much celebrated in the North America of the 1980s, and which resulted in a cover-up technique which in practice only hid conflicts under the carpet.

77. Miranda is also affected by a strange condition—variously called later on in the novel as the "memory disease" or the "dreaming disease"—which in her is manifested as a strange and pungent odour that emanates from her every pore. This condition is said to be the result of her mother eating an extraordinary durian, which upon ingestion prepares the woman's body for conception. The image of the durian as a forbidden fruit, which is reminiscent of Adam and Eve's eating of the apple and their transgression in the Christian tradition, appears recurrently and with different meanings throughout the novel.

78. Their situation is even worse than that of immigrant workers in the novel, since the Sonias are not only hybrid but queer. Moreover, as Wong points out: "Working in domestic spaces, these women are often excluded from the protections to which all citizen-workers should be entitled" ("Troubling Domestic Limits" 121).

79. Moreover, and as Wong claims, "*Salt Fish Girl* is deeply inflected with a sense of history repeating itself, materializing in contemporary forms. The mythical, the historical, and the futuristic conjoin in the novel, making home a multiple time zone, that is, a simultaneity of past and present stories as new immigrants experience hardships comparable to those experienced by members of earlier generations" ("Troubling Domestic Limits" 112).

80. Sturgess tackles the question of identity in Lau and explores how it is connected to her particular use of language: "Female identity as a problem explicitly centred within language and the symbolic relation of 'self' to 'Other' within representation" (77). Language mediates between life (dim, morbid, disgusting most times) and self in Lau's writing. At the same time, language is for her the sign of otherness: her devotion to writing since early childhood was instrumental in her development; this inclination for the written word became in her case the only true means of communication, as well as the trait of her character that made her different, an "other."

81. One might wonder to what an extent her writing a bestseller and her decision to reveal scandalous material about her life affect the status of the autobiographical voice and the political function of the literary form.

82. The case was profusely publicized in newspapers and magazines. See, for example, *The Globe and Mail* (Toronto, March 4, 1998) and *Maclean's* (March 16, 1998).

83. Language is variously described as the tool to conceal, as in alchemical texts containing the formula of Jin Dan elixir (142).

84. For further information on the (mis)fortunes of the Japanese Canadian community in the first half of the twentieth century, see Ken Adachi, *The Enemy that Never Was* (1976).

85. Both *Chorus of Mushrooms* and *The Electrical Field* won the Commonwealth Writers Prize for Best First Book and the Canada-Japan Literary Award.

86. To the best of our knowledge, only Kerri Sakamoto's *The Electrical Field* has been translated into several languages: Japanese, Dutch, German, French, and Czech. None of these other writers' works are currently available in widely-spoken languages like French or Spanish.

87. On the significance of *Obasan*, particularly in relation to the construction of Asian Canadian/American literary criticism, see Guy Beauregard's "After *Obasan*: Kogawa Criticism and Its Futures" (2001); in relation to the construction of Japanese Canadian identity, see Marlene Goldman's "A Dangerous Circuit: Loss and the Boundaries of Racialized Identity in Joy Kogawa's *Obasan* and Kerri Sakamoto's *The Electrical Field*" (2002).

88. See Introduction for further comment on the development of this academic field of research.

89. The term "Sansei" refers to the third generation of citizens of Japanese ancestry; "Nisei" to the second, and "Issei" to the first.

90. This chapter only covers adult fiction, even though, like other Japanese Canadian writers, Hiromi Goto has successfully written fiction for young readers. On the subject of fiction for children from the Japonese Canadian perspective, see Teresa Gibert's article "Representing War Trauma in Children's Fiction: *A Child in Prison Camp* and *Naomi's Road*" (2007).

91. The term "Nikkei" refers to diasporan or foreign-born Japanese.

92. See below for the politics of homosexual relations in Japanese Canadian women's writing.

93. The unreliability of Ishiguro's narrators has attracted much critical attention over the years. See, for instance, Kathleen Wall's "*The Remains of the Day* and Its Challenges to Theories of Unreliable Narration" (1994), and Molly Westermann's "Is the Butler Home? Narrative and the Split Subject in *The Remains of the Day*" (2004).

94. Once more, this has been read by critics as "talking back" to *Obasan*, where "female sexuality is repressed, unspoken, and troubled" (Ty, *Politics* 161).

95. This subject will be further examined below.

96. See below for Goto's use of myth as a stylistic feature.

97. Latimer has pointed out further connections between food and self-hatred in this novel, particularly in the way that memories of food and eating are juxtaposed with incidents of violence and racism (http://www.thirdspace.ca/journal/article/view/latimer/129 10/10/2009).

98. Goto has discussed these aspects and given examples, including this particular story, in her essay "Alien Texts, Alien Seductions: The Context of Colour Full Writing" (1998).

99. Kobayashi's first publication, *All Names Spoken* (1992), was written in collaboration with Mona Oikawa.

100. On this subject, see Belén Martín-Lucas, *Género literario, género femenino: veinte años del ciclo de cuentos en Canadá* (1999). On the use of this form by Asian Canadians, see Rocío Davis, *Transcultural Reinventions* (2001).

101. *Obasan* criticism is overwhelmingly large. For a comprehensive account of critical approaches to the novel, see Guy Beauregard, "After *Obasan*: Kogawa Criticism and Its Futures" (2001).

102. On this topic, see in particular Chapter 12 of *Itsuka*.

103. Visvis does not explicitly mention how the fact that the plot is set in the 1970s, that is, prior to the success of the Redress Movement, fits into this reading.

104. For more on the subject of Asako and Eiji's relationship, see Stone, "Internalized Racism."

105. Stum is technically still a Nisei like his sister, but it is true that he is closer to the Sansei because he has no conscious knowledge of wartime experiences.

106. For a comparative North American perspective on this subject, see Pilar Cuder-Domínguez's essay "Facing Japan: Homelands, Affiliations, and Gendered Identities in North American Nikkei Writers" (2009).

107. See Libin's "Lost in Translation" for an insight into how a white reader may cope with the untranslated Japanese sections in Goto's novel, as well as for how this affects classroom politics.

108. Yoshio Iwamoto has pointed out the "ample science fiction elements" in "*The Kappa Child*" (102).

109. The location suggests the notion of space travel, and therefore highlights the science fiction ties of the tale. It is noteworthy too, that the narrator's mother later claims to have been an alien abductee for many years.

WORKS CITED

Adachi, Ken. *The Enemy that Never Was: A History of the Japanese Canadians.* Toronto: McClelland & Stewart, 1976.

Agnew, Vijay. "Gender, Home, and Nation: A Century of Writings by South Asián Women in Canada." Research Report. Toronto: Centre for Feminist Research, York University, 2003. http://www.yorku.ca/gmcr/full_text_bibs/South%20Asian%20 Bibliography.pdf. 03/03/2008.

Almeida, Sandra RG. "Strangers in the Night: Hiromi Goto's Abject Bodies and Hopeful Monsters." *Contemporary Women's Writing* 3.1 (2009): 47–63.

Amoko, Apollo O. "Resilient ImagiNations: *No-No Boy, Obasan* and the Limits of Minority Discourse." *Mosaic* 33.3 (2000): 35–55.

Anthias, Floya and Nira Yuval-Davis. *Racialized Boundaries.* London and New York: Routledge, 1992.

Badami, Anita Rau. *Tamarind Mem.* Toronto: Penguin, 1996.

———. *The Hero's Walk.* Toronto: Vintage, 2000.

———. *Can You Hear the Nightbird Call?* Toronto: Knopf, 2006.

Baldwin, Shauna Singh. *English Lessons and Other Stories.* New Delhi: HarperCollins, 1996.

———. *What the Body Remembers.* Toronto: Vintage Canada, 2000.

———. *The Tiger Claw.* Toronto: Vintage Canada, 2005.

———. *We Are Not in Pakistan.* Fredericton: Goose Lane, 2007.

Beauregard, Guy. "Hiromi Goto's Chorus of Mushrooms and the Politics of Writing Diaspora." *West Coast Line* 18 (29/3) (1995–96): 47–62.

———. "The Emergence of 'Asian Canadian Literature': Can Lit's Obscene Supplement?" *Essays on Canadian Writing* 67 (1999): 53–75.

———. "Unsettled, Unsettling". Review of Kerri Sakamoto's *The Electrical Field. Canadian Literature* 163 (1999): 191–93.

———. "After *Obasan:* Kogawa Criticism and Its Futures." *Studies in Canadian Literature* 26.2 (2001): 5–22.

———. "What is at Stake in Comparative Analyses of Asian Canadian and Asian American Literary Studies?" *Essays on Canadian Writing* 75 (2002): 217–39.

Beeler, Karin. "Visual Texts, Textual Visions: Hypertext, Resistance, and Contemporary Asian-Canadian Writing." *Canadian Review of Contemporary Literature* 27.1–2

(2000): 181–96.

Begamudré, Ven. *Extended Families*. Toronto: Viking/Penguin, 1997.

Bernier, Lucie, ed. *Aspects of Diaspora: Studies in North American Chinese Writers*. Bern: Peter Lang, 2000.

Braidotti, Rosi. *Metamorphoses: Towards a Materialist Theory of Becoming*. Cambridge: Polity, 2002.

Bringas-López, Ana, and Belén Martín-Lucas, eds. *Reading Multiculturalism: Contemporary Postcolonial Literatures*. Vigo: Universidade de Vigo, 2000.

Bromley, Roger. *Narratives for a New Belonging: Diasporic Cultural Fictions*. Edinburgh: Edinburg University Press, 2000.

Brouillette, Sarah. "South Asian Literature and Global Publishing." *Wasafiri* 22.3 (2007): 34–38.

Brownmiller, Susan. "Making Female Bodies the Battlefield." *Newsweek* 4 Jan 1993, 37.

Brydon, Diana, and Jessica Schagerl. "Empire Girls and Global Girls: A Dialogue on Spaces of Community in the Twentieth Century." Kanagayakam 27–45.

Campbell, Sue. "Women, 'False' Memory, and Personal Identity". *Hypatia* 12.2 (1997): 51–83.

Chao, Lien. "Constituting Minority Canadian Women and Our Sub-Cultures: Female Characters in Selected Chinese Canadian Literature." *Silvera* 333–54.

———. "Anthologizing the Collective: The Epic Struggles to Establish Chinese Canadian Literature in English." *Essays on Canadian Writing* 57 (1995): 145–70.

———. *Beyond Silence: Chinese Canadian Literature in English*. Toronto: TSAR Publications, 1997.

Chariandy, David. Review of Dionne Brand's *What We All Long For*. *New Dawn* 1.1 (2006): 103–109.

Cheung, King-Kok. "Of Men and Men: Reconstructing Chinese American Masculinity." *Other Sisterhoods: Literary Theory and US Women of Color*. Ed. Sandra Kumamoto Stanley. Urbana: University of Illinois Press, 1998. 173–99.

Cho, Lily. "Diasporic Citizenship: Contradictions and Possibilities for Canadian Literature." *Trans.Can.Lit: Resituating the Study of Canadian Literature*. Ed. Smaro Kamboureli and Roy Miki. Waterloo: Wilfrid Laurier University Press, 2007. 93–109.

Chua, Cheng Lok. "Witnessing the Japanese Canadian Experience in World War II: Processual Structure, Symbolism, and Irony in Joy Kogawa's *Obasan*." *Reading the Literatures of Asian America*. Ed. Shirley Gek-lin Lim and Amy Ling. Philadelphia: Temple University Press, 1992. 97–108.

Coleman, Daniel, and Donald Goellnicht. "Introduction: 'Race' into the Twenty-First Century." *Essays on Canadian Writing* 75 (2002): 1–29.

Condé, Mary. "An Interview with Evelyn Lau." *Etudes Canadiennes/Canadian Studies* 38 (1995): 105–11.

Cuder-Domínguez, Pilar. "The Laundry and the Restaurant: Judy Fong Bates' Stories of

Chinese Canadian Community." Bringas-López and Martín-Lucas 117–23.

———. "Surviving History: Kerri Sakamoto Interviewed by Pilar Cuder-Domínguez." *Journal of Commonwealth Literature* 41.3 (2006): 137–43.

———. "The Politics of Gender and Genre in Asian Canadian Women's Speculative Fiction: Hiromi Goto and Larissa Lai." *Asian Canadian Literature Beyond Autoethnography.* Ed. Eleanor Ty and Christl Verduyn. Waterloo: Wilfrid Laurier University Press, 2008. 115–31.

———. "Facing Japan: Homelands, Affiliations, and Gendered Identities in North American Nikkei Writers." *The Dialectics of Diasporic Identification.* Ed. Mar Gallego Durán and Isabel Soto. Valencia: PUV, 2009. 89–104.

———. "Nation, Narration, and the Abject Self in Japanese Canadian Women Writers." *Her Na-rra-tion: Women's Narratives of the Canadian Nation.* Ed. Françoise Lejeune and Charlotte Sturgess. Nantes: CEC-CRINI et Université de Nantes, 2009. 171–80.

Darias Beautell, Eva. "Hiromi Goto's *Chorus of Mushrooms:* Cultural Difference, Visibility, and the Canadian Tradition." *Revista Alicantina de Estudios Ingleses* 16 (2003): 6–50.

Davis, Rocío G. *Transcultural Reinventions: Asian American and Asian Canadian Short Story Cycles.* Toronto: TSAR Publications, 2001.

Deer, Glenn. "Editorial." *Canadian Literature* 163 (1999): 5–15.

Dhaliwal, Sarindar. "Shani Mootoo. Shifting Perceptions, Changing Practices. Interview." *Fuse* 22.2 (1999): 18–25.

Dhruvarajan, Vanaja. "People of Colour and National Identity in Canada." *Journal of Canadian Studies* 35.2 (2000): 166–75.

Downes, Gwladys. "Contrasts in Psychic Space." *in the feminine. women and words/les femmes et les mots.* Ed. Anna Dybikowski et al. Edmonton: Longspoon, 1985. 117–121.

Fetterley, Judith. *The Resisting Reader: A Feminist Approach to American Fiction.* Bloomington: Indiana University Press, 1977.

Fu, Bennett Yu-Hsiang. "Meta-Morphing T'ien Hu: Sexual Transgression and Textual Transposition in *When Fox is a Thousand.*" *West Coast Line* 44 (2004): 147–63.

Ghatage, Shree. *Awake When All the World is Asleep.* Toronto: House of Anansi Press, 1997.

———. *Brahma's Dream.* Toronto: Doubleday Canada, 2004.

Gibert, Teresa. "Representing War Trauma in Children's Fiction: *A Child in Prison Camp* and *Naomi's Road.*" *Stories for Children, Histories of Childhood.* Ed. Rosie Findlay and Sebastien Salbayre. Tours: Presses Universitaires Francois Rabelais, 2007. 267–83.

Giles, Wenona, and Jennifer Hyndman, Eds. *Sites of Violence: Gender and Conflict Zones.* Berkeley and Los Angeles: University of California Press, 2004.

Gilmore, Leigh. *The Limits of Autobiography: Trauma and Testimony.* Ithaca, NY: Cornell University Press, 2001.

Goellnicht, Donald C. "A Long Labour: The Protracted Birth of Asian Canadian Literature." *Essays on Canadian Writing* 72 (2000): 1–41.

Goldman, Marlene. "A Dangerous Circuit: Loss and the Boundaries of Racialized Identity in Joy Kogawa's *Obasan* and Kerri Sakamoto's *The Electrical Field*." *Modern Fiction Studies* 48.2 (2002): 362–88.

Gonick, Marnina. "Canadian=Blonde, English, White: Theorizing Race, Language and Nation." *Atlantis* 24.2 (2000): 93–104.

Goossen, Theodore. "Writing the Pacific War in the Twenty-First Century: Dennis Bock, Rui Umezawa, and Kerri Sakamoto." *Canadian Literature* 179 (2003): 56–69.

Goto, Hiromi. *Chorus of Mushrooms*. Edmonton: NeWest, 1994.

———. "Alien Texts, Alien Seductions: The Context of Colour Full Writing." *Literary Pluralities*. Ed. Christl Verduyn. Peterborough: Broadview, 1998. 263–69.

———. *The Kappa Child*. Calgary: Red Deer Press, 2001.

———. *Hopeful Monsters*. Vancouver: Arsenal Pulp Press, 2004.

Gunew, Sneja, and Anna Yeatman, eds. *Feminism and the Politics of Difference*. Boulder and San Francisco: Westview Press, 1993.

Gunew, Sneja. "Operatic Karaoke and the Pitfalls of Identity Politics." Verduyn 254–62.

Gupta, Nila. *The Sherpa and Other Fictions*. Toronto: Sumach Press, 2008.

Handa, Amita. *Of Silk Saris and Mini-Skirts" South Asian Girls Walk the Tightrope of Culture*. Toronto: Women's Press, 2003.

Haraway, Donna J. "A Manifesto for Cyborgs: Science, Technology, and Socialist Feminism in the 1980s." Kirkup, Janes, Woodward, and Horenden 50–57.

Härting, Heike. "Diasporic Cross-Currents in Michael Ondaatje's *Anil's Ghost* and Anita Rau Badami's The Hero's Walk." *SCL/ÉLC*. 28.1 (2003): 43–70.

Hilf, Susanne. *Writing the Hyphen: The Articulation of Interculturalism in Contemporary Chinese-Canadian Literature*. Frankfurt am Main: Peter Lang, 2000.

Hodgson-Blackburn, Jacqueline. "Indigestible Secrets: Female Melancholia in the Work of Evelyn Lau." http://extra.shu.ac.uk/wpw/femprac/blackburn.htm. 23/11/2004

Howells, Coral Ann. *Contemporary Canadian Women's Fiction: Refiguring Identities*. London: Palgrave, 2003.

Huggan, Graham. *The Post-colonial Exotic: Marketing the Margins*. London and New York: Routledge, 2001.

Irigaray, Luce. *This Sex Which Is Not One*. Trans. Catherine Porter. Ithaca: Cornell University Press, 1985.

Ito, Sally. "Issues for the Writer of Colour." Special issue "Colour: An Issue." *West Coast Line* 13/14 (1994): 172–78.

———. *Floating Shore*. Toronto: Mercury Press, 1998.

Iwama, Marilyn. "Transgressive Sexualities in the Reconstruction of Japanese Canadian Communities." *Canadian Literature* 159 (1998): 91–110.

Iwamoto, Yoshio. "The Kappa Child." *World Literature Today* 77.1 (2003): 102.

Kamboureli, Smaro. *Scandalous Bodies: Diasporic Literature in English Canada*. Don

Mills, ON: Oxford University Press, 2000.

Kanagayakam, Chelva, ed. *Moveable Margins: The Shifting Spaces of Canadian Literature.* Toronto: TSAR Publications, 2005.

Karmali, Sikeena. *A House by the Sea.* Montreal: Véhicule Press, 2004.

Kearns, Emily. "Indian Myth." *The Feminist Companion to Mythology.* Ed. Carolyne Larrington. London: Pandora, 1992. 189–226.

Kelley, Paul. "Out of Bounds." Special issue "Colour: An Issue." *West Coast Line* 13/14 (1994): 179–87.

Khajatt, Didi. "The Boundaries of Identity and the Intersection of Race, Class, and Gender." *Canadian Woman Studies/Les cahiers de la femme* 14.2 (1994): 6–12.

Kirkup, Gill, Linda Janes, Kath Woodward, and Fiona Horenden, eds. *The Gendered Cyborg: A Reader.* London: Routledge, 2000.

Kobayashi, Tamai. *Exile and the Heart.* Toronto: Women's Press, 1998.

Kogawa, Joy. *Obasan.* Toronto: Penguin, 1981.

———. *Itsuka.* New York: Doubleday, 1992.

Kwa, Lydia. *This Place Called Absence.* Manitoba: Turnstone Press, 2000.

———. *The Walking Boy.* Toronto: Key Porter Books, 2005.

———. "The Walking Boy." www.lydiakwa.com/books.html. 22/11/2006.

Kwa, Lydia, Fionna Cheong, and Shirley Geok-lin. "Singapore of My Mind." *The Women's Review of Books* 19.10-11 (2002): 24–25.

Kristeva, Julia. *Powers of Horror: An Essay on Abjection.* New York: Columbia University Press, 1982.

Ladha, Yasmin. *Women Dancing on Rooftops: Bring your Belly Close.* Toronto: Coach House Press, 1997.

Ladha, Yasmin. *Lion's Granddaughter and Other Stories.* Edmonton: NeWest Press, 1992.

Lai, Larissa. *When Fox is a Thousand.* Vancouver: Press Gang, 1995.

———. "Political Animals and the Body of History." *Canadian Literature* 163 (1999): 145–54.

———. "Corrupted Lineage: Narrative in the Gaps of History". *In-Equations: can asia pacific.* Ed. Glen Lowry and Sook C Kong. West Coast Line 33 (34/3) (2001): 40–53.

———. *Salt Fish Girl.* Toronto: Thomas Allen, 2002.

———. "Future Asians: Migrant Speculations, Repressed History and Cyborg Hope." *West Coast Line* 44 (2004): 168–75.

———. "Interview with Tamai Kobayashi." http://www.eciad.bc.ca/~amathur/writers/tamai-int.html. 01/03/2007.

Lal, Malashri. "Politics of Self-Definition: Mapping Asian-Indians in Canada". *Mapping Canadian Cultural Space: Essays on Canadian Literature.* Ed. Danielle Schaub. Jerusalem: The Hebrew University Magnes Press, 2000. 54–70.

Latimer, Heather. "Eating, Abjection, and Transformation in the Work of Hiromi Goto." *Third Space* 5.2 (2006). http://www.thirdspace.ca/journal/article/view/latimer/129.

10/10/2009.

Lau, Evelyn. *Fresh Girls and Other Stories.* Toronto: HarperCollins Canada, 1993.

———. *Other Women.* London: Minerva, 1995.

———. *Inside Out:* Reflections on a Life So Far. Toronto: Anchor, 2001.

Layoun, Mary N. *Wedded to the Land? Gender, Boundaries and Nationalism in Crisis.* Durham and London: Duke University Press, 2001.

Lee, C Allyson. "Is There a Mind without Media Any More?: Sky Lee Talks to C Allyson Lee." *Silvera* 382–403.

Lee, Tara. "Mutant Bodies in Larissa Lai's Salt Fish Girl: Changing the Alliance Between Science and Capital." *West Coast Line* 44 (2004): 94–109.

Libin, Mark. "Lost in Translation: Hiromi Goto's Chorus of Mushrooms." *Canadian Literature* 163 (1999): 121–40.

———. "Some of My Best Friends . . .': Befriending the Racialized Fiction of Hiromi Goto." *Essays on Canadian Writing* 73 (2001): 93–121.

Lim, Shirley Geok-lin. "Feminist and Ethnic Literary Theories in Asian American Literature." *Feminist Studies* 19.3 (1993): 70–75.

Lundgren, Jodi. "Writing 'in Sparkler Script': Incest and the Construction of Subjectivity in Contemporary Canadian Women's Autobiographical Texts." *Essays on Canadian Writing* 65 (1998): 233–247.

Lynch, Gerald. *The One and the Many: English-Canadian Short Story Cycles.* Toronto: University of Toronto Press, 2001.

McAllister, Kirsten Emiko. "Held Captive: The Postcard and the Internment Camp." *West Coast Line* 34 (35.1) (2001): 20–40.

McCullough, Steve. "'Trust Me': Responding to the Threat of Writing in Chorus of Mushrooms." *English Studies in Canada* 29.1–2 (2003): 149–70.

McGifford, Diane. "Introduction." *The Geography of Voice: Canadian Literature of the South Asian Diaspora.* Ed. Diane McGifford. Toronto: TSAR Publications, 1992. vii–xviii.

McGoogan, Kenneth. "Cross-Country Check-Up (Calgary Herald)." *Books in Canada* 21.1 (February 1992): 11–12.

Maclear, Kyo. "Diss-Orient-ation." *Fuse* 16.5–6 (1993): 25–27.

Makabe, Tomoko. *The Canadian Sansei.* Toronto: University of Toronto Press, 1998.

Mannur, Anita. *Culinary Fictions: Food in South Asian Diasporic Culture.* Philadelphia: Temple University Press, 2010.

Mansbridge, Joanna. "Abject Origins: Uncanny Strangers and Figures of Fetishism in Larissa Lai's Salt Fish Girl." *West Coast Line* 44 (2004): 121–33.

Mara, Rachna. *Of Customs and Excise.* Toronto: Second Story Press, 1991.

Martín-Lucas, Belén. "Psychic Spaces of Childhood: Jamaican-Canadian Short Story Cycles." *International Journal of Canadian Studies/Revue Internationale d'Etudes Canadiennes. Special Issue on Diaspora and Exile/La diaspora et l'exil.* 18 (1998): 91–109.

———. *Género literario, género femenino: veinte años del ciclo de cuentos en Canadá.* Oviedo: KRK, 1999.

———. "Metaphors of the (M)Other land: The Rhetoric and Grammar of Nationalism." *Her Na-rra-tion: Women's Narratives of the Canadian Nation.* Ed. Françoise Le Jeune. Nantes: Editions du CRINI (Centre de Recherches sur les Identités Nationales et l'Interculturalité), 2009. 105–117.

———. "'Mum is the word': Gender Violence, Displacement and the Refugee Camp in Yasmin Ladha's Documentary-Fiction." *Feminism, Literature and Rape Narratives: Violence and Violation.* Ed. Zoe Brigley and Sorcha Gunne. London: Routledge, 2009. 239–271.

———. "'Grammars of Exchange': The 'Oriental Woman' in the Global Market". *Cultural Grammars of Nation, Diaspora and Indigeneity in Canada.* Eds. Melina Baum Singer, Christine Kim, and Sophie McCall. Waterloo, ON: Wilfred Laurier University Press. Forthcoming.

Mehta, Gita. *Karma Cola: Marketing the Mystic East.* New York: Vintage, 1994.

Memba, Javier. «Cómo se hacen los libros (VI). La promoción, el arma clave». 2000. http://www.el-mundo.es/elmundolibro/2000/07/09/anticuario/962962416.html. 11/03/2005.

Miki, Roy. *Broken Entries: Race Subjectivity Writing.* Toronto: The Mercury Press, 1998.

———. "Altered States: Global Currents, the Spectral Nation, and the Production of 'Asian Canadian'." *Journal of Canadian Studies* 35.3 (2000): 43–72.

Mistry, Rohinton. *Such a Long Journey.* Toronto: McClelland & Stewart, 1991.

Mittapalli, Rajeshwar. "Global Temptations and Local Loyalties: Indian Fiction in English and Regional Literatures". *Global Neo-Imperialism and National Resistance: Approaches from Postcolonial Studies.* Ed. Belén Martín Lucas and Ana Bringas López. Vigo: Universidade de Vigo, 2004.

Mookerjea, Sourayan. "Some Special Times and Remarkable Spaces of Reading and Writing thru 'Race'." *West Coast Line* 15 (1994–95): 117–29.

Mootoo, Shani. *Out on Main Street.* Vancouver: Press Gang Publishers, 1993.

———. *Cereus Blooms at Night.* Vancouver: Press Gang Publishers, 1996.

———. *He Drown She in the Sea.* Toronto: McClelland & Stewart, 2005.

Morris, Robyn. "Making Eyes: Colouring the Look in Larissa Lai's *When Fox is a Thousand* and Ridley Scott's *Blade Runner.*" *Australian Canadian Studies* 20.1 (2002): 75–98.

———. "Revisioning Representations of Difference in Larissa Lai's *When Fox is a Thousand* and Ridley Scott's *Blade Runner.*" *West Coast Line* 44 (2004): 69–86.

———. "'Sites of Articulation': An Interview with Larissa Lai." *West Coast Line* 44 (2004): 21–30.

Moure, Erín. *Teatriños ou Auturuxos Calados.* Trans. María Reimóndez. Vigo: Editorial Galaxia, 2007.

Nakagawa, Anne Marie, dir. *Between: Living in the Hyphen.* National Film Board of Canada, 2006.

Navarro-Tejero, Antonia. *Gender and Caste in the Anglophone-Indian Novels of Arundhati Roy and Githa Hariharan: Feminist Issues in Cross-Cultural Perspectives.* Lewiston, Queenston, and Lampeter: The Edwin Mellen Press, 2005.

Nguyen, Viet Thanh. *Race and Resistance: Literature and Politics in Asian America.* Cary, NC: Oxford University Press, 2002.

New, WH. *Dreams of Speech and Violence: The Art of the Short Story in Canada and New Zealand.* Toronto: University of Toronto Press, 1987.

Niessen, Sandra, Ann Marie Leshkowich, and Carla Jones. *Re-Orienting Fashion: The Globalization of Asian Dress.* New York: Berg Publishers, 2003.

Oikawa, Mona. "My Life is Not Imagined: Notes on Writing as a Sansei Lesbian Feminist." *Open Letter* 8.4 (1992): 100–104.

Oliver, Kelly, ed. *The Portable Kristeva Reader.* New York: Columbia, 1997.

Omatsu, Maryka. *Bittersweet Passage: Redress and the Japanese Canadian Experience.* Toronto: Between the Lines, 1992.

Pandey, Beerendra. "A Paradigm Shift in the Representation of Violence in Partition Short Stories by Women: Political Irony in Shauna Singh Baldwin's 'Family Ties.'" *The Atlantic Literary Review. Special Issue on Indian Women's Short Fiction* 5.3–4 (2004): 105–112.

Parameswaran, Uma. "Let Us Sing Their Names: Women Writers in South Asian Canadian Literature." *Intersexions: Issues of Race and Gender in Canadian Women's Writing.* Ed. Coomi S Vevaina and Barbara Godard. New Dehli: Creative Books, 1996. 142–155.

———. *What Was Always Hers.* Fredericton: Broken Jaw Press, 1999.

———. *The Sweet Smell of Mother's Milk-Wet Bodice.* Fredericton: Broken Jaw Press, 2001.

———. *Mangoes on the Maple Tree.* Fredericton: Broken Jaw Press, 2002.

———. *Riding High with Krishna and a Baseball Bat and Other Stories.* Bloomington, IN: IUniverse, 2006.

———. *Fighter Pilots Never Die.* Winnipeg: Larkuma, 2007.

———. *The Forever Banyan Tree.* Winnipeg: Larkuma, 2007

Park, Shelley. "False Memory Syndrome: A Feminist Philosophical Approach." *Hypatia* 12.2 (1997): 1–50.

Pearson, Wendy Gay. "'Whatever That Is: Hiromi Goto's Body Politic/s." *Studies in Canadian Literature* 32.2 (2007): 75–96.

Peepre, Mari. "Crossing the Fields of Death and Kerri Sakamoto's The Electrical Field." *Missions of Interdependence.* Ed. Gerhard Stilz. Amsterdam: Rodopi, 2002. 51–62.

Rahman, Shazia. "Mingling the Margins: Yasmin Ladha's *Lion's Granddaughter and Other Stories.*" *Open Letter* 10.2 (1998): 95–100.

———. "Marketing the Mem: The Packaging and Selling of a First Novel." *The Toronto Review of Contemporary Writing Abroad* 18.1 (Fall 1999): 86–99.

Ralston, Helen. "Identity and Lived Experience of Daughters of South Asian Immigrant Women in Halifax and Vancouver, Canada: An Exploratory Study." International Migration and Ethnic Relations Conference. "Youth in the Plural City: Individualized and Collective Identitites." Rome: Norwegian Institute, May 25–27, 1999. http://pcerii.metropolis.net/Virtual%20Library/ConferencePapers/ralston99.pdf. 01/21/2008.

Rushdie, Salman. *Imaginary Homelands: Essays and Criticism 1981–1991.* London: Granta Books, 1991.

Said, Edward. *Orientalism.* 1978. London: Penguin, 1995.

Sakamoto, Kerri. *The Electrical Field.* Toronto: Vintage Canada, 1998.

———. "A Canadian sansei in Tokyo." National Post, March 6, 1999: 6.

———. *One Hundred Million Hearts.* Toronto: Alfred A Knopf, 2003.

Sarbadhikary, Krishna. "Indian English Literature at the Turn of the Century: Challenging National Identity and Cultural Homogeneity." *Challenging Cultural Practices in Contemporary Postcolonial Societies.* Ed. Belén Martín Lucas and Ana Bringas López. Vigo: Universidade de Vigo, 2001. 205–215.

Sasano, Mari. "'Words Like Buckshot': Taking Aim at Notions of Nation in Hiromi Goto's *A Chorus of Mushrooms.*" Open Letter 10.3 (1998): 38–53.

Sato, Gayle K Fujita. "Momotaro's Exile: John Okada's *No-No Boy.*" *Reading the Literatures of Asian America.* Ed. Shirley Gek-lin Lim and Amy Ling. Philadelphia: Temple University Press, 1992. 239–58.

Seidler, Victor. *Man Enough: Embodying Masculinities.* London: Sage, 1997.

Selvadurai, Shyam. "Introducing Myself in the Diaspora." *Story-Wallah: Short Fiction from South Asian Writers.* Ed. Shyam Selvadurai. New York: Mariner Books, 2005. 1–14.

Silvera, Makeda, ed. *The Other Woman: Women of Colour in Contemporary Canadian Literature.* Toronto: Sister Vision Press, 1995.

Stasiulis, Daiva. "'Authentic Coice': Anti-racist Politics in Canadian Feminist Publishing and Literary Production." Gunew and Yeatman 35–60.

Stone, Andrea. "Internalized Racism: Physiology and Abjection in Kerri Sakamoto's *The Electrical Field.*" Canadian Literature 193 (2007): 36–52.

Sturgess, Charlotte. *Redefining the Subject: Sites of Play in Canadian Women's Writing.* Amsterdam: Rodopi, 2003.

"Tiptree Award to Hiromi Goto." Science Fiction Chronicle 24.7 (2002): 4.

Tourino, Christina. "Ethnic Reproduction and the Amniotic Deep: Joy Kogawa's *Obasan.*" Frontiers: a Journal of Women's Studies 24.1 (2003): 134–53.

Ty, Eleanor. *The Politics of the Visible in Asian North American Narratives.* Toronto: University of Toronto Press, 2004.

————. *Unfastened: Globality and Asian North American Narratives.* Minneapolis: The University of Minnesota Press, 2010.

Ty, Eleanor, and Donald C Goellnicht. "Introduction." Ty and Goellnicht 1–14.

————, eds. *Asian North American Identities: Beyond the Hyphen.* Bloomington, IN: Indiana University Press, 2004.

Van Leuven, Lynne. "Trading Identities in Canadian Fiction." Bernier 39–47.

Verduyn, Christl, ed. *Literary Pluralities.* Toronto: Broadview Press, 1998.

Visvis, Vikki. "Trauma Remembered and Forgotten: The Figure of the Hysteric in Kerri Sakamoto's *The Electrical Field.*" *Mosaic* 40.3 (2007): 67–83.

Wall, Kathleen. "The Remains of the Day and Its Challenges to Theories of Unreliable Narration." *Journal of Narrative Technique* 24.1 (1994): 18–42.

Warriar, Nalini. *Blues from the Malabar Coast.* Toronto: TSAR Publications, 2002.

West, Lois A, ed. *Feminist Nationalism.* London and New York: Routledge, 1997.

Westermann, Molly. "Is the Butler Home? Narrative and the Split Subject in *The Remains of the Day.*" *Mosaic* 37.3 (2004): 157–70.

Wolmark, Jenny. *Aliens and Others: Science Fiction, Feminism and Postmodernism.* Hemel Hemsptead: Harvester Wheatsheaf, 1994.

Wong, Rita. "Jumping on Hyphens: A Bricolage Receiving 'Genealogy/Gap,' 'Goods,' 'East Asian Canadian,' 'Translation' and 'Laughter.'" Silvera 117–53.

————. "Market Forces and Powerful Desires: Reading Evelyn Lau's Cultural Labour." *Essays on Canadian Writing* 73 (2001): 122–40.

————. "Troubling Domestic Limits: Reading Border Fictions Alongside Larissa Lai's *Salt Fish Girl.*" *British Columbia Studies* 140 (2003–04): 109–24.

Yamamoto, Traise. *Masking Selves, Making Subjects: Japanese American Women, Identity and the Body.* Berkeley: University of California Press, 1999.

Yeh, William. "To Belong or Not to Belong: The Liminality of John Okada's *No-No Boy.*" *Amerasia Journal* 19.1 (1993): 121–33.

Yuval-Davis, Nira. *Gender and Nation.* London: Sage, 1997.